The Book of
THE THAMES

The Book of
THE THAMES

ALAN JENKINS
With photographs by
DERRY BRABBS

M

Macmillan London

Copyright © Text by Alan Jenkins 1983
Copyright © Photographs by Derry Brabbs 1983
All rights reserved
No part of this publication may be
reproduced or transmitted, in any form
or by any means, without permission.

First published 1983 by
MACMILLAN LONDON LIMITED
London and Basingstoke
Associated companies in Auckland, Dallas,
Delhi, Dublin, Hong Kong, Johannesburg, Lagos,
Manzini, Melbourne, Nairobi, New York,
Singapore, Tokyo, Washington and Zaria

This book was designed and produced by
The Rainbird Publishing Group Ltd,
40 Park Street, London W1Y 4DE

ISBN 0 335 36049 4

Editor: Georgina Evans
Designer: Martin Bristow
Indexer: Diana LeCore

Text set by Oliver Burridge and Co Ltd, Crawley, England
Illustrations originated by Adroit Photo Litho Ltd,
Birmingham, England
Printed and bound by Industria Gráfica Barcelona, D.L. 28840-1983

Frontispiece: The infant Thames by Lechlade

ILLUSTRATION ACKNOWLEDGMENTS

The Mary Evans Picture Library *half-title, frontispiece*, 15, 19, 21, 27
The Mansell Collection 11, 18, 23, 28, 31, 162
The Rainbird Picture Library 12 (from the Pepys Library)
The Tate Gallery, London 25

Contents

Author's Acknowledgments

There are hundreds of books about the River Thames, and my excuse for adding to their number is that the river is changing all the time, and books about it quickly go out of date. I have striven to make this book as up-to-the-minute as I could, but changes may have taken place even during the writing of it. It follows that many books have had to be consulted and checked by personal observation.

My thanks are due to my wife and my daughter for help with research; to my editor, Georgina Evans, for ideas and encouragement; to Christopher Jennings for reading the manuscript and for his invaluable knowledge of the non-tidal Thames; to John Yeoman for his specialized knowledge of the Thames painters, James McNeill Whistler and Walter Greaves; and to Ian and Jenny Nicoll, of the Rose Revived, for providing a comfortable background to part of my research and much local information. My collaborator Derry Brabbs, that fine photographer, has been a pleasure to work with. Of official sources of information, I must single out Laurie Moles, Public Relations Manager, Thames Water; the River Thames Society; the information department of the Port of London Authority; and the National Trust.

The most useful of many books consulted were:

The Book of the Thames (Mr & Mrs S.C. Hall), Virtue & Co, 1859; new edition published by Charlotte James, 1975

Dictionary of the Thames (Charles Dickens Jr) Macmillan, 1888

The Stripling Thames (Fred S. Thacker) 1909

The Thames Highway (Fred S. Thacker) (2 vols) 1914, 1920; new edition David and Charles, 1968

Sweet Thames Run Softly (Robert Gibbings) Dent 1940

A Land (Jacquetta Hawkes) Cresset Press 1951

Time on the Thames (Eric de Maré) Architectural Press 1952

Thames Estuary (William Addison) Hale 1954

Till I End My Song (Robert Gibbings) Dent 1957

Oxford Dictionary of Place Names (E. Ekwall) O.U.P. 1960

The Thames (A. P. Herbert) Weidenfeld & Nicolson 1966

An Eye on the Thames (Alan Wykes) Jarrolds 1966

Portrait of the Thames (from Teddington to Source) (J.H.B.Peel) Hale 1967

The Upper Thames (J.R.L. Anderson) Eyre & Spottiswoode 1970

Holiday Cruising on the Thames (E. & P.W. Ball) David & Charles 1970

Berkshire (Roger Higham) Batsford 1977

The Companion Guide to London (David Piper) (6th edition) Collins 1977

A View of the Thames (Norman Shrapnel) Collins 1977

London's River (Philip Howard) Hamish Hamilton 1975

The Shell Book of English Villages (ed. John Hadfield) Michael Joseph 1980

The New Shell Guide to England (ed. John Hadfield) Michael Joseph/Rainbird 1981

A Thames Companion (Mari Prichard & Humphrey Carpenter) (2nd edition) O.U.P. 1981

The Thames from Source to Tideway (Peter H. Chaplin) Whittet Books 1982

The Buildings of England series — *Oxfordshire, Buckinghamshire* and *Surrey* (ed. Nikolaus Pevsner) Penguin Books 1974, 1960, 1971

A.J.

CHAPTER ONE

Poseidon to Tamesis

A River is Born

In the beginning, when Earth was half as old as the solar system, about 3,000 million years ago, the moon parted from the earth, and gas and liquid began cooling into rock. There was no life on Earth for another eighteen million years, and no creature like man for nearly 1,200 million years after that. In what geologists call the Cambrian Age, all Britain lay under an ocean (known as Poseidon) stretching to the present-day Pacific – there were no land masses, such as America, in between. Poseidon ceased when a vast continent emerged linking South America, Africa, India and Australia which geologists named Gondwanaland.

North of Poseidon was another continent, embracing Scandinavia and Canada, called Atlantis. Land and sea rose and fell, volcanoes erupted, and about seven million years ago the continent of Europe began to assume something like its present shape, with Britain as a peninsula at its northwest corner. Ice Ages came and went, and the southern limit of the ice was the Thames Valley. The Thames was joined to the river Rhine, and their combined flood entered the North Sea somewhere off the coast of Norfolk. This has encouraged a pretty speculation that 'if the Thames had entered the sea at Clacton, the capital of England would have been Colchester'. There is also some evidence that the Thames was joined, earlier, to the Bristol Channel in the west.

Homo sapiens sapiens arrived about 30,000 years ago. During the warmer intervals of the Ice Ages prehistoric man lived in southern England leaving traces of himself in the Thames Valley. He came on foot, for the Channel did not yet exist, from as far away as Africa, from Germany and France: tall, fair, warlike Celts; small, dark Iberians with engineering skills; and Mediterranean men, greedy for gold and tin. About 7,000 years ago the melting ice swelled the North Sea and the warm Gulf stream, and formed the English Channel. Henceforth all foreign invaders had to sail to Britain. Sooner or later they all went up the Thames Valley.

The Thames is the longest river in England – 215 water miles from Thames Head to the Nore – but in Britain, the Severn, which rises in Wales, beats it by 5 miles. Such a little river compared to the Nile (4,150 miles), the Amazon (3,900 miles), the Missouri and Mississippi (3,800 miles) or the Yangtze (3,400 miles). Yet it is part of the English island consciousness. 'The sea is all about us,' said T. S. Eliot, 'the river is within us.'

I first met the Thames at the wrong end – its Estuary. My boyhood holidays were mostly spent on the north Kent coast. By day it looked like any other seaside coast (though in clear weather you could just see, on the horizon, a faint rumour of Essex 15 miles away). By night, how different! Flashing coloured lights, lightships and buoys guiding ships to the Port of London, riding on shoals with memorable names like Nore, Mouse, Girdler, Kentish Knock, Shivering Sand, Edinburgh, Maplin, and Tongue. From this I learned that the Thames, for a good part of its length, was a working river. I did not see the Source until I was nearly fifty.

Without the Thames there might have been no England; certainly no London beyond a Celtic village with a ford. Here, more than a thousand years ago, the English language was born, helped by Alfred the Great, around Wantage and Faringdon and Wallingford. Most of the events that made English history happened near, or were affected by, the Thames. It once

London grew because it was situated on the River Thames

had great strategic importance: its upper reaches were the frontier between Mercia and Wessex, and the southern limit of Danelaw. Here, tiny bridges were fiercely fought over in the Civil War.

How to define the unique charm of this river? Its beauty is seldom dramatic like that of the Rhine: it has no fairy-tale castles built precariously on cliff-sides by mad Bavarian Kings. 'It's the *trees*,' says a well-known Thames photographer. 'Trees *are* the Thames.' Beech-covered chalk hills, lines of Lombardy poplars, weeping willows at water's edge. The river's beauty is – I am striving to avoid the word *cosy* – intimate, perhaps? (Another word I promise to avoid is *picturesque*, the adjective beloved of Dr Syntax when writing up his tours nearly 200 years ago: 'I'll *picturesque* it everywhere.') The Thames does not disturb. It soothes, as Soames Forsyte, hero of Galsworthy's *Forsyte Saga*, discovered. We feel it belongs to us. Like our national character, it has streaks of sheer vulgarity. In order to enjoy the Thames you must learn to love the squalid, or see it as a nocturne, like Whistler or Monet. You must become a connoisseur of gasworks, power stations and bungalows, exercising your riverman's right to peer nosily into people's back gardens.

Its character changes as it flows, whether you are an up-streamer or a downstreamer. It is possible to divide the river into architectural sections: Victorian castellated fantasy, Edwardian turrets and balconies, post-1918 shacks (don't worry – there is plenty of Georgian too). Or to characterize Teddington-to-Staines as 'urban', Staines-to-Reading as 'sophisticated', Reading-to-Oxford as 'rural', and all above Oxford as 'remote'. Is it possible to sail between Boulter's Lock and Marlow without memories of faded photographs, of punts and parasols, girls in enormous hats and men in straw boaters? To John Buchan, the writer, the whole river above Oxford was 'medieval', for here is one of the few parts of the country where today we can see some of the self-same things that our forebears saw a millennium ago.

The Invaders

When the Romans first saw the Thames at London, the forests came down to the marshy banks. We get some idea of this from Samuel Pepys, who records, in September 1665, that 'in digging the late Docks [in what is now Blackwall] they did twelve feet underground find perfect trees over-covered with earth. Nut trees, with the branches and the very nuts upon them.' And in 1882, workmen excavating what was to be the Inner Circle Underground line found Roman pavements on oak piling – and the oaks had roots.

The Romans, like all the successive waves of invaders, penetrated the Thames Valley. They came as conquerors and colonizers, and were able to hold the colony for 400 years. But the problem of sailing up the Thames was always that, as you came upstream, your rear was vulnerable to more invaders unless you defended it. So the Romans appointed a 'Count of the Saxon shore' with armed galleys and 10,000 men to protect the southeast coast from Shoreham by Sea (West Sussex) to Brancaster (Norfolk). One of their fortresses, Regulbium, survives today as Reculver, a ruined Saxon-Norman church 3 miles east of Herne Bay.

The Romans found previous invaders occupying definite areas in tribes. The Dobunni were around what is now Gloucestershire, centred on Cirencester, which the Romans called Corinium Dobunnorum. The Belgae, who included the Catuvellauni and came from Eastern France, frequented the area between Winchester and Bath; and the Atrebates had their capital at Calleva Atrebatum (Silchester), 10 miles from Reading. Along the marshy estuary were the Trinovantes in Essex, and the Cantii in Kent.

The Romans, their over-extended empire unable to hold back the barbarians, began to leave England and the country was at the mercy of a series of fresh invasions. The Jutes stayed mainly in Kent (yet their leader Hengist may have given his name to Hinksey, near Oxford, which seems to mean Hengist's island or ford). Throughout the Thames Valley were Romano-British farms, villas and estates, which the Saxons took over. Towards the end of the sixth century a new kind of invasion began: Christianity was introduced to the Thames Estuary and gently penetrated the river and its surrounding lands.

This happened more quickly than an age of violence could have imagined. In 596 St Augustine landed in Thanet with forty monks, 'Frankish interpreters, relics and manuscripts, painted banners and silver crosses.' The following year, on Whit Sunday, he baptized Ethelbert of Kent in the river Swale (between Sheppey and the mainland). It is reputed that 12,000 of Ethelbert's subjects were baptized on Christmas Day 598. The Essex side of the Estuary had to wait another fifty years for St Cedd to land at Bradwell-on-Sea. (His tiny chapel, St Peter's-on-the-Wall, is still there, somewhat overshadowed by a nuclear power-station.)

In the upper Thames, St Birinus had arrived in 635. For some time he made little progress among the pagan West Saxons, until King Cynegils asked for instruction in the faith. He and his family were baptized in the Thames (or it may have been the Thame). So to the ultimate glory of Wessex, the magnanimous conqueror, Alfred the Great, first king of all England, the educated educator, whose father had taken him on a pilgrimage to Rome. Meekly paying Danelaw when he had to, he bided his time and eventually captured London and the whole Danish fleet. His capital had been Winchester, but he was, however, born within 9 miles of the Thames. He did not found Oxford University, but there is a homely tradition that he had a royal longboat made to his own design, at Reading, and used it to take him to Oxford to discuss with scholars his plans for the spread of learning. (It has been pointed out that, since there were then no locks, the boat must have been manhandled up the rapids.)

William the Conqueror's drive up the Thames Valley to Wallingford and the building of Windsor Castle were part of his

St Augustine brought Christianity to the Thames Estuary. In 597 he baptized King Ethelbert of Kent

plan to establish a chain of castles which dominated the valley enabling him to control southeast England. The Normans built castles, abbeys and monasteries throughout England. They were the first conquerors to plan military defence on a national scale. They realized that the Thames was a tremendous asset — for trade as well as defence. Richard the Lionheart also understood the importance of the river: he vested, by royal charter, responsibility for conservancy in the Corporation of London. By Edward I's time, the wool trade was England's main industry. It was carried on along the whole length of the Thames, whose mouth faced those of the hungry rivers Scheldt, Meuse and Rhine, where the weavers lived. The Thames was a *short* river, and was therefore able to transport goods more cheaply than continental rivers.

One clause in Richard I's royal charter had insisted that 'all weirs within the Thames shall be removed'. Weirs were useful

The Queen's Journey from Hampton Court to Whitehall on 23 August 1662

for navigation, but often became choked with dead fish or flooded; when the barons presented their demands to King John on an island by Runnymede, weirs (specifically fishing weirs, using the medieval Latin word *kidelli*) were to be 'utterly put down'. So it is that the foundation of British democracy, in Clause 23 of Magna Carta which listed the liberties granted by King John to the English people in 1215, is all mixed up with fish and navigation of the Thames.

In the next century the voice of the peasants demanded to be heard and it was along the sides of the Estuary that they came in 1377, marching on London – Wat Tyler from Essex, camping in Mile End Fields, and John Ball from Kent, camping on Blackheath, where, seventy-three years later, Jack Cade was to register his protest at the desperate state of the country after the French Wars. The French had attacked the coast of southeast England, Gravesend had been sacked and burned, and the mouth of the Thames was guarded by timber booms to hinder enemy shipping.

Royal River

The Thames was a highway, and with the Tudors it became royal. There is no longer a State Barge; the last, built in 1689, known as Queen Mary's Shallop, was used by George V and Queen Mary finally at Henley Royal Regatta in 1912. It is now in the National Maritime Museum at Greenwich. When the river was the chief 'road' from east to west the State Barge was essential. It was by water that Anne Boleyn went to her coronation in 1533 from Greenwich to the Tower. As she stepped from her barge she was received amid fanfares by the King who wore a gold and crimson doublet, his shoes studded with diamonds. On this fair May morning they led a procession of fifty barges carrying the Lord Mayor and aldermen wearing scarlet gowns and gold chains. Anne was to make another river journey in 1536 to the Tower for her execution.

Elizabeth I, as a young princess, on the orders of her sister Mary, was taken to the Tower by water and made to disembark at Traitor's Gate. As Queen, she regarded the river with loving possessiveness: in 1592, on her way to Cirencester, she insisted on being carried from Lechlade to the Source so that she could see 'the very first trickle of my fine Thames'. When she died at Richmond Palace, her body was taken by barge at night to Whitehall Palace. The secret funeral of Charles I after his execution was also carried out at night, in freezing February weather, amid ice-floes: his headless body was brought by Bishop Juxon of London to St George's Chapel at Windsor.

With the Restoration in 1660 came pageantry too: Catherine of Braganza's entry into London by river was deemed by John Evelyn 'finer than . . . the espousal of the Adriatic at Venice'. Shortly afterwards, a vast crowd gathered at Westminster to welcome the King and Queen home to London from Hampton Court. Samuel Pepys watched them from the top of the new Banqueting House in Whitehall: the river was jammed with boats and barges – 'ten thousand . . . I think, for we could see no water for them'. Charles II was luckier than George I, who disembarked at Greenwich Pier in thick fog to take up his new throne, only to find that the Royal welcome had already been given to his son who had arrived before him.

The Lord Mayor's Show began on the Thames in 1453 when Sir John Norman, having built himself a ceremonial barge, was rowed by watermen using (we are told) silver oars, and led a procession of City Companies in their own barges. This event was marred for thirty years by a dispute about precedence between the Merchant Taylors and Skinners, but the show went on as a river pageant for more than four centuries until 1857. There was an attempt to revive it in 1953, the 500th anniversary of its beginning and the year of Elizabeth II's coronation. Inspired by the Lord Mayor, Sir Rupert de la Bere, and organized by the Port of London Authority, a 3-mile procession of 150 craft came up the river from Greenwich to Westminster.

Royal honeymoons nowadays tend to be taken on the Royal Yacht *Britannia*, sometimes departing from London River (the Thames); and in 1945 there was a Victory celebration when the King of Norway and Marshal Tito arrived by water and George VI sailed up the Estuary from Southend to Parliament Buildings. Pageantry at its most solemn is reserved for State funerals: Nelson, in 1805, rode upon the Thames (in a hailstorm) on his way to St Paul's, and Sir Winston Churchill, on 30 January 1965, after his funeral service at St Paul's, was borne to Tower Gate, placed upon the barge *Havengore* and taken upstream to Waterloo Pier, the dockyard cranes dipping in salute, guns firing, bosun's whistles piping grief; then he was taken by railway from Waterloo Station to the tiny churchyard at Bladon, Oxfordshire. The date was important, for on that day high water in King's Reach was at 1 p.m. precisely. 'A week before, we couldn't have done it,' the Duke of Norfolk, in charge of all arrangements, told Sir Alan Herbert.

The River at War

Sir Alan Herbert is our chronicler of the Thames at war. With the rank of Petty Officer he commanded his own motor-launch *Water Gipsy* from 1938 onwards, as a unit of the River Emergency Service, which became the R.N. Thames (Auxiliary) Patrol and carried an armament of one rifle and fifty rounds of ammunition. For some time *Water Gipsy* was posted to Westminster Pier, which was convenient for the House of Commons (A.P.H. was M.P. for Oxford University). Then he went downstream to the Estuary, where the action was. He had pulled a few bodies out of the Thames and conveyed them to hospital ships, but there had not really been much excitement. Now, in 1940, he witnessed the air raids on Dockland (weird, sickly smells of burning wheat, rubber, barrels of rum, drums of paint) and Woolwich Arsenal (firemen working among boxes of live ammunition and crates of nitro-glycerine). Further downstream, *Water Gipsy* watched for parachute-mines, some magnetic. Many fell around Southend Pier which, code-named HMS *Leigh*, was the organizing point for convoys of troopships and for transports massing for D-Day in 1944. Meanwhile the same creeks along the Thames which had supplied 'small vessels' for the 'amateur Armada' at Dunkirk now concealed concrete caissons which would become Mulberry Harbours. The hero of the war, Herbert maintained, was Southend Pier, 'she should have got the George Medal'.

Sporting River

Sir Alan Herbert, *Punch* staff writer, lyricist, librettist and an honorary Conservator of the Thames, loved everything about the river; above all, the Oxford and Cambridge Boat Race, for which, every year, he gave a party at his riverside house, at Nos. 12 and 13 Hammersmith Terrace, just above Hammersmith Bridge in London, in a row of narrow Georgian houses, backing onto the river, which were said to have been built for the mistresses of George II. Here, in the 1920s, actors, authors, painters, and sculptors assembled – from H. G. Wells to a then unknown Major Bernard L. Montgomery.

The Boat Race is part of the Pleasure River, now that the Working River has moved so far down the Estuary. (But pleasure is also an industry on the Upper Thames.) The first such race, using boats containing eight oarsmen, was from Hambleden Lock to Henley Bridge ($2\frac{1}{4}$ miles upstream) in 1829; after a false start, in which the two boats collided, Oxford won. The next inter-University race was rowed along the Westminster–Putney course in 1836: this time Cambridge won. Oxford rowed in dark blue: Cambridge attached a light blue ribbon to their boat as a sort of mascot, and so a tradition was started. The river at Westminster was becoming too full of commercial traffic to be comfortable for sporting events, and so it was in 1845 that the course Putney Bridge-to-Mortlake Church was adopted. In 1846 the finishing point, Mortlake Church, was altered to the Ship Inn, and this, giving a length of just under $4\frac{1}{4}$ miles, has been the course ever since.

Two more famous boat-race meetings, localized to Oxford, are Eights Week (May–June), the annual college champion-ships, and Torpids (once unofficially called Toggers, February–March) 'for less advanced oarsmen'. These start at Iffley Lock and finish at Folly Bridge. Like all Oxford boat races they began in the early 1800s, when undergraduates enjoyed rowing down to the King's Arms at Sandford for dinner and, elevated by wine, rowed back to Oxford. Only one boat at a time could leave Iffley Lock, so those behind tried to draw alongside, or at least bump, the one in front. Thus bumping races began, and led to a strange parlance which could make assertions like 'Balliol bumped Jesus in the Gut', and also to the Viking revels of Bump Suppers, which have been known to end with a burning boat in the Quad, and much broken glass.

In the summer, regattas are held along the river between Oxford and London. The most celebrated, of course, is Henley Royal Regatta – Royal since 1851 when the Prince Consort became its patron. Although Henley is the 'Holy City' of rowing, it would be untruthful to say that people swarm there, every first week in July, to *see* the races. It is almost as much a fashion parade as the races at Royal Ascot. Old men, some in bath chairs, some with clerical collars because they are bishops, sport faded 'Leander pink' blazers and ties, with shrunken Leander caps on their heads. A military band plays selections from *Oklahoma!* and *The Gondoliers*. It is another world, despite the women coxswains and scullers of today.

Rowing clubs from all over the globe send crews to Henley. American colleges and schools (and Russians too) have carried off trophies. Those trophies (some of them as old as the Regatta itself) have famous names such as the Grand Challenge Cup, Stewards' Challenge Cup, Wyfold, Silver Goblets, and Diamond Sculls. In recent years there has been some falling off in entries from schools, because Henley often clashes with examinations. The course – a good straight one of 1 mile 550 yards – begins at Temple Island and ends opposite Phyllis Court, just below

The Oxford and Cambridge Boat Race has run the same course since 1846. Here, Oxford, the winning crew in 1863, come ashore at Mortlake

Henley Bridge. Thus it is rowed upstream against a current, in summer estimated at 0.7 m.p.h., and a prevalent northeast breeze. The Regatta has been held here, except in wartime, since 1839, when a meeting of Henley businessmen resolved that such an annual event would be 'productive of the most beneficial results to the town of Henley'. There are regattas along most of the river – such as those at Reading, Wallingford, Abingdon, Marlow, Maidenhead, Staines, Walton and Wargrave; and there is a feeling in many quarters that the river needs more regattas and fireworks, like the 1975 Thames Regatta, held two hundred years after the last great Ranelagh Regatta; and the Thames Clipper Regatta where more than sixty sailing ships from several nations – including the ketch *Arethusa*, the schooner *Sir Winston Churchill*, the Russian barque *Tovarishch* and the West German Navy training ship *Gorch Fock* – assembled, in the Upper Pool below London Bridge, for the start of the Round-the-World Race.

There are also Head races such as Reading Head and Putney Head and recently an Abingdon Head race. The English Tourist Board gives its support to all attempts to brighten up the river. A Thames Barge Driving Race, from Greenwich Pier to Westminster, has been taking place each June since 1975, involving 'twenty Thames working barges manned by Freemen and Apprentices of the Watermen's Company'. It is organized by the Transport on Water Association. Today, each September there is Thames Day, inspired by the Greater London Council, when for one day, between Westminster and Hungerford Bridges, the public is invited to take part in, or at least watch, 'Fun On the River' with power-boat races, barge driving, canoeing, Royal Marines rescue displays, and fireworks.

All this may make you yearn for the peace of the Upper Thames; but there is one traditional event on London's river that you should see once in a lifetime. Thomas Doggett, an Irish comedian who flourished about 1700, was grateful for the services of Thames watermen, of whom there were a great many as there was no bridge but London Bridge; to get to a theatre people had to be ferried (or wherried) across the Thames. Doggett was also a fervent Royalist, and in 1715 he founded a Coat and Badge Race for young watermen; according to the announcement made annually from Fishmongers' Hall, these men will row from the Swan Inn by London Bridge to the Swan Inn at Chelsea (a very long course, just short of 5 miles, which has been completed in the record time of 23 minutes 22 seconds) 'for the Livery and Badge provided yearly under the Will of the late Mr Thos Doggett, a famous Comedian, in commemoration of the happy Accession of His Majesty George the First to the Throne of Great Britain in 1714.' The race has a reasonable claim to be the oldest surviving sporting event in the country if not in the world, and it happens annually in July. The original prize was a scarlet skirted coat with a large silver arm-badge bearing the Horse of Hanover. Competitors use racing sculls.

Keeping Swans

Travelling upstream, you will probably see your first swans somewhere about Putney (you may, however, see them as far east as Blackfriars). Swans, as the Three Men in a Boat discovered, are not particularly friendly unless they think you are going to feed them, and there is a strong case for leaving them well alone. They are mute swans, but they can hiss like anything. The Thames swans belong to the Queen and to two City Companies, the Vintners and the Dyers. The Vintners' swans may be recognized by two nicks cut in the upper beak while the Dyers' birds have only one; the Queen's (she owns about 500) have none at all. The nicks are made painlessly when the birds are very young, and this is done at the annual Swan Upping ceremony in the third week of July. A team of eighteen watermen today is led by Mr John Turk, the Royal

Henley Regatta began in 1839 but was not given royal patronage until 1851. It is one of the oldest regattas in the world

Swan Keeper, whose father held the job before him (the Turks have been Thames Watermen since 1760). There have been Royal Swan Keepers since about AD 1300 or even earlier.

Turk's Boat Yard, a weatherboarded building near Cookham Bridge, is John Turk's headquarters. He spends much of his time answering distress calls from the public and police about injured or lost swans. Swans in flight are always mistaking the M40 motorway for water and landing on it, to the peril of traffic. Swans also suffer from fishermen's weights and floats which cause lead pollution and a consequent reduction in swan flocks. They are much disturbed too by the 20,000 or so pleasure boats using the river every year. Mr Turk wears a special uniform (a red and white jersey and white trousers) to distinguish him from the Dyers' Swan Keeper (who wears blue) and the Vintners' (green and white). Swan Upping has taken place for more than 700 years.

Keeping Locks

Cruising about the river, you cannot fail to notice the cheerful brightness, colour and general attractiveness of the locks, their keepers' cottages and the gardens. This is partly because lock-keepers and their families are house-proud people, and partly due to the City Challenge Cup for the best-kept lock. This was first competed for in 1957, the centenary of Thames Conservancy (now amalgamated with the Thames Water Authority); and the Hanson Cup for the best lock garden was founded in 1904 by Sir Reginald Hanson, Lord Mayor of London. Bray and Sonning Locks have been among the most frequent winners.

Many lock-keepers come from families that have served the river for several generations. Although in 1980 there was a dispute about a claim for a five-day week, shorter hours and better pay for weekend working (which involves closing locks earlier), most lock-keepers enjoy their job and the way of life,

The official source of the river is at Thames Head, near the village of Coates in Gloucestershire

even at the height of the holiday season when, at Boulter's Lock for example, many hundreds of craft pass through. The lock-keepers' main job, however, is to trim the weir levels and so carry out vital flood control. They also telephone water levels to Thames Water every three hours (this can give early warning of floods), and inform Mr Turk about any maltreatment of swans. Above all, lock-keepers live 'over the shop', and have no rent, rates or repairing leases to worry about.

Weirs were the forerunners of locks. They were made chiefly for the benefit of millers who needed water-power to drive the grindstones, and for fisheries, since fish were bottled up in the weir-pool. The flow of water was controlled by removable 'paddles' held in place by 'rymers'. These were 'flash weirs' (in medieval times made of stakes and brushwood, with eel traps like long nose-bags) which enabled downstream boats to 'shoot the rapids' and upstream traffic to be either manhandled or hauled by horses. They also enabled millers to charge exorbitant tolls. Hence Clause 23 of Magna Carta. The last 'flash', Medley Weir, disappeared in 1937. (There are still rollers at some locks where you can manhandle a small craft.)

How to make the river navigable for larger craft? In Tudor times the river's importance for trade (coal upstream, food downstream) was increasing, and most goods were carried on barges. The two monarchs who best understood the importance of the Thames were James I and Charles I. In 1605 James I appointed eighteen men, to be known as the Oxford-Burcot Commissioners, to improve the river between Oxford and Burcot, a village just above Dorchester. The University, which would benefit most by them, promoted the idea of pound-locks, in which water is held in a pound or pond — by gates, mechanically operated, not by paddles — until it can be released. The Thames falls from its source at an average rate of 15 feet 5 inches per mile, so there was a demand for pound-locks once a few experimental ones had been tested. The first three, completed in the 1630s, were at Iffley, Sandford-on-Thames and Abingdon.

A Thames waterman in Doggett's Coat and Badge

Who invented pound-locks? It seems that they were already in use in fifteenth-century Italy when Leonardo da Vinci made some drawings of them for a Milan canal project.

Thames locks are soundly built in stone and well maintained. Most keepers' cottages are twentieth-century, or at least Victorian; but as recently as thirty years ago there were still a few with no running water or indoor sanitation. If you have patience and enjoy watching people, locks can be fun. Each has its own personality. Lock dues were once collected in a bag at the end of a long pole, like church offertories, but today each boat has to have an up-to-date Thames Conservancy plate. You may be lucky enough to find a lock-keeper's wife who will sell you home-made pies and home-grown vegetables. There are still one or two locks in the Upper Thames which are not automatic or electrified, and if the lock-keeper is not on duty you may have to open and close them yourself. Look about you among the bollards for big boats and chains for small ones; notice the Thames Water (and sometimes the Trinity House) emblems, the flood high-water marks. You may even share Sir Alan Herbert's delight in discovering by-laws about swearing.

Many lock-keepers before World War II were retired Royal Navy petty officers. Others came from families that had served the river for generations. Within living memory (that is in the 1950s) the keeper at King's Lock, one Fred Smith of Rotherhithe, had served a five-year apprenticeship as a lighterman. His indentures insisted that he should not 'commit fornication or matrimony within the said term . . . shall not play at cards, dice, tables . . . shall not haunt taverns or playhouses, or absent himself from his master's service.'

Literary River

What art has the Thames inspired? Only a little music of any quality; occasional spurts of poetry, though (like the river itself) not much of grandeur; some vivid narrative prose; and a good deal of painting. Probably the best-known line about the Thames in all poetry is 'Sweet Thames, run softly till I end my song'. Before 1941, when Robert Gibbings published his whimsical, digressive book, *Sweet Thames Run Softly*, illustrated with his own exquisite engravings (a cheering, best-selling labour of love in time of war), it is probable that only students of English Literature were familiar with it as the refrain of Spenser's *Prothalamion*. For Matthew Arnold, the river was always 'youthful', the stripling of Bablockhythe. For Francis Thompson, by the Embankment, it was a river where he could imagine 'Christ walking on the water, Not of Gennesareth, but Thames!' The cliché about 'liquid history', comparing our river to the 'muddy' Mississippi and the 'crystal' St Lawrence, is attributed to John Burns, the first working-class Cabinet Minister. For William Morris, 'the clear Thames bordered by its gardens green' (and he lived beside it for twenty-five years) was the symbol of an idealized, un-megalopolitan, smoke-free future. For Sir John Betjeman, it is summed up nostalgically by Henley Regatta in wartime, where 'beefy A.T.S.' disport themselves. For Alexander Pope, the river was a comfortable setting for translating Homer (at Stanton Harcourt) or for writing about Miss Blount (at Mapledurham).

No poet has found truly epic qualities in the Thames; but Spenser's contemporary Michael Drayton, in that curious topographical poem about England, *Polyolbion*, found it always 'great'. (He lived in an age which had seen few longer rivers.) He apostrophizes its source:

> But, Cotswold, be this spoke to th'only praise of thee,
> That thou, of all the rest, the chosen soil shouldst be,
> Dame Isis to bring forth (the mother of great Thames),
> With whose delicious brooks, by whose immortal streams
> Her greatness is begun.

Can this be the sonneteer who wrote 'Since there's no help, come let us kiss and part'? He goes on to give all the tributaries human personalities, relationships and stock epithets:

The lock-keeper's cottage at Boveney Lock, 1857

> . . . to guide,
> Queen Isis on her way, ere she receive her train,
> Clear Colne and lively Leach have down from Cotswold's
>   plain,
> At Lechlade linking hands, some likewise to support
> The mother of great Thames.

The Windrush joins in:

> . . . and with herself does cast
> The train to overtake; and therefore hies her fast
> Through the Oxfordian fields; when (as the last of all
> Those floods that into Thames out of our Cotswold fall,
> And farthest unto the north) bright Evenlode forth doth
>   bear . . .

At Reading, 'clear Kennet overtakes her lord, the stately Thames', who receives her 'with many signs of joy'. Notice that Thames is always male, his tributaries (usually) female. For

Drayton, however, the Thame is (at one point) the 'bridegroom' of the Thames. For Thomas Warton, in the eighteenth century, the Thames is a 'silver-slippered virgin'. And Spenser got confused about the Thame: 'But much more aged was his wife than her, The Ouse, whom men do Isis rightly name.'

For Kipling, it was the history — and pre-history — that mattered. The river speaks:

> . . . I'd have you know that these waters of mine
> Were once a branch of the River Rhine,
> When hundreds of miles to the East I went
> And England was joined to the Continent.

If there be a true poet of the Thames (the Upper Thames, anyway) it is perhaps Robert Bridges:

> There is a hill beside the silver Thames
> Shady with birch and beech and odorous pine . . .

(Well, the Thames is seldom silver, just as the Danube is never blue; but never mind.) More romantically recognizable is:

> A rushy island guards the sacred bower
> And hides it from the meadow, where in peace
> The lazy cows wrench many a scented flower,
> Robbing the golden market of the bees.

For Masefield the sailor, the Thames is:

> The great street paved with water, filled with shipping,
> And all the world's flags flying, and the seagulls dipping.

Back to Pre-Raphaelite Morris for a similar approach, but more historic-literary than Masefield's 'Cargoes':

> . . . treasured scanty spice from some far sea,
> Florence gold cloth and Ypres napery
> And cloth of Bruges and hogsheads of Guienne,
> While nigh the thronged wharf Geoffrey Chaucer's pen
> Moves over bills of lading.

For W. E. Henley, memories of Kew:

> On the way to Kew,
> By the river old and grey,
> Where in the Long Ago
> We laughed and loitered so.

Each according to his temperament. Tragic John Davidson, about the turn of the twentieth century, became the only man ever to write a poem about the Isle of Dogs, which, by social reform, could give him a splendid vision of Millwall Docks as 'A green isle like a beryl set in a wine coloured sea.' And was Wilfred Owen the only poet to address verses — very sinister ones — to Shadwell Stair?

We go back to the eighteenth century (and the Upper Thames marshes) for a more normal reaction:

> Here Thames slow gliding through a level plain
> Of spacious weeds, with cattle sprinkled o'er,
> Conducts the eye along its sinuous course,
> Delighted . . .

The Thames may not have its own poet of the first rank, but it has a lively poetaster. John Taylor, born about 1580, was a Thames waterman who, after being press-ganged into the Navy at the age of sixteen and, coming out of it with an injured leg, made his living ferrying (or wherrying) people over the river to and from the Bankside playhouses and bear-gardens in London. He was a fearless, slightly crazy character who called City merchants 'fur-gowned money-mongers' to their faces, and was once arrested on his own wherry as a pirate. An excellent showman, he somehow came by the job of master of river pageants, notably one to celebrate the marriage of James I's daughter, Elizabeth, to the Elector Palatine. By this time he liked to call himself the Royal Poet, and could claim Ben Jonson among his

Swan Upping in 1874 — it dates originally from about 1295

friends. Much of his verse was topical, such as an account of his own voyage by sea and river from London to York and back, called *A Very Merry Wherry-Ferry Voyage*. He retired to an inn, the Crown, in Long Acre, and, being a devout Royalist, renamed it the Mourning Crown after Charles I's execution. Cromwell does not seem to have minded.

The river has perhaps inspired better prose than poetry; and often it is the more squalid and workaday features that have done so, especially in the London Tideway and the Estuary. There is Dickens's love-hate of the river in *Our Mutual Friend*, which begins with the filth and crime and floating corpses of a city where the river is a symbol of all that is wrong with society; Daniel Quilp, too, in *The Old Curiosity Shop*, inhabits a fearful wharf where any evil thing could happen. (These were the years of the Thames-as-sewer, called The Great Stink.) Withal, the river, by Wapping and Limehouse, has its consolation, such as crooked inns like the Six Jolly Fellowship Porters, 'a tavern of dropsical appearance [which] had long settled down into a state of hale infirmity. In its whole constitution it had not a straight floor, and hardly a straight line. . . . The whole house . . . impended over the water, but seemed to have got into the condition of a faint-hearted diver who has paused so long on the brink that he will never go in at all.'

Charles Dickens Jr, son of the novelist, favoured the Thames above Kingston: his *Dictionary of the Thames* is a practical guidebook for its time, the 1890s, of which he gives a vivid and detailed picture as seen from the river.

There is Joseph Conrad too who wrote about the Thames in his novel *Mirror of the Sea* – a skipper for whom the river was always a little claustrophobic, 'oppressed by bricks and mortar and stone'. Estuaries 'appeal strongly to an adventurous imagination. . . . The estuary of the Thames is not beautiful; it has no noble features, no romantic grandeur of aspect, no smiling geniality; but it is wide open, spacious, inviting, hospitable' as your pilot 'steers through one of the lighted and buoyed passageways of the Thames, such as Queen's Channel, Prince's Channel, Four Fathom Channel . . .'

For Arthur Morrison, pioneer of the detective story and, like Thomas Burke, explorer of the East End riverside, a pub called the Hole in the Wall gave him the title of a story. It may or may not be based on the Prospect of Whitby in Wapping:

It was wooden and clap-boarded, and like others of its sort was everywhere larger at top than at bottom . . . not only top-heavy but also most alarmingly lop-sided. By its side, and half under it, lay a narrow passage through which we saw a strip of the river and its many craft, and the passage ended in Hole-in-the-Wall Stairs . . . I decided that what kept the Hole in the Wall from crashing into the passage was nothing but its countervailing inclination to tumble into the river.

Dockland was the province of W. W. Jacobs, whose father was manager of the old South Devon Wharf. He grew up among old salts ashore, listening to tales of sea-captains and firstmates aboard cargo-ships and barges; his tales, often told by his famous night-watchman, full of pawky humour (but sometimes macabre), appeared regularly in the old *Strand* magazine.

Even Henry James, of all fastidious people, loved 'the brown, greasy current, the barges and the penny steamers, the black, sordid, hetero-geneous shores.'

Comedy and Fantasy

Strange that the two most famous books about the Thames should be, respectively, a comic masterpiece and a fantasy for children: *Three Men in a Boat* and *The Wind in the Willows*. In the early 1880s Jerome K. Jerome took river holidays with two friends, a bank manager named George Wingrave and Carl Hentschel, who is 'Harris' in *Three Men in a Boat*. Jerome, a struggling journalist, was asked to write a serious guide to the river, to be serialized in a weekly magazine. As he turned in his copy, he found that the editor was deleting a lot of the serious

Jerome K. Jerome's *Three Men in a Boat* on the River Thames

information and asking for more funny bits. The result of this we know and love today.

The Wind in the Willows began as bedtime stories about animals for Alastair, the young son of Kenneth Grahame, Secretary of the Bank of England, who lived at Cookham Dean. When it was published in 1908, a reviewer – was he leg-pulling? – thought the book 'negligible' as a work of natural history. Perhaps he was confused by the sheer oddity of the book. For is it really a children's book? Like all 'messing about in boats' it is an escape. 'Beyond the Wild Wood comes the Wide World', says Rat. 'I've never been there, and I'm never going.' The river, to Kenneth Grahame, as to Soames Forsyte, is time, and bears all our cares away. The book contains more descriptive writing than children can usually tolerate: 'Green turf sloped down to either edge, brown snaky tree-roots gleamed below the surface of the quiet water, while ahead of them the silvery shoulder and foamy tumble of a weir, arm-in-arm with a restless dripping mill-wheel, that held up in its turn a grey-gabled mill-house, filled the air with a soothing murmur of sound . . .' That's the Upper Thames all right.

Mole, who has never seen a river before, reacts more simply. 'Oh, my! Oh, my!' But Rat, of all the river animals, is a kind of religious poet, a very un-Bank-of-England pantheist or Pan worshipper. The animals moor their boat at an island, looking for the baby otter. 'Here, in this holy place', cries Rat, 'here if anywhere, we shall find Him!' Him is the Friend and Helper, with curved horns, pan-pipes, shaggy limbs, and hooves, protecting the lost baby otter. And the animals fall down and worship Him. In the next chapter we return to farce, with Mr Toad escaping from prison disguised as a washerwoman.

Perhaps, after all, Galsworthy is the writer to whom the Thames meant most. He was born at Kingston upon Thames. All through *The Forsyte Saga* the river is a linking symbol of life-flow and change. Again and again Soames returns to his Thames-side estate at Mapledurham. Here the unsuspected poetry of the man comes out. While gazing down on the Thames Valley he thinks: 'Look at the Ganges — monstrous great thing, compared with that winding silvery thread down there! The St Lawrence, the Hudson, the Potomac . . . had all pleased him, but, comparatively, they were sprawling pieces of water.'

Soames even wonders what it is like to be a lock-keeper, and imagines Fleur, his daughter, as an improbable lock-keeper's daughter. At crises in his life he fishes from a punt, taking notice of things like water-rats and dragonflies and flowers — 'something of Nature's calm entered his soul'.

Michael Mont, who marries Fleur, also seeking comfort, tears down to the towpath at Pangbourne, just to smoke a pipe by the water's edge. Warmson, James Forsyte's butler, when his master dies, takes a pub, the Pouter Pigeon, at 'Moulsbridge . . .

on the Berkshire side'. And, of course, it is at Mapledurham (I have known people look for the grave) that Soames Forsyte is buried, as he wished, under a crab-apple tree by the water.

Music? You would think that some composer — Elgar, Walton, Britten, Vaughan Williams perhaps — would have written a major work about the Thames. Is there no Smetana, who wrote that grand tone-poem *Vltava* about a mere tributary of the Elbe? Elgar would have done it superbly, in his Cockaigne manner; but he was a man of the Severn. Holst, born at Cheltenham so near to Seven Springs? Too preoccupied with the Planets. Vaughan Williams, born at Down Ampney 3 miles from the infant Isis, made his home in Surrey and wrote 'Norfolk Rhapsodies'. No opera about the river, not even a comic one? But yes: Charles Dibdin, singing actor and composer of sea-songs (among them 'Tom Bowling') — and river-songs too — wrote one in 1774 called 'The Waterman' whose leading aria began: 'Then farewell my trim-built wherry, oars and coat and badge farewell!' Modern songs? A few. Two old ladies won a song competition with a waltz, 'Cruising Down the River' (on a Sunday afternoon). And, a year or two before World War II, a cheerful song, 'Old Father Thames', heartily sung by Peter Dawson. We are left with Handel's splendid 'Water Music' and the 'Music for the Royal Fireworks' . . .

The River in Painting

Every weekend a party of painters turn out and paint the riverside at Wapping. It is seldom the prettiest stretches of the river that attract artists of today. In the seventeenth century it was the shipping that fascinated them. The Van de Veldes, father and son, brought to England by Charles I and given studios in the Queen's House at Greenwich, influenced all other marine painters. Canaletto, in the next century, left us pictures of the Thames at Westminster and Greenwich. J. M. W. Turner, born in Maiden Lane, London, had his first view of the river by the Savoy. Later he investigated the Thames Valley, often staying

Turner was much inspired by the Thames. His view of 'Richmond Hill, on the Prince Regent's Birthday', was exhibited at the Royal Academy in 1819

with his uncle at Brentford and at Sunningwell, near Abingdon; he sketched all round here, especially distant views of Oxford. He was a true Thamesman. His first drawing, exhibited at the Royal Academy in 1790, when he was only fifteen, was of 'The Archbishop's Palace at Lambeth'. He lived at several riverside addresses – Upper Mall in Hammersmith, Sion Ferry in Isleworth, Twickenham and Cheyne Walk, Chelsea – and made studies of Windsor Castle, Walton Bridge and 'Richmond Hill, on the Prince Regent's Birthday (1819)'. And in 1838, boating with friends, he saw the *Fighting Téméraire* being towed into a shipbuilder's yard at Rotherhithe to be broken up. One of his friends said, 'There's a fine picture, Turner!' It was, and is.

Constable sailed down to Gravesend in 1803 in the East Indiaman *Coutts*, trying to escape from his rural image; he also made several attempts to paint Waterloo Bridge, not very successfully. Both Constable and Turner, like good news photographers, were present with their sketchbooks at the burning of Parliament Buildings in 1834.

For Whistler, and the friend whose simple work he spoiled by imposing his own ideas on him, Walter Greaves, the river was at its most attractive at Chelsea in winter. Greaves, whose forte was naïve fidelity, used to say, 'To Mr Whistler a boat was a tone, but to me it was always a boat . . . Mr Whistler put his boats in wherever he wanted them, but we [Walter and his brother] left them just where they were.' Above all, the Thames was Greaves's whole life: 'I never seemed to have any ideas about painting. The river *made* me do it.' The son of a boat-builder, he has left us a wonderful record of the Victorian river, in snow and ice, lots of people, Battersea Bridge (the old rickety one which was replaced in the 1880s), and the last Chelsea Regatta which took place in 1871 before the Embankment spoiled the old waterfront.

Warehouses, Rotherhithe, Wapping, 'The Thames in Ice' (painted on Christmas Day 1860), etchings and oils: Whistler was seldom far from the river, which he translated into titles like 'Nocturne in Blue and Gold'. He said: 'And when the evening mist clothes the riverside with poetry, as with a veil, the poor buildings lose themselves in the dim sky, and the tall chimneys become *campanili*, and the warehouses are palaces in the night.'

For Alfred Sisley, in the 1870s, the Thames yielded clear riverscapes around Hampton Court, but for Claude Monet, who came here several times at the turn of the twentieth century, London smog was an obsession: it gave weird light effects and distortions which, since the Clean Air Act, no longer exist. His favourite subject was the Houses of Parliament seen from below Westminster Bridge. And Waterloo Bridge – why has it attracted so many foreign artists, Kokoschka among them? In 1903 Monet chose 'A Grey Day' to paint it. Monet, then being sixty-three and fairly comfortably off, stayed at the Savoy Hotel in London and there he painted the riverscape from his bedroom window.

For that strange genius Stanley Spencer the river, localized to Cookham, yielded Biblical characters for his religious paintings, and his swan uppers might have peopled Galilee.

Enjoying the River

Most people's first experience of Thames navigation is on board a pleasure steamer or launch; or, in the Upper Thames, in a rowing boat or canoe. (The punt is less universal than it used to be.) Alan Wykes, author of *An Eye on the Thames*, and his artist friend John Worsley used a land-or-water vehicle called an Amphicar: this is rare. Down the Estuary there used to be stately vessels with names like *Golden Sovereign* and *Royal Daffodil*, taking Londoners to such faraway places as Southend and Ramsgate. Up-river, the best-known name in pleasure-boats of all kinds is Salter's boatyard by Folly Bridge in Oxford. (There is a list of all boatyards along the Thames, and most amenities and items of information the Thames cruiser is likely to need, in Stanford's Map of the River Thames From Lechlade to Richmond.) Salter's, established in 1858, pioneered passenger travel on the river, and around 1900 was running a twice-a-day service from Oxford to Kingston and return. The voyage, which used to take two-and-a-half days each way, was discontinued in 1973. Today there are only smaller trip boats on sections of the river.

Not that Salter's was first in the field: as early as 1826 there were big pleasure-craft with bands on board plying between Queenhithe Dock (above Southwark Bridge) and Richmond. The first steamboat appeared in 1865, and until 1878 there was a regular service both upstream to Richmond, and below London Bridge to Gravesend and points east. But the *Princess Alice* disaster (*see* Woolwich) shook public confidence in the service. The London County Council's paddleboat service ('Penny Steamers') between Hammersmith and Greenwich looked promising, but eventually failed.

The exploitation of the Thames for pleasure grew spectacularly in the last thirty years of the nineteenth century – steamboats, punts, skiffs (especially those with awnings under which you can sleep, as Jerome and his friends did), and a proliferation of rowing clubs. The 1920s saw a trend towards cruiser-hiring or owning. At the end of World War II there were only about 1,900 pleasure craft on the river. In the next twenty-five years the total number of registered launches increased to more than 12,000. And today, if we can be guided by the throughput at Boulter's Lock, the total number of craft is over 19,000.

Inexperienced cruising people (I am among them) need advice on how to hire (or, if you can afford it, buy) a cruiser. A good first step is to contact the Chief Navigation Officer, at Thames Water (Nugent House, Vastern Road, Reading) or the Thames and Chilterns Tourist Board in Abingdon. Some things you will discover for yourself, such as the sex discrimination by which there are gentlemen's lavatories at *all* locks, but ladies' at only *some*. You probably also need advice on where to start from and where to go, bearing in mind that if you start from Kingston or Windsor, do not try to get beyond Oxford at the most, since you can only cruise at a certain speed, there are dozens of locks to get through, and your boat has to be returned within a certain time. If you are in a hurry, you shouldn't come on this sort of holiday at all.

A special word on punting. It was all the rage in Edwardian times ('spooning') and in the 'twenties and 'thirties ('heavy necking'), and has always been a feature of Oxbridge life; but, strangely, though so useful for seeking the peace of willow-fringed backwaters, it is less often seen on the Thames. Punting as a sport was put on the athletic map by the 1st Lord Desborough, greatest amateur punter of his day. He was also President of both the MCC and of the 1908 Olympic Games, and Chairman of Thames Conservancy from 1904 to 1937. He would have enjoyed a recent book, *Punts and Punting*, by R. T. Rivington, an Oxford bookseller. Mr Rivington goes deeply into postures, delicately relaxed fingers, and style. He says that there is a profound difference of style between Oxford and Cambridge: Oxford goes stern first, Cambridge bows first. And he reveals

Boulter's Lock, popular in the nineteenth century, is still a crowded spot on the river today

London's working river – 'View of Old London Bridge' by Claude de Jongh 1650, the only road across the Thames until 1738

that there is a club at each university for 'punters who have entered the river involuntarily fully clothed' – the Charon Club at Oxford, the Dampers at Cambridge.

Since pleasure is work, the Thames can be described, for most of its length, as a working river. But that is not what the Port of London means by the expression. Today, largely because of 'containerization', most of Dockland has moved downstream to Tilbury. But in Queen Anne's time, food, drink and timber were transported by water to London, and London sent back

Tyneside coal and imports from Europe all the way down the Thames and its tributaries below Oxford. Abingdon and Reading, centres of agriculture, sent farm produce to the capital. Until Westminster Bridge was built in 1738, London Bridge was the only road across the river. As we have seen from the life of John Taylor, boatmen and barges thronged the river, plying for hire. Between London Bridge and Westminster Stairs there were more than thirty landing places. The London River at this time gave employment to about 40,000 people.

As Nonconformist earnestness spread, it need not surprise us that in 1761 fines for bad language were instituted (half-a-crown per oath), and some twenty-five years later on a 'Society for Promoting Morality among Watermen' was formed — with a floating chapel!

As recently as the 1900s, barges still went up to Lechlade. Now the barge is almost extinct, and splendid old sailing barges are kept alive by the sort of enthusiast who cherishes vintage cars. The last considerable barge-owner, affectionately known as 'Mother Thames', died in 1974 aged (it is believed) over eighty. Dorothea Woodward-Fisher, educated at Cheltenham Ladies' College, married a Thames Waterman named Billy, bringing as her dowry a forty-foot barge. Together they built up a fleet of more than a hundred barges and a dozen tugs. Then came the 'container revolution . . .'

There is always a lobby for 'using the river'. Alan Herbert spent half a lifetime promoting the idea of Thames water-buses, driving down to the House of Commons from Hammersmith in his own launch to make his point. In the early 1970s the Greater London Council subsidized a 'commuting by water' experiment with hydrofoils — Greenwich to the Tower in ten minutes, Greenwich to Westminster in fifteen minutes, with a 'request stop' at Charing Cross. But the idea was abandoned for the speed spoiled the journey, and bad weather caused delays.

Cleaning the River

'Filthy river, filthy river, Foul from London to the Nore!' sang *Punch* in 1858. This was the year of the Great Stink, when what were referred to in Parliamentary language as 'noisome effluvia' from the river made sessions of both Lords and Commons intolerable; so bad was the smell that curtains soaked in disinfectant had to be hung over the windows. The following year, *The Oarsman's Guide* complained furiously: 'The enormous traffic of London, its increased dirt . . . its sewage, coal-smoke and coal gas, tiers of barges and steamboat piers, have done

their work; but not so the Corporation of London . . . Fishes, wiser in their generation than ourselves, have forsaken in disgust a medium which in these latitudes has long since ceased to be a definite element . . . Odours that speak aloud stalk over the face of the so-called "waters". The Avernus of the Fleet Ditch find articulate echo in the Cocytus of the great Effra Sewer . . .'

Cholera epidemics hit London every few years; London's drainage was either by cesspool or by direct discharge into the river and its tributaries; and in 1861 the Prince Consort was to die of typhoid fever caused, it was believed, by defective sewage disposal at Windsor Castle. But help — slowly — was on the way, in the shape of Sir Joseph Bazalgette, creator of London's modern sewage system. (He also built the Thames Embankment and designed Hammersmith Bridge.) The immediate results of his work could be seen in 1867, when a Master Fishmonger wrote to *The Times* (11 May): 'As a proof of the improved condition of the Thames I beg to inform you that a fine, well-conditioned sturgeon, upwards of 60 lb weight, was caught this morning at Westminster Bridge, and is now alive in a tank in my shop.' Pollution is a recurring problem in the river and needs the strict regulation which the Thames now has.

In 1856 the Corporation of London, lacking the money for its huge responsibilities along the river, said it could no longer shoulder them alone. So 1857 saw the formation of Thames Conservancy to control the river between Staines and Yantlet Creek, at the mouth of the Medway near a marsh known as Bishop Ooze. Nine years later the old Commissioners, 600 of them, who since 1770 had administered the Thames to within a few miles of its source, abolished themselves and their powers were transferred to Thames Conservancy. Today the supreme controlling body is the Thames Water Authority, which took over the Thames Conservancy as a Division in April 1974, and in April 1982 this Division finally disappeared. Nevertheless the work of the pioneering Commissioners and the conscientious

Conservators (Alan Herbert was one of them) should always be remembered. The Golden Age of the Conservators was probably in the reign of Lord Desborough (1904–37), whose punting prowess we have already noted. In addition to his innumerable sporting achievements with oar and punt-pole, he rowed in two Boat Races, and twice swam the pool below Niagara Falls – the second time to convince journalists that he had done it the first time. He is commemorated by the Desborough Cut near Weybridge, a channel dug below Shepperton Lock.

In the early 1960s there was still a faint 'bad-eggs' smell from Westminister to Woolwich; and ten years before that, ships painted white for the Festival of Britain began to blacken as hydrogen sulphide attacked their lead-painted hulls. Today, the Chairman of Thames Water can claim with pride that 'we may now look upon a river which is perhaps the cleanest metropolitan estuary in the world.' The credit is due to many bodies and people besides the Authority, whose present Chief Executive, named Hugh Fish, is a water chemist of vast experience. 'In the 1950s', the Chairman says, 'the river was completely devoid of oxygen, and fish put into the water would literally choke to death.' (New detergents and what was called 'industrial effluent' were partly to blame.) 'Today we have over ninety species recorded in the Tideway and more are confidently predicted.'

River management necessitates interfering with the river's natural courses so that it carries the right amount of water. Ditches and streams must be straightened and cleared. Obstructions and silt must be removed to help navigation. Locks and weirs need maintenance. For most of us, drinking and household water comes from rivers – about 1,000 million gallons a day are taken from the Thames, and each of us uses on average 35 gallons a day. We make water dirty, so it is then cleaned in sewage treatment works; every day Thames Water pours back 940 million gallons of 'cleaned effluent' into its rivers. Solid sewage, called sludge, is treated to remove harmful substances and then either used as fertilizer (called Thamesgrow) or dumped at sea: a favoured place for this is Barrow Deep, in the Estuary. It is not easy to define 'pure water', but a lot depends on how much oxygen it contains: oxygen promotes useful bacteria and enables fish and plants to breathe.

No water is taken from the Thames below Teddington Weir; beyond this point the river is tidal and mixes with sea water. At various points along the river you will notice reservoirs, especially around Staines: the total storage capacity of Thames region reservoirs is about 54,000 million gallons. This guards against drought. All the way along the line, water samples are taken and tested in Thames Water's quality control laboratories.

If you are managing a river, you are managing everything that happens on or beside it: water sports, navigation, angling, sailing (you can sail on seven of the Authority's reservoirs). More than 500,000 fishermen use the Thames, and one of Thames Water's tasks is to maintain, restock and develop fisheries. It runs fish nurseries to supply fish for restocking. In the tidal Thames there are now nearly one hundred species of fish – also exotic visitors (nobody seems quite sure how they got there) like the seahorse and the Chinese Mitten crab. The return of edible fish such as salmon and trout, helped by fish nurseries, has now happened. The last time a salmon was landed by rod and line from the Thames was in 1833. The Thames may not be as clear as the Dee or the Wye, but it was a proud day (30 July 1982) when Mr Hugh Fish was able to announce that twenty salmon had been caught (electronically) from the Thames at Molesey Weir pool near Hampton Court in the last three days. And in that year a competition was held to catch the first live salmon in the river.

You must observe Thames Water by-laws about fishing: there are eighteen of them, followed by notes – about reporting all catches of salmon and trout, about close seasons, the kinds of bait you must use, the precise dimensions of undersized fish, and special rules about eels and crayfish.

The Frost Fair on the Thames in 1683, by Jan Griffier the Elder

The return of fish to the river, by pollution control, has also meant the return of the fish-eating birds. This has been recognized as wildfowl conservation of international importance. The most spectacular riverside areas are below Barking Creek with mallard, shelduck, pintail, lapwing, and in the marshes near Gravesend, teal, widgeon, ringed plover and redshank. By Bow Creek, attracted by a grain wharf, there is a flock of 345 swans.

Thames Water considers it has a responsibility for the behaviour and good manners of river users. They are: people in private cruisers and hired craft, yachtsmen, oarsmen, canoeists, swimmers and sub-aqua people, fishermen, walkers, campers, naturalists and the wildlife they are observing. They all threaten to hinder each other. Boating and fishing in particular can cause extreme hostility, hence rules like 'don't steer through fishing lines', and 'cruising speed should not exceed walking pace'. All these points – most of them based on commonsense safety – are summed up in the useful booklet called the *Thames River Users' Code*.

The Port of London

In 1909 the Port of London Authority (P.L.A.) was created to take over from Thames Conservancy the whole administration of the tidal river below Teddington – in effect, 95 miles of water. Despite the decay in the twentieth century of Dockland below Tower Bridge, London is still Britain's biggest port, especially for timber, pulp and paper, bulk wine and grain imports. The London Docklands Development Corporation was set up in 1981 to coordinate the development of 2,000 hectares of dockland. The West India and Millwall Docks, on the Isle of Dogs, are to be given a special status as an Enterprise Zone.

The Port deals with about 1,000 ships a week. The P.L.A.'s Thames Navigation Service uses radar, radio and tide gauges and has stations at Gravesend, Woolwich Reach and Warden Point on the Isle of Sheppey. There are VHF broadcasts to all shipping every half-hour, and a Hydrographic Service monitors water-depths which are maintained by dredgers.

The river can also be a dangerous enemy. Hence the Greater London Council's great Barrier, which spans 1,700 feet across Woolwich Reach at Silvertown – the world's largest movable flood barrier. It consists of a series of enormous steel gates between concrete piers which house the hydraulic lifting machinery. Under normal conditions the gates lie in the river bed so that shipping can pass above them. But in the event of a 'surge tide' from the North Sea, the Barrier can be closed within thirty minutes of a 'surge' warning, turning the gates through 90 degrees so that they stand 52 feet above the river bed.

London has been sinking for 2,000 years, and it is a miracle that it has survived all the Thames floods so far. (Rufus, Lord Noel-Buxton, discovered this in the 1950s when, attempting to wade the river by Westminster to show that it had once been fordable, he was compelled, despite his 6 feet 3 inches height to swim for a few yards in mid-stream.) On 6 June 1972 Mr Christopher Tugendhat, M.P. for the Cities of London and Westminster, rose in the House of Commons to say that 45 square miles of London (and the lives of 800,000 people) were at risk because they all lived on ground lower than the river's highest recorded level. Only the top floors of Buckingham Palace would escape, said another Member, and the London Underground would be inundated. 'We have a 1-in-30 chance of being drowned during one of our debates!' Mr Tugendhat said dramatically. Mr Wellbeloved, Labour M.P. for Erith and Crayford, added that 'London's dream town of Thamesmead' was being, but should not be, built on Erith Marshes, which were known to be at risk.

There were floods in 1894, 1915, 1928, 1929, 1947, 1953, and 1963. In January 1928 lives were lost in Rotherhithe and Pimlico, and there was 6 feet of water in A.P. Herbert's Hammersmith basement. The disastrous floods of 1953 were due to a combination of a surge tide in the North Sea, a higher spring tide up the river, and land water (swollen by snow and rain) from tributaries. On the 8,000 devastated acres of Canvey Island, Essex, 58 people were drowned, many of them in their own homes: others were rescued by a 'Dunkirk fleet' of small boats.

These dangers had been foreseen centuries before. In December 1663, Pepys tells us, 'all Whitehall drowned'; and among many flood-prevention plans was that of Herbert Spencer, the Victorian philosopher, who – being by profession a civil engineer – designed a barrage with locks for the tidal control of the whole river.

The Thames used to freeze almost as often as it flooded. When Old London Bridge was the only road across the river its narrow arches obstructed its flow. There were Frost Fairs in 1683, 1698, and 1740: Evelyn tells us that coaches and horses were driven on the ice by Temple Stairs. (The same thing happened at Oxford in 1895 when a coach and six paraded up and down by the college barges below Folly Bridge.) That year, too, the

The lock-keeper's cottage and garden at Bray Lock. There is keen competition among lock-keepers to have the best-kept garden

breaking ice smashed barges in the Pool of London and the wreck-fragments floated down the Estuary. The Frost Fair of 1814 was the most elaborate on record. It was held between Blackfriars and London Bridges. Whole sheep were roasted. There was dancing, and huge fires were lit to keep people warm. There were skittles and gambling games; and as if to offset all this frivolity, there were printing presses running off souvenir copies of poems and the Lord's Prayer. On Saturday, 5 February, the thaw began, the fires sank hissing into the water, and some people were drowned.

For centuries people have wanted to develop the Thames, alter it, make it more spectacular, more enjoyable. (Lovers of the Upper Thames tend to feel that any change would be destructive.) Sir John Soane, in the early years of the nineteenth century, designed a Corinthian Triumphal Bridge across the river, to celebrate the British victory over Napoleon: it was to have been where Lambeth Bridge now is. Someone else wanted to build a railway (suspended) down the middle of the Thames. In the 1980s there is a scheme for a new Thames bridge carrying shops and offices, flats and pubs. It is designed by Richard Seifert and Partners, and would link London Bridge Station to the City, would be half as wide as it is long, and its amenities would include 'an 80-foot high suspended atrium with a skating rink'. Cost: escalating from £200 million. Material: mirror glass, like hundreds of diamonds joined together.

A new 1,200-foot bridge, at a height of more than 150 feet, from Beckton to Thamesmead, 11 miles downstream from London Bridge, is planned as a contribution to the national road network. Alternatively, a third under-river tunnel at roughly the same place . . .

Simpler, more down to earth, and certainly nearer to the heart's desire, are plans like the Thames National Park, inspired by the 1949 National Parks and Access to Countryside Act and

HMS *Belfast*, a veteran of World War II, lies beside London Bridge; she is now a floating naval museum

promoted by the photographer and writer about the river, Eric de Maré, and others, including Sir Alan Herbert. This was sometimes known as the Thames Linear Park, which was to contain a continuous 135-mile riverside walk all the way from Teddington to Cricklade. There are a number of conflicting reasons (many of them financial) why it has never been possible to realize this ideal completely; one of them is that the towpath is sometimes interrupted, and changes to the other side of the river. It is increasingly difficult to follow the towpath now that most of the ferries have disappeared. There is also a stretch, within sight of Windsor Castle, where for the Royal Family's security you must make a 1½-mile detour through Datchet.

Problems like these are very much the concern of the River Thames Society and the Ramblers' Association, who have for some years been trying to persuade the Countryside Commission (successors to the National Parks Commission) to adopt a Thames Walk as part of their official policy. So far they have not done so; but enthusiasts for the scheme have been greatly encouraged, since 1980, by the Thames Water Authority's 'general support, in broad principle, to the concept of a continuous Thames Walk'.

We are almost ready to start our journey down the Thames from Source to Estuary. I choose this way because rivers do not flow backwards, and I am a man who temperamentally wants to begin with peace and solitude and end among the human throng, and what A. P. Herbert, in his description of Gravesend Reach, calls 'the beauty peculiar to business on the water'. Others choose the opposite way: I shall not attempt to read anything womb-seeking or Freudian into this. After all, you have got to come back again! Do not look to me for advice on boatmanship, on which I am not an expert (there is an admirable body of specialist literature on it). Since cruising speed is not supposed to exceed walking pace, we shall have plenty of time for observation; and so it would be well to take with us a few books on plants, birds and natural history generally — for it is probable you will see kinds of dragonfly you have never seen before. (Why did that fool Swinburne say rivers were weary and found safety only in the sea? The sea is never safe, and rivers are alert things teeming with life.)

There are birds to see too (again, I am no expert): sandpipers in summer, snipe in winter; courtship of the crested grebe, if you're lucky and swans, of course. We have seen how a cleaner river has attracted new bird-life to Dockland: the old Surrey and Commercial Docks are now infested with ornithologists (and botanists too). Skylarks and goldfinches have been seen around Beckton gasworks. Ducks, of course, some of them rather cantankerous, but able to lose their dignity in a second (think of Kenneth Grahame's Ducks' Ditty, 'Up tails all!'). Moorhen and coot – you can confuse the two – the coot is charming but ruthless about raiding grebe's eggs. In the Middle and Upper Thames, large flocks of Canada geese, and heron. Among the reeds, sedge and reed warblers. Kingfisher – not common, yet not so timid as he is made out to be; he lives often in a disused vole-hole (Ratty, in *The Wind in the Willows*, is more than likely a vole).

Plants – in the water and on the banks. Willowherb and purple loosestrife (believed anciently to have the power of 'taking away strife or debate between beasts') everyone can recognize. There may not be quite so many species as when Mr and Mrs S. C. Hall came down the river more than 120 years ago and wrote their classic *Book of the Thames* in 1859 (the year after the Great Stink), but many survive. Nor are there quite so many water-lilies as when Charles Dickens, about the same time, wrote to Angela Burdett-Coutts: 'The rowing down from Oxford to Reading, on the Thames, is more charming than one can describe in words. I rowed down last June, through miles upon miles of water-lilies, lying on the water close together, like a fairy pavement.'

The Halls noted American weed which chokes rivers unless it is controlled; the arrowhead whose bulbs, we are told, are eaten in China; purple and white flowering rushes; and ivy-leaved snapdragons 'on the walls of old locks' (the Halls noticed *everything*); persicaria, with floating green and red leaves and pink flowers; and the purple-flowered meadow cranes-bill. You will discover many others.

One thing remains to be done which should perhaps have been done at the beginning: to tell how the Thames gets its name (in the next chapter we shall see that there is a case for calling it the Churn). Tam, Tame, Team, Teme, Thame, Tamar all these are names of English rivers, and the philologist Eilert Ekwall, the great authority on place names, connects it with the Sanskrit word *tamasa*, which is also the name of a tributary of the Ganges. It means 'dark river'. Whatever the Ancient Britons called our river, the Romans pronounced it *Tamesis*, which is how it appears in Julius Caesar's *De Bello Gallico*. In Anglo-Saxon documents the name is Temes, and during Norman times an H crept in and the first vowel became *a*. When did the custom of using the name Isis to denote the section of river below Oxford begin? It isn't just an Oxford fad. We find a fourteenth-century historian Ranulf Higden, in his *Polychronicon*, also calling the mainstream Isis and the source Thames. The statute of James I setting up the Oxford-Burcot Commission (1605) regulating navigation writes about 'river of Thames'; but a statute of George II (1751) calls it Isis again.

Who (you may well ask) cares? Scholars do; and some others have introduced a fresh red herring by referring to the river as the Isis all the way down to Dorchester, where it is joined by a tributary confusingly called the Thame. And Dorchester is mostly on the Thame, not the Thames. Very unscholarly is the attempt to derive Caesar's *Tamesis* from Thame-Isis. Isis has nothing to do with the Egyptian goddess: it makes more sense to derive it (like Ouse, Usk, Exe) from the Celtic *uisge* meaning water, as in *uisge beatha* (whisky). Let our verdict be that Caesar, and to some extent Higden, were right; and hurry on to the river's Source.

CHAPTER TWO

The Infant Thames

'Is this little wet ditch the Historical Thames?' asks a character in an H. G. Wells novel, looking incredulously at an undignified dribble in a Gloucestershire meadow. We are standing in Trewsbury Mead, 3½ miles southwest of Cirencester. In a dry summer the dribble disappears.

We know this is the Thames because a block of stone marks the spot, and there is also an ash tree two centuries old inscribed with the letters T.H. for 'Thames Head'. Until 1974 a statue of Old Father Thames stood here, surrounded by railings to protect him from graffiti. But vandals laugh at railings, and Father Thames had to be removed to St John's Lock, below

The statue of Old Father Thames at St John's Lock — vandals caused him to be moved from the Source at Thames Head

Lechlade. At Trewsbury he used to stare out from behind the railings, rather crossly, as if meditating escape. He had been there since 1958, when the Conservators of the River Thames (the inscription tells us) wished to 'mark the Source' as well as their own centenary, and also to settle for ever the ancient dispute about the real source. The 3-ton sculpture was given by Mr H. Scott Freeman, one of the Conservators; it also bore the name of the then Chairman of the Conservators, Mr Jocelyn Bray, D.L., J.P.

For many years Old Father Thames lived at the Crystal Palace, until 1936, when that splendid symphony in glass was gutted by fire. The London County Council then sold him to the Honourable Michael Berry, son of Lord Camrose, the newspaper proprietor, for his garden at Whitchurch, near Aylesbury. From here he was acquired by the philanthropic Mr Scott Freeman.

For centuries there was a well nearby, and romantic lovers of the river (such as the late Sir Alan Herbert, who wrote a poem on the Source) liked to imagine the Romans coming down from their camp at nearby Trewsbury Castle to fill their ewers. Sir Alan also planned to glorify the 'little wet ditch' with an ambitious 'Thames Head Park'.

The Source is not particularly easy to find. We shall do well to begin at the Thames Head Inn (formerly the Railway Inn) where we may as well refresh ourselves for the first part of our downstream journey, which must be on foot. Approaching from Cirencester along the A429, we follow the Fosse Way, part of the Roman road system connecting Lincoln, Leicester, Bath and Exeter.

The pub is about 1 mile west of the Thames Head Bridge, where the streamlet flows under Fosse Way (which has now branched out to the right and become the A433). I am nervous

Seven Springs, at Coberley, is often thought to be the source of the Thames; it is instead the source of the Churn, a tributary

about giving too precise instructions on how to find the Source because it is too easy to mislead people (as I was misled myself on my first visit). The safest policy is to ask at the pub unless you are very good with large-scale Ordnance Survey maps. You will find the Source at the end of a path in a tree-sheltered hollow. Just behind you will see the embankment of the old disused Thames and Severn Canal.

Before starting our downstream journey, it is our duty to examine the *other* source of the Thames, 15 miles north, about 3 miles out of Cheltenham, at Seven Springs. Take the A435 north from Cirencester (it bends as it follows the river Churn) to Coberley, and turn left onto the A436. Soon you come to a lay-by and below this a steep hollow with a pool watered by several springs, marked by a stone bearing a superior Latin inscription: *Hic Tuus O Tamesine Pater Septemgeminus Fons*

('Here, O Father Thames, is Thy Sevenfold Source'). To be honest, it does look rather more like the start of a great river than Trewsbury Mead, and it does not dry up in summer.

Back in 1937, when the nation might have been expected to concentrate its worries on Hitler, the Spanish Civil War and the imminent Coronation of the unexpected George VI, there was a gentlemanly altercation in the House of Commons about this place. Barbed yet not without schoolboy giggles, it was conducted in rather more elegant prose than the House enjoys today. On 25 February the Member for Stroud (Glos.), a Mr Perkins, asked that in the next Ordnance Survey Seven Springs should be recognized as the true source of the Thames. His stonewalling opponent, Mr W. S. Morrison, Minister of Agriculture was M.P. for Cirencester and Tewkesbury and knew the terrain well. It was, Mr Morrison said, 'not an invariable rule in geographical practice to regard as the source of a large river the source of the tributary most distant from its estuary.' (*Laughter*).

MR PERKINS: 'Is my right Hon. friend aware that the source known as Thames Head periodically dries up?'

AN HON. MEMBER: 'Why don't you?'

MR PERKINS: '. . . as in 1935, for instance?'

MR MORRISON: 'That does not alter my view that the river Thames rises in *my* constituency.' (*Laughter*).

LORD APSLEY (Bristol Central): 'Probably the real Thames is a stream known as the Swill Brook, which rises in the constituency of the Hon. Member for Chippenham (Wilts.), Captain Cazalet.'

Against Mr Perkins it was argued that Seven Springs was the source of the Churn, not the Thames. The Churn had always (or anyway since Roman times) been known as the Churn, or something like it. It had given its name to Corinium, now Cirencester, and to the villages of North and South Cerney. Two thousand years of history would have had to be rewritten, and the same number of maps redrawn if Mr Perkins had had his way. He fought heroically, but lost.

So let us stick to tradition, and accept the statement of John Leland, the sixteenth-century topographer, that 'Isis riseth at three miles from Cirencester, not far from a village called Kemble, within half a mile of the Fosseway, where the very head of Isis is.'

We are back at Trewsbury Mead, looking for that trickle of mud among the harebells, clovers and vetches. Preferably in gum-boots, we can track it ½ mile or so towards Kemble, which it bypasses, and Ewen (the name itself means 'spring' or 'source') where the stream is already 3 feet wide.

Do not attempt this journey in winter when the fields tend to be flooded. There is much to be said for cheating, and going by car to meet the river in one of the villages, such as Somerford Keynes, 4 miles from the Source – it is here that the first footpath begins, and where the first ford crosses the river. Between Poole Keynes and Somerford Keynes the stream divides, comes together again, and sometimes almost disappears. Here the river is rich in, indeed almost choked by, bulrushes. At Ashton Keynes, 2½ miles below Somerford, the river, now 9 feet wide, flows past some twenty houses each of which has its own bridge (of stone, brick or wood) across the water to the lane. (Yet even here the stream is occasionally reduced to a bed of damp pebbles.) Soon we are joined, on the right, by Swill Brook, the product of many streams; and the Thames begins to be a serious river. But still its fields are subject to flooding in winter, and at Waterhay Bridge (just before Cricklade) you might not know that a river is there.

Cricklade is the first township on the Thames, with little more than 2,000 people, and the first point at which the river becomes truly navigable, at least for canoes and punts. Before and after the town we are joined by numerous tributary streams. Some with names, like the Churn (on the left), Derry Brook, the Ray, and the Key, others anonymous even on the Ordnance Survey Map. We can therefore understand the bewilderment of Daniel Defoe, who came here in 1724 and reported that 'we very remarkably crossed four rivers . . . and the country people called them every one the Thames.' We are now, by the way, in Wiltshire, which we entered just below Kemble. Pre-Roman Ermine Street (the A419 from Cirencester to Swindon) crosses the river at Cricklade, which was forded in AD 878 by Alfred the Great in his war with Guthrum, King of East Anglia. This was probably the westernmost point in England to be penetrated by the Vikings.

The next 11½ miles, to Lechlade, show the Upper Thames at its most peaceful, not to say sleepy. By now our eyes are accustomed to the colours of the country, the yellows of cinquefoil, ragwort and wild mustard, deep blue of bugle, white meadowsweet, mauve and purple of willowherb and loosestrife. There is still no towpath (nor any need for one), and at times the river bank is so high that if you are in a boat you must tie it up and climb out to see over the top. On the right is Castle Eaton, and on the left, 1 mile beyond, is Kempsford with its fat church tower. The Thames here is 21 feet wide; hardly a cottage to be seen; meadows, willows, hawthorn hedges come right down to the water, all put there by agricultural man, yet populated only by cows.

Other creatures we may see now are the shy vole or water-rat, the mallard duck and the moorhen. If you spot the blue-green flash of a kingfisher, write to *The Times* about it. It is supposed to be a timid bird; yet Robert Gibbings, engraver, author of two of the most beguiling books on the Thames, swore that a kingfisher perched on the end of his fishing rod, waiting to steal his catch. If you see an otter, no one will believe you: there are only about 300 or so left in Britain, and none has been seen here for many years.

A mile above Lechlade, Inglesham Church can be seen in the trees on the right; and from the left the river Coln enters the Thames after its 20-mile journey from the Cotswolds, taking in on the way Bibury (one of the contenders for 'the most beautiful village in England') and the comely country town of Fairford.

Kempsford's fine perpendicular church tower was built by John of Gaunt in 1390 as a tribute to his first wife

The Coln, like the Churn, is best explored by canoe. Near here, too, is a channel to the now disused Thames and Severn Canal (we saw a bit of it at Thames Head): a canal bridge, a wooden footbridge and a cottage which was once a stable for barge-horses, and many poplars and willows point the way. Canals can be as beautiful as rivers. If you decide to explore it on foot, a walk of $2\frac{1}{2}$ miles brings you to Sapperton Tunnel, one of the engineering wonders of 1789 when the Canal was opened.

Four counties meet at Lechlade (Berkshire, Oxfordshire, Wiltshire and Gloucestershire), but the town itself is in Gloucestershire. Here we may expect to see the first motorboats, usually small cabin cruisers, for above Lechlade the river is only 2 feet deep. Here it starts to matter whether you fall in the water, and cruising families should adopt the discipline of wearing life-jackets. You will want to explore Lechlade, for it is the very expression of rural England. Meanwhile, study Halfpenny Bridge, a humpback bridge built in 1792 to replace a ferry and to make way for the voluminous traffic expected at Lechlade Wharf from the new Thames and Severn Canal. It was a toll bridge until 1839 (you can see the toll house at one end of it) and acquired its name because a halfpenny was the standard charge for a human being, while an animal cost a penny. Robert Gibbings, who sailed down the Thames in 1939, was puzzled by the bridge's unbevelled keystone: how did it stay in position? By faith? By friction? I leave the problem to civil engineers.

Just below Lechlade Bridge the river Cole (distinguish this from the Coln) enters from the right, and within $\frac{1}{2}$ mile we are at St John's Lock. This first lock of the downstream still has its paddles raised by a windlass which is operated by an L-shaped iron handle. Plenty of moorings hereabouts, and a good pub, the Trout, in the backwater below St John's Bridge (narrow — approach gingerly). It is the first of several Trout Inns on the Thames: it was called the St John the Baptist's Head until 1704. A medieval hospital once stood here, then a priory, and later a workhouse. The remains of the priory (and its well and fish-pond) can still be seen. The foundations of the bridge are thirteenth-century, but the superstructure is Victorian.

Just before you enter St John's Lock (where Old Father Thames now sits, safe from vandals), look back at Lechlade in the distance. I promised, at the beginning of this book, that I would never use the words *picturesque*, *pretty* and *charming*. How then am I to describe this view, whose composition is held together by the focus of the church spire? The answer is, I cannot: it is one of the great healing sights of England, full of a peace we can usually only imagine, seen across grazing fields.

We are now entering Oxfordshire. The river Leach or Lech, from which Lechlade obviously takes its name, enters from the left, about 15 miles from its Gloucestershire source. The Thames now bends southeast, and 1 mile further on is Buscot Lock. You may have to work this yourself: its paddles are lifted by geared wheels, and the gates are self-closing. Buscot, like other Upper Thames places, was once an important inland wharf, specializing in the transport of cheese. You will probably want to visit the village ($\frac{1}{2}$ mile) and also Buscot Park ($1\frac{1}{2}$ miles), the mansion owned by the National Trust, on the right bank.

Another $1\frac{1}{2}$ miles brings us (on our left) to Kelmscot, with good moorings, shops and pubs — the one on the river is the Anchor, standing in mid-stream among trees on the site of the last of the primitive 'flash locks' which disappeared in 1936. Cross the footbridge to visit Kelmscott Manor, the home of William Morris from 1871 to 1896, and now cared for by the Morris Society.

The towpath is now on the left bank. On the opposite side we can see, among several farms, the hamlet of Eaton Hastings, just before we reach Grafton Lock. A further mile brings us to Radcot Bridge (single-arched) which, we are advised by experts, is 'possibly the most hazardous on the river, being very narrow and set at an angle' — both current and wind can take you by surprise. What is claimed to be the oldest bridge on the river (it

The Trout Inn beside Tadpole Bridge near Bampton

crosses the backwater here) has a stone socket which used to hold a cross: bridges in medieval times were blessed, being built as much for the glory of God as for the convenience of the public. The other bridge, built in 1787 when a new cut was dug in expectation of increased traffic from the Thames and Severn Canal, is marked for miles around by two dramatic poplars.

Radcot, which was also a key point in one phase of the Civil War, is a convenient place from which to visit Faringdon, $2\frac{1}{2}$ miles away on the right bank. Radcot has a good inn, the Swan, whose exhibits of stuffed fish show that it is favoured by anglers. It is difficult to imagine that this tiny place, with its boatyard, was the wharf from which Cotswold stone was shipped to build St Paul's Cathedral in London. After $\frac{1}{2}$ mile comes Radcot Lock and Weir.

Sharney Brook goes off to the left: it will return at Rushey Lock, where it connects with Great Brook, which eventually rejoins the river at Shifford. We pass under Old Man's Bridge.

This is a typical strongly built footbridge of which there are many on the Thames, of a pleasing functional design which enhances the view. Burroway Brook leads off to the left and returns $\frac{1}{2}$ mile later.

The countryside is now of a flatness which makes one welcome a prosaic landmark coming up on the left, the masts of Bampton radio station. After Rushey Lock (notice the lock-keeper's fine, possibly prize-winning, garden and his sturdy 1896 cottage) the towpath, which crossed to the right bank at Radcot, now returns to the left. (Towpaths keep changing sides because of ancient landowning rights.) Now that there are no regular ferries across the Thames, these changes are a great nuisance to walkers.

Tadpole Bridge, whose single wide stone arch was built in 1802, welcomes you at another Trout Inn, where you can obtain permission to fish. Its bar used to boast a stuffed freak trout with teeth in its tongue. Bampton, 2 miles away on the left, is a sleepy, largely eighteenth-century, market town relatively unspoiled by traffic, and Tadpole Bridge is the place to disembark for it.

Tenfoot (timber) Bridge is 2 miles on. Here, on the right, the terrain changes and the Berkshire Downs come into view. You cannot fail to notice a new landmark, Faringdon Clump with its tall (140 feet) folly, a brick tower built by the eccentric Lord Berners in 1936 (to a design by the 8th Duke of Wellington) with the laudable object of providing work for the unemployed and to house his own body when he died – stuffed and sitting at a piano. Today these benevolent men would probably be refused planning permission. Still on the right, we can see, on the Downs, Buckland House (*circa* 1760), built in stone by John Wood the Younger, who designed the famous Royal Crescent at Bath.

As we approach Shifford Lock through tall willows, the hamlet of Chimney (two or three houses and a farm) is on the left, and the weir stream flows to the right (it is navigable by small boats for about $\frac{1}{2}$ mile to Duxford village). Shifford means simply 'sheep ford' and the ford is still there today. This is the youngest lock on the Thames, built in 1898; and also the loneliest. So isolated is it that the lock-keeper, whose cottage is on an island, has to walk $1\frac{1}{4}$ miles along a path to Chimney Farm to collect his milk and groceries and $2\frac{1}{2}$ miles to Cote village or Aston to do his shopping or post a letter. (His coal supplies, however, are brought by water.) This remoteness has its attractions for the holiday cruiser, who, in the cut above Shifford Lock, will find himself among trees in a silence which, except for birdsong, is total.

Is it conceivable, as certain ancient historians claim, that this spot was once a Royal Borough, with sixteen churches and at least as many taverns? That King Alfred held his first parliament here? Today Shifford consists of a handful of cottages, a farm and a tiny Victorian church on the site reputed to be of a thanksgiving monument set up by Alfred. Equally difficult to imagine is the warfare that once raged along the Upper Thames: the Civil War saw battles, or at least skirmishes, at Radcot, Faringdon, Bampton and Newbridge, all subservient to the two big battles at Edgehill and Newbury, only 25 miles away.

Half a mile past Shifford village, on the right, we are within sight of Harrowdown Hill (only 325 feet high, but looks higher); it is the last hill we shall see for several miles as the Berkshire Downs recede behind us. Past a couple of farms on the right, and Standlake Common on the left, we reach Newbridge; but a few yards before we do, the river Windrush joins from the left. You can, if you are so minded, canoe for 21 miles up the Windrush, past Witney and Burford to Bourton-on-the-Water in Gloucestershire, where the stream is 30 feet wide and only 6 inches deep.

OPPOSITE The church of St Lawrence at Lechlade can be seen across the water-meadows for many miles
OVERLEAF Kelmscott Manor was the home of William Morris; it has been carefully restored to preserve it as it was in his lifetime

The six-arched bridge at Newbridge (another contender for 'the oldest bridge on the Thames') is thought to be of mid-thirteenth-century foundation, rebuilt in the fifteenth century and repaired in 1801. Much of the old stonework bears the scars of 700 years of weather. The arches (cruisers should use the two middle ones) are pointed and ribbed, and the piers act both as 'cutwaters' and as V-shaped niches for pedestrians to avoid the traffic and to stand and stare at the river. Newbridge was captured by Cromwell in 1644 in a battle which forced the King, with his headquarters at Oxford, to retreat north.

The bridge carries the A415 from Witney to Abingdon. Standlake is 1 mile to the north. The charm of Newbridge is that there is really nothing there but the bridge and two famous pubs, the Rose Revived (left bank) and the May Bush (right bank). The former, rebuilt in Cotswold stone, is nowadays more of an hotel, from whose quiet terrace you can sit and watch the river-life.

We are now 8 miles from Oxford, as the crow flies. We are, thank God, not crows, and by keeping to the water we have another 11 miles to Folly Bridge. The country is flat and agricultural again, and we observe that the towpath, which from Duxford weir stream to Newbridge changed to the right bank, has returned to the left. We pass under the footbridge that marks the old Hart's Weir, where there was once a flash lock: on the right you can still see the thatched roof of the keeper's cottage. This is the beginning of Matthew Arnold's 'stripling Thames'. It may appear, to foreign eyes, too flat and uneventful: Eric de Maré, in one of his books on the river, believes that we have to be *taught* by poets and painters how to love this type of scenery. All manmade, drained, hedged and farmed, it has that rich quality of peace and 'cosiness' which the German word

Gemütlichkeit only approximates and the French *confortablement* gets nowhere near.

Hart's Weir was also known as Rudge's Weir. Generations of Rudges and Harts have served the river, and in 1766 Betty Rudge, daughter of the ferryman at Bablockhythe, was spotted there by young Lord Ashbrook, an undergraduate of Christ Church College, Oxford, who had come there to fish. He courted Betty, and had her educated, and married her — a socially almost impossible alliance in those days — and one of her grand-daughters married a Duke of Marlborough. When Ashbrook died in 1784, Betty married a theologian, Dr John Jones of Jesus College. If you hear church bells across the meadow on the left striking the hour, they certainly come from Northmoor Church where Betty Rudge was married. Northmoor village (1 mile) is best approached from Newbridge as there is no road from the lock.

At Northmoor Lock, almost as remote as Shifford, there are good moorings. The village of Appleton (which has a good pub called the Thatched Tavern) is 1 mile away on the right side. The river banks are now wooded. Bablockhythe, 1½ miles farther on, is today not quite as Matthew Arnold (or Betty Rudge) saw it. The Thames still 'stripples' here, and, set about by poplars, it does indeed appear narrow; but the scene is rather spoiled by houses and caravans and car parks. The old chain ferry has not functioned since 1965, to the relief of cruisers that used to be delayed by it. The Chequers Inn and the Ferry Inn provide good refreshment; and if you go ashore, Stanton Harcourt and Cumnor are within easy walking distance. A little beyond Cumnor is Eaton village, with a pub, the Eight Bells.

Between Bablockhythe and Eynsham the river becomes deceptively tortuous in a generally northeast direction; so much so that it has been claimed that just below Pinkhill Lock the towpath (which returned to the right bank at Bablockhythe) 'takes 300 yards to advance 100 feet'. Approaching Pinkhill (there is a farm but no village) we pass Farmoor Reservoir on

OPPOSITE Newbridge, *circa* 1250, is reputed to be one of the oldest bridges on the river
PREVIOUS PAGE The cold but peaceful Thames near Radcot flows through flat and remote countryside

the right. The lock has a neat garden with topiary. Just below it, on the right, is the first fully-equipped cruiser station we have encountered since Lechlade. The road beyond, now running almost parallel to the winding river, is the A4141 from Eynsham to Oxford, with Beacon Hill (an ancient British camp, probably also used as a beacon to warn of the coming of the Spanish Armada in 1588) above – a welcome protuberance amid so much flatness, despite the intrusion of a neo-Georgian water-works in the foreground.

The A4141 eventually crosses the river at Swinford Bridge, described by architects as 'noble': its stone arches, biggest in the middle and tapering off at the sides, make it probably the most elegant of the classical parapeted Thames bridges. It was built in 1769 by Lord Abingdon, who was certainly reimbursed several times over from the tolls he collected on it. It is one of the two surviving toll-bridges on the Thames (the other is at Whitchurch). The original toll was two pence for vehicles. The stone shingled toll house is still there.

Immediately we come to Eynsham Lock, with two inns handy, the Swan Hotel and the Talbot. Eynsham village, 1 mile north of the river, regarded by some as a mere 'suburb of Oxford', is well worth a visit.

There can be no more talk of 'suburbs of Oxford' as Wytham Great Wood looms up on the right. For the next 3 miles or so we shall see few houses, no roads, railway or pubs. The land-scape seems not to have changed for two hundred years. The Great Wood is one of the remaining tracts of the dense forest that in ancient times followed the Thames for most of its course. At its centre is Wytham Hill (540 feet), part of a defence mound used by Cynewulf, King of the West Saxons, in his war against Offa and his Mercians.

On the left, the Cassington Cut joins the Thames, closely followed by the river Evenlode, which rises in the Cotswolds

The Ferry Inn, Bablockhythe, is named after the ferry that used to carry towing-horses where the tow-path changed banks

near Moreton-in-Marsh: you can canoe up it for 25 miles as far as Charlbury. Three miles upstream it joins the old Cass-ington Canal; and as the Thames turns south, just before King's Lock, you can see behind you, among the willows, the old spire of Cassington Church, 2 miles from Eynsham. The greenery on our left is Yarnton (or West) Mead, separated from Pixey Mead by Duke's Cut. These meads are tracts of grazing land which, by ancient ceremony dating back to the Middle Ages, were drawn by lot every July at Mead Farm. Duke's Cut, though rather weedy, is a convenient point of entry to James Brindley's Oxford Canal, which connects up with almost all other working waterways in England.

On our right, by Hagley Pool, is a channel called the Sea-court Stream, which we shall meet again by Osney Lock. At King's Lock the river begins to clutter up: we are now only about $4\frac{1}{2}$ miles from Folly Bridge, and there are still some flashes of beauty ahead before the uglier parts of Oxford start coming at us fast. We have been through four locks in 5 miles, and within $\frac{3}{4}$ mile we shall enter another at Godstow. Just before it, we pass under a road carrying the A34 which becomes the Ring Road round Oxford. On the left is the famous Trout Inn, scene of many dawn bacon-and-egg breakfasts after all-night Commemoration Balls at the Oxford colleges. The Trout, with its lovely gardens and harsh peacocks, once the guesthouse of Godstow Nunnery, was modernized some twenty years ago by Messrs Bass Charrington, but it is still a fine place to take re-freshment among swarms of undergraduates in term-time. Fishermen catch real trout here, and fat ones too. You can see them just below the pub's terrace wall. Beyond the Inn, across the cut in Wolvercote, is the first glimpse of industry we have had – the Oxford University Press papermills. On the right are the ruins of Godstow Nunnery, and the narrow road over the old bridge leads westward to Wytham and its Abbey ($\frac{3}{4}$ mile). The old bridge gives us, framed by its central arch, our first view of the distant spires of Oxford.

Once through the lock, we are in Port Meadow where, in 1862, the Reverend Charles Dodgson and his friend Robinson Duckworth (afterwards Dean of Westminster) took three little girls rowing and told them the stories that became *Alice in Wonderland*. Port Meadow (440 acres) has been free grazing land since the reign of Edward the Confessor, and is theoretically the property of the Freemen of Oxford. The river now widens a little: this is one of the few good places on the Thames for dinghy sailing – and for watching wild geese which nest here. On the right the scene is becoming – perhaps the polite word would be 'urban'. Binsey has the Perch Inn, a few houses and a Norman church, and some factories, but is worth a visit.

The river narrows by Fiddler's Island: this is the last greenery before the smelly industrial part of Oxford, the like of which we shall not see again until Reading. I must remind you that I said at the beginning of this book that the Thames at times makes a ruthless demand on us, that we strive to see the beauty in all things, even gasworks, which (I am told by painters) can look dramatic by dawn or sunset. For the moment, we must see the river as a canalscape. We must be serendipitous: thus it is a pleasure to see, on the left, the graceful little single-span iron Medley footbridge carrying the towpath, which chooses this, of all places, to change to the left side of the river. The bridge (1865) is functional in a Victorian way, criss-cross latticed and usually painted white. Opposite, on the right bank, is Medley Manor Farm, once an oratory for Godstow Nunnery.

Osney Bridge, a humdrum affair carrying one of the main roads into Oxford, should be approached gingerly if your craft is tall: there is only 7 feet 6 inches headroom. Once there was an Abbey here, but it vanished in the Dissolution of the Monasteries. Its largest bell, now known as Great Tom, hangs at Christ Church College: so loud is it that in World War I it was muffled for fear it should guide Zeppelins to the University.

Round a bend and under a railway bridge, we arrive at what was once the worst of Oxford. There used to be a feast of gas-works here but in recent years they have been demolished. Fear not, I shall not abandon you here. There are moorings (rather crowded in summer) just below Folly Bridge, with Salter's Boat-house nearby. This is also the terminus for many boat trips.

Folly Bridge was built in 1828 on the site of a Norman *Grand Pont* which, we are told, had eighteen arches and a fortified gateway or defensive tower. This tower was once the study and observatory of Friar Roger Bacon, the thirteenth-century savant who foresaw the advent of gunpowder, aircraft and the nature of the solar system; a man so learned and ahead of his time that he was thought to be in league with the Devil. The gateway was repaired by a certain Mr Welcome, who added an elaborate additional storey which became known as Welcome's Folly. The Folly was pulled down in 1779 and its stones sold for £13, but the name remained. There is a Victorian near-folly on almost the same site, built in a quasi-Venetian style in 1849, with terracotta statuettes all round. We are now truly in Oxford, and 41 river miles from the 'little wet ditch'.

The Source to Oxford - 41 river miles

BAMPTON (*Oxfordshire*)

The name derives from the Saxon *beam-tun* meaning 'tree enclosure'. Situated 3½ miles northeast of Radcot, Bampton was once known, 200 and more years ago, as Bampton-in-the-Bush because, though it was a market town, there were no good roads leading to it. Its significance as a market was at its height in the eighteenth century, although it is referred to as such much earlier in Domesday Book. For centuries its local industry was 'fellmongering' — making leather and sheepskin jerkins and breeches.

Today this attractive small town of gamboge-coloured stone is famous for its Whit Monday (we must now call it Spring Bank Holiday) carnival, which is well worth seeing, but if you are interested in quieter things, such as buildings, you should probably choose another day. The holiday is dominated by Morris dancing, very correct and classical, enlivened by a traditional Fool (for some irreverent local reason known as 'the Squire') who bops people on the head with a bladder; a swordbearer and a fiddler. Two teams of dancers, all in white with coloured ribbons and streamers, and jingling bells on their legs, take to the streets. The swordbearer carries a plum cake impaled on his sword and (in exchange for suitable donations to his 'treasury') distributes pieces of it to the crowd: it brings luck. There are also two pubs named after the two Morris sides; there is much rivalry in the town over Morris dancing.

There is a horse fair in the last week of August which dates back to Edward I's reign: again, it is more of an excuse for jollification than a serious mart (do not confuse this Bampton with its Devonshire namesake which also has a horse fair).

Apart from these two annual events, Bampton is a peaceful, even sleepy, place far enough off the main road to be relatively traffic-free, with good shops and a number of Georgian houses (some of the shop-fronts are Georgian too). The parish church of St Mary the Virgin, in a melange of styles from the eleventh to eighteenth centuries, has an octagonal 170-foot thirteenth-century spire with four projecting statues, rising out of a mainly Norman tower, whose herringbone stonework hints that it may once have been the West tower of a Saxon church. It is a landmark for many miles around which no amount of pre-eighteenth-century 'bush' could ever have hidden and in those days it guided travellers to the town.

The spire of Bampton parish church guided travellers to the once-isolated market town

Inside the church is a fourteenth-century reredos carved from one piece of stone with primitive dwarf-like figures of Christ and the Apostles. Notice a profusion of Crusader crosses, all about 3 inches high, near the south transept; also two thirteenth-century piscinas, some brasses, and a curious recess in the fourteenth-century chapel leading off the north transept – it looks like a tomb but is more probably an Easter Sepulchre. The chancel pews are *circa* 1500 and include four misericords with carved seats. One bench end bears the initials T H (probably for Thomas Harris, precentor of Exeter 1509–11, who held the living here).

The Deanery, west of the church, is a rambling but impressive fourteenth-century manor originally built by the See of Exeter as a summer residence for its deans: a wing was added *circa* 1660 and restored in the eighteenth century. The Manor House, standing in its own grounds northwest of the church, has a stuccoed Georgian front but is basically seventeenth-century; and north of the church is Southside, late-seventeenth-century, with dovecots over the stables (there are some good examples of dovecots in Oxfordshire: *see* Kelmscot).

Bampton Castle, in Mill Street ($\frac{1}{2}$ mile west of the church), was built by Aylmer de Valence, Earl of Pembroke, in the thirteenth century. Only the west gatehouse and a bit of wall remain. Inhabited until the Commonwealth, it is 'one of the ruins that Cromwell knocked about a bit'. Today, merged into an old farmhouse, it is a private residence known as Ham Court.

Probably the most attractive part of the town is the little close of houses round the church, but the outlying streets are full of interest to the architectural eye. There are two grammar schools here, one founded by Robert Veysey, a wool merchant, in 1635, the other (single-storey Gothic Revival) in Church Lane, was built in 1871. The Italianate town hall (1838) is pleasing, as are many houses and shops in the main street, Bridge Street – notice, for example, how Dotton's Stores has been fashioned out of a row of seventeenth-century cottages.

BINSEY (*Oxfordshire*)

From 'Byni's island'. It is 2 miles northwest of Folly Bridge, Oxford, opposite Port Meadow and is near enough to Oxford to be thought of as a suburb, but it is still 'villagey', with a green across which there is a peaceful view of cottages and farms. It is well worth going ashore to look at it. There is a thatched pub, the Perch, but the outstanding pleasure is the lane, which becomes an avenue of chestnuts, leading to the little church. In the churchyard is the holy well of St Margaret, which, legend says, was miraculously found in AD 730 by St Frideswide, virgin patron of Oxford, who was being pursued through Binsey forest by an unwanted suitor. The suitor was struck blind, but his sight was restored by St Margaret's well water; whereupon he gave up the chase. For centuries the healing waters (they were good for eyes, the stomach, and fertility) attracted pilgrims, and there is an odd tradition that a town called Seckworth of 65,000 people grew up here, with eleven churches and twenty-four inns. In 1158 Seckworth strangely disappeared. The story is as elusive as St Margaret herself: she was probably St Margaret of Antioch. Her well is still there, and many visitors believe in its healing waters and their powers.

Why did Mr and Mrs Hall in their book on the Thames, more than 120 years ago, think that the tiny church of St Margaret had 'a heartbroken look'? It is very much a country church, the oldest parts being the twelfth-century south door and the porch. The rest of the church is mostly thirteenth- to fifteenth-century, with some medieval stained glass in the east window of the chancel. There is a carving of two figures, one of which may be St Margaret. The first vicar of Binsey of whom we have any record was Nicholas Breakspear, Adrian IV, the only English Pope ever elected.

Gerard Manley Hopkins wrote a poem in 1879 lamenting the felling of all the riverside poplars here, along the 'wind-wandering weed-winding bank'; and it is recorded that three poets, Louis MacNeice, W. R. Rodgers and Dylan Thomas,

Blenheim Palace, built for the 1st Duke of Marlborough, between 1705 and 1722 at Woodstock

spent some weekends here during the late 1940s — mostly at the Perch, the village pub, I guess.

BLADON (*Oxfordshire*)

It takes its name from the river Bladon, which was the old name for the Evenlode. About 8 miles northwest of Oxford, just off the A34 Woodstock road on the left (down the A4095), it could be visited as part of an excursion to Woodstock and Blenheim Palace since it lies at the south end of the Great Park and is a little way from the river. You are unlikely to go there for the quarries which have yielded forest marble, a stone much used in Oxford (for buildings like the new Bodleian Library) during the past fifty years. Rather you will want to make a pilgrimage to Sir Winston Churchill's simple grave in the churchyard of St

47

Martin, which until the eighteenth century was the parish church of Woodstock. Sir Winston is buried near his parents, Lord and Lady Randolph Churchill and other members of his family. The church itself is pleasant but of no great interest: a medieval foundation with much nineteenth-century rebuilding.

BLENHEIM PALACE (*Oxfordshire*)

At Woodstock, 8 miles north-northwest of Oxford on the A34, it is a 'must' if you find yourself in Oxford with transport of some kind. Vanbrugh's masterpiece it may be, but many people have disliked it, including Alexander Pope, who complained: ''Tis very fine, But where d'ye sleep, and where d'ye dine? I find by all you have been telling that 'tis a house and not a dwelling.' Where ye dine is clear enough; but so far from the kitchens that the food had to be reheated several times on its journey (*see* the autobiography of Consuelo Vanderbilt for the true awfulness of living at Blenheim). As successive Dukes of Marlborough have found, it is not easy, and fearfully expensive, to live in a national monument, which took seventeen years to build. Intended as a gift to a brilliant general, John Churchill, 1st Duke of Marlborough, from a grateful nation which believed he had broken the power of France, its costs escalated and, by the time it was completed, the Duke was dead, his Duchess had quarrelled with Vanbrugh the main architect, and the Churchill family were dipping into their own pockets to pay for it. The Duchess did not even like Blenheim: 'I mortally hate all gardens and architecture,' she said. All she wanted was 'a clean sweet house and garden, be it ever so small.'

Small Blenheim is not. Let us begin with the exteriors, in particular the Great Park. The Palace, despite its hugeness (it occupies 3 acres) is nothing if not seen in its huger setting. The grounds are largely attributable to Lancelot 'Capability' Brown (1715–83); we should not forget, however, that the original layout was devised by Queen Anne's own gardener, Henry Wise. This was adapted by Brown to suit the fashion of the day, which was largely his own creation. Military historians can amuse themselves by testing the tradition that Brown's avenues followed the plan of the battle of Blenheim in 1704. The great lake was formed by damming the little river Glyme which flows through the 2,500-acre park and eventually joins the Evenlode and finds its way into the Thames. The lake demonstrates Brown's genius for creating 'naturalness', of which it is perhaps the supreme example. The bridge that divides it was designed by Vanbrugh (nearly 400 feet long). The pivot or focus of the whole design is the Column of Victory on which the 1st Duke stands dressed as a Roman. We do not know how Marlborough felt about this monument, but we do know that he wished his defeat of Louis XIV to be symbolized in some way, and to this end he captured a colossal bust of the Sun King from Tournai in 1709 and put it above the south front of Blenheim like a traitor's head on old London Bridge.

Inside this vast building, with its four main towers surmounted by pinnacles, is the Great Court, with the Stable and Kitchen Courts extending to the northeast and northwest. The Great Hall has a 'Roman' effect, and the Corinthian columns at the corners have cornices carved by Grinling Gibbons, whose work can also be seen elsewhere in the Palace. The Saloon beyond has a ceiling painted by Sir James Thornhill: it depicts Marlborough presenting Britannia with a plan of the battle of Blenheim. The rest of the Saloon, decorated by Laguerre, deliberately follows Versailles styles, to drive home the idea of victory over Louis XIV.

Even the tapestries in the State Rooms (either side of the Saloon) celebrate Marlborough's victories. They were woven by J. de Vos of Brussels, after L. de Hondt, and one panel shows him receiving the surrender of Marshal Tallard after the battle of Blenheim. The Long Library, running for 180 feet along the West Front, was originally meant to be a picture gallery. It is

Swinford Toll Bridge, built in 1767, still charges a toll. Its toll-house can be seen on the Eynsham bank of the river

dominated by a statue of Queen Anne; the decoration is by Hawksmoor, who employed other artists for the plasterwork and for carving the doorcases. Various sculptures, mostly busts of the Marlborough family, are by Rysbrack, who also executed the statue of Queen Anne. At the north end is a large organ: the 8th and 9th Dukes were fond of organ music, and an organist used to travel from Birmingham to play to the Marlboroughs' guests during dinner.

The Chapel to some extent continues the style of the Library, with columns and plasterwork. Even here there is a monument to the Duke and Duchess (by William Kent and Rysbrack) and their sons, with a relief showing the surrender of Tallard. There are also monuments to the 7th Duke (d. 1883) and Lord Randolph Churchill (d. 1895).

For many visitors it is a relief to enter the small room on the ground floor where Sir Winston Churchill was born in 1874 – prematurely after his mother Jennie had been out riding. A bed, chest of drawers and framed exhibits on the walls are all the furniture. Just before you reach this room there is a permanent exhibition of Churchill's letters including those heartrending ones sent home from school to his neglectful parents, begging them to come and see him on sports days, speech days, any days. But only his Nanny Everest was faithful.

The Palace is open to the public (under a fairly rigid guided-tour system) from April to late October. The gardens are open most of the year.

BUSCOT (*Oxfordshire*)

The name stems from 'Burgweard's cot, cottage or sheep-pen'. It lies between Lechlade and Faringdon on the A417. The park, lake, water-garden, house, village and 3,863 acres of farmland and woods all now belong to the National Trust — right down to the willow-lined Thames, here little more than a stream. The

St Mary's Church at Buscot has two windows by Sir Edward Coley Burne-Jones and some painted panels by Andrea Mantegna

house and park (open at stated times from April to October) were creations of the eighteenth century: the house was built in Adam style by Edward Loveden Townsend *circa* 1780. The exterior is not impressive but the inside is worth a visit. In 1889 a large new Victorian wing was added, but it was pulled down and both interior and exterior were restored to their original state by the 2nd Lord Faringdon in 1938. This was the eccentric Socialist-Pacifist peer, identified with every possible peace-loving movement, who, in the darkest days of 1943, rose to address the Upper House as 'My Dears . . .' His son, the 3rd Baron, still lives at Buscot House.

As with other buildings in this part of the Upper Thames region, the presence of the Pre-Raphaelites is strongly felt. The lovely furniture and ceilings are mostly Regency, and the rich Faringdon collection of pictures includes Italian, Dutch, Flemish and Spanish masters, together with many English, among them Lawrence, Reynolds, Gainsborough — and Sir Edward Burne-Jones. His series of paintings of Briar Rose (1890) — the Sleeping Beauty story — in their original ornate gilded frames, designed by the artist, dominate the centre saloon and were commissioned by the 1st Lord Faringdon.

A short distance from the house, two classical ranges have been added, in weird contrast to everything else. Known as Marx House, they contain paintings of the Labour Party and the History of Socialism, executed by Lord Huntingdon, the left-wing muralist, in the 1930s. The park and lakes were landscaped in the eighteenth century, and the Italian-style water-gardens, with fountains, waterfalls and statues, were designed some fifty years ago by Harold Peto.

St Mary's Church, by the river outside the village, has a Perpendicular west tower with west doorway and window. The chancel arch is Norman, *circa* 1200; and the Pre-Raphaelite movement confronts us again as we come upon two windows by Burne-Jones, one of them (the east window) of the Good Shepherd (1891). There are also monuments to the Loveden family, who once owned Buscot Park, and an astonishing seventeenth-century Spanish lectern of carved wood. The sixteenth-century pulpit, given to the church in 1908, has three painted panels which have been ascribed to the Italian painter, Andrea Mantegna, but are now thought to be by the Flemish artist Jan Gossaert. Carpets and curtains were designed by William Morris. The handsome eighteenth-century headstones in the churchyard are carved in Cotswold stone.

The Old Rectory nearby is a fine house of about 1700. Buscot Old Parsonage (National Trust), an early eighteenth-century house of Cotswold stone with a small garden, can be visited on Wednesday afternoons by written appointment. Buscot village, built in Cotswold stone, is a 'model settlement' of cottages laid out in 1879. There is also a Victorian parish hall, a well with a

The seventeenth-century Spanish lectern in Buscot Church

pump and a four-gabled roof of a pleasantly 'twee' design popular in the 1890s.

Connoisseurs of the sinister may like to be reminded that Buscot Park, in the 1870s, was owned by a family named Campbell, whose daughter Florence, better known as Florence Bravo, is generally thought to have poisoned two husbands in Balham, London, while having an adulterous affair with one of the most fashionable physicians of the day, Dr James Manley Gully.

CASTLE EATON (*Wiltshire*)

From *ea-tun* meaning 'riverside homestead'. About 4 miles downstream from Cricklade; one of several Eatons near the Upper Thames (or Isis, on some maps), it has no castle. It does have a Georgian brick pub, the Red Lion, whose gardens overlook the infant river. You will probably visit it on foot from Cricklade; there is no towpath here yet. At least you can cross the river, albeit by a rather ugly iron bridge.

St Mary's Church, also overlooking the rivulet, is nicely situated. Its Norman foundation survives in two Norman doorways. The chancel is late thirteenth-century. In the north aisle, a line of wooden posts mounted on stone: what were they for? Surely not for tethering horses? The church was restored (not too drastically) by Butterfield in the 1860s: he added a small corbelled bell-turret and a spire. Inside it, an old fourteenth-century bell was discovered in 1900. Was this the original Sanctus Bell, which was tolled during the most sacred part of the service (as Eric de Maré has suggested), so that people who could not come to church could pray in the fields or in their own homes, saying, 'Holy, holy, holy, Lord God of Hosts' (but in Latin).

CRICKLADE (*Wiltshire*)

The only Wiltshire town on the River Thames, if you can dignify it by the name of river here, so shallow a trickle is it so near to the Source. Yet this agreeable market town (population 2,000), which the Romans knew merely as a Dobunni village, was important in Saxon times for its strategic position, the river being the frontier of Wessex. In 1016 (says the Anglo-Saxon Chronicle) 'came King Canute with a force of 160 ships, and Ealdorman Edric with him over the Thames at Cricklade'; they then went up into the Midlands 'burning and stealing as is their wont'. (The word 'ships' is surely a mistranslation? One cannot imagine that there was ever enough water to carry them upstream.)

In Edward the Confessor's time the town had its own mint, and in Stephen's reign a castle was built — no trace of it remains, though there are fragments of fortifications. Cricklade is mentioned in Domesday Book as a 'borough' — probably reflecting Alfred the Great's policy of building defences along southern England, having observed the ease with which the Danes had overrun the country when there were no permanent garrisons to stop them. Recent excavations have revealed what is believed to be a Saxon defensive *burh*, a large square enclosure surrounded by an embankment of earth and timber and a ditch, with traces of eleventh-century masonry. The town museum (at the west end of the main street) has exhibits dating back to the Roman occupation.

The town today has some attractive seventeenth- and eighteenth-century houses, especially at the south end of its broad High Street — notice particularly one in stone, dated 1708, which overlooks St Sampson's churchyard. Just outside the town is the Priory, built *circa* 1230 as a Hospital of St John (not for the sick, but a guesthouse for poor travellers). The few remains of the original building have been converted into a row of houses. Local legend asserts that St Augustine once came here from Canterbury, and at Braydon, about 5 miles southwest there is a Gospel Oak where he is supposed to have held a conference of bishops. It is also claimed that Robert Canutus of Cricklade, Prior of St Frideswide (*see* Oxford), was one of the first Chancellors of Oxford University.

St Mary's Church, Castle Eaton, by the Thames

The great feature of the town is the parish church of St Sampson, a Welsh-Breton saint whom we are surprised to find in such a non-Celtic district. Its pinnacled, richly decorated late Gothic tower (built by the Duke of Northumberland in 1553), rising from the crossing point of nave, chancel and transepts, looks as if it belonged to a cathedral, almost too heavy for the infrastructure, having much in common with the 'wool churches' of the area (Lechlade, for example), and partly Norman (the arches are thirteenth-century). It was built by the Duke of Northumberland and the local Hungerford family at the time of the Reformation. Below it is an unusual lierne vault (cross-ribbed) with rich carved heraldic decorations. The tower looks most impressive from a distance, and certainly dominates the wooded landscape. Inside, the church has traces of all the centuries from the twelfth to the sixteenth, including a late fifteenth-century south chapel. Some windows are modern, designed by Martin Travers in 1930.

The smaller church of St Mary, in the High Street, is basically Norman, with a fine chancel arch; but it may be on the foundations of a gatehouse chapel which was part of the Saxon town wall. It has a good Norman chancel, a Jacobean pulpit and a circular thirteenth-century font. In the churchyard is a fine fourteenth-century cross.

CUMNOR (*Oxfordshire*)

From 'Cumma's hill-slope' – possibly referring to Cumma, Abbot of Abingdon in the eighth century. It is 4 miles west-southwest of Oxford by the A420 turning right onto the B4017, or 1 mile from Bablockhythe. You need to visit this village in a spirit of literary and historical nostalgia, for if you expect to see Cumnor Place, scene of Amy Robsart's mysterious death in Scott's *Kenilworth*, you will be disappointed – the last stones of the house were taken away to Wytham in 1811 by the Earl of Abingdon, who used them to rebuild Wytham Church.

Amy was found dead at the foot of some stairs at Cumnor Place, with her neck broken; rumour – and Sir Walter Scott – concluded that she had been murdered by order of her husband Robert Dudley, Earl of Leicester, because he wanted to be free to marry Queen Elizabeth I. Dudley would have been about twenty-eight at this time. The Queen admired him and gave him titles and favours: it was common gossip at Court that he would marry her, and this was reported by the Spanish Ambassador who referred to Dudley as 'the future King'.

Anthony Forster, Dudley's steward, rented Cumnor Place for him, and Amy was installed there in the company of Mrs Pinto, Amy's maid. Dudley himself was at Windsor with the Queen. On 8 September 1560 the household staff and servants went to Abingdon Fair: when they returned, Amy's body was discovered. One rumour had it that Dudley had ordered Forster to throw her downstairs. This unreliable method of murder strains belief. Mrs Pinto, at the inquest, said she had overheard Amy praying for deliverance from an undefined 'desperation'. But

Cumnor Village has many pretty grey-stone houses

there was no further evidence, and motive was not enough. Verdict: accidental death.

The story has rather swamped the village, which can be appreciated for itself. It spills down the side of Hurst Hill (520 feet) with the church on a ridge near the top, and has mainly stone houses most with magnificent rose gardens. The village feels healthy: you can understand why the Abbots of Abingdon liked to come here when they were ill. The church contains a seventeenth-century spiral staircase of oak leading to the belfry; a carved Jacobean pulpit (the central part is signed by its maker TB. GN. 1685) and many reminders of the Amy Robsart story. In the vestry is a rare statue of Queen Elizabeth I (believed to have been carved for the Earl of Leicester), discovered in an outbuilding of Wytham Abbey and brought here in 1888. On the wall nearby are frames containing Amy's letters and other relics. The imposing tomb of Anthony Forster (1572) shows him kneeling with his wife and children. The church also possesses a Bible published in 1611. The main structure of the church is a mixture of Transitional and Decorated, and the tower is *circa* 1200. If you climb it — or even if you don't — you can enjoy splendid views of Oxford in one direction and the Cotswolds in another. A few stones in the churchyard wall show roughly the site of Cumnor Place. Cumnor Hill was one of the places where Matthew Arnold's Scholar Gypsy used to wander 'in days when wits were fresh and clear, and life ran gaily as the sparkling Thames,/Before this strange disease of modern life . . .'

EATON HASTINGS (*Oxfordshire*)

This village, reached by the A417 road between Lechlade and Faringdon, lies almost opposite Kelmscot (on the left bank) and just east of Buscot Park. From the river you see its small, isolated church and a few scattered farms. It gets its name from Ralph de Hastings, who owned the village in the twelfth century. Why is the thirteenth-century Norman church so small, and why is it isolated? Is this an instance (and there are many in the country) of a 'village that vanished'? Was there a plague that wiped out most of its population? The Black Death was by no means the only scourge of its kind. The village has no true centre — there does not seem to have been a manor house.

Eaton Hastings had one of the last flash weirs which survived until 1937. It was sometimes known as Hart's Weir, called after a lock-keeper's family who looked after it for several generations. Today the site is marked by a small footbridge, and a pub called the Anchor (badly damaged by fire in 1980).

EYNSHAM (*Oxfordshire*)

The name may mean 'Aegan's ham'. It is 7 miles northwest of Oxford on the B4044, and does not like to be thought of as a suburb of Oxford though it undeniably is a dormitory for many people who work in the city. The township is unspoiled at the centre, which is the Market Square, surrounded by grey-stone

Eynsham town centre still retains some of its old buildings

cottages in several streets. The commuter dwellings are on the outer fringe. There is a small seventeenth-century Market House, or Hall, which is a single room above arches that were filled in so that it could be used as a jail. It was also formerly used as a Roman Catholic chapel, and is now a public library. The thirteenth-century church of St Leonard, rather over-restored in Victorian times, faces directly on to the Square. Chancel, north and south aisles and nave are thirteenth-century, the west tower is fifteenth-century, and the northwest tower has battlements with gargoyles. On one wall of the chancel are the remains of fourteenth-century paintings of the life of St Catherine. Near the church is a fourteenth-century cross.

Wandering round this typically Oxfordshire town, we notice the Queen Anne vicarage in Mill Street (enlarged in Regency times), and nearby Myrtle House, early Georgian. Wintle's

Farm, early fifteenth-century, The Gables in Newland Street (seventeenth-century) and Murray House in Aere Street (early Georgian) are among many modest but handsome houses worth looking at. About 3 miles northwest is Eynsham Park, a mansion, originally designed by Sir Charles Barry in Italian style, and rebuilt in the early 1900s in Jacobean style.

Near St Leonard's Church is the site of Eynsham Abbey, founded in the eleventh century for the Benedictine order. We do not know what it looked like, for only two ruined towers and a few windows survived the Dissolution; but it had great importance in its day. There is also an excavated Saxon village (sixth- or seventh-century) at New Wintles Farm, about 1 mile northwest of the town. There are two good pubs: the Talbot, a seventeenth-century coaching inn, and the Swan Hotel, believed once to have been a guesthouse for the old Abbey.

Eynsham has one of the two remaining toll-bridges on the Thames (the other is at Whitchurch, Pangbourne). A small shingled toll-house stands at the Eynsham end. It is known as **Swinford Bridge**, built of stone, 80 yards long, with parapets, by the Earl of Abingdon in 1769. His descendants collected tolls (for four-wheeled vehicles – stagecoaches, hearses, lorries and cars) at a flat rate of four old pence or two new ones until 1981, when a new owner sparked off a local row by trying to raise the toll to five pence. Under the original Act, claimed the protesters, the toll for any coach, chariot, Berlin, chaise, wagon, wain, dray, cart or carriage could never exceed Lord Abingdon's first charge. It would need a new Act of Parliament to change it. Swinford Bridge is used by some 15,000 vehicles a week. Police, ambulances, Royal Mail vans and bicycles cross for nothing.

Travellers were a lot worse off before the bridge existed. A rather unsafe ferry caused a number of deaths by drowning; and in 1764 John Wesley, riding from Oxford to Witney in bad weather, found himself astride a swimming horse as the ferry became inundated: 'after one or two plunges, we got through and came safe to Witney.'

FARINGDON (*Oxfordshire*)

A stone town, and not quite so old as it looks, for most of it is no earlier than seventeenth-century.

In Saxon times Faringdon was of great strategic importance, being at one point of the triangular West Saxon kingdom (the other two were Hinksey and Wallingford); and Alfred the Great is said to have had a palace on the site of the Salutation Inn. Faringdon was also the scene of skirmishes in the eleventh-century civil wars, and was eventually presented by King John to the monks of Beaulieu Abbey, Hampshire. The town was also badly knocked about in the struggle between King and Parliament in the seventeenth century (*see also* Radcot): the church steeple was smashed by a cannon ball, and Sir Robert Pye, brother-in-law of the famous Parliamentarian, John Hampden, found himself in the unenviable position of having to storm his father's home, Faringdon House, which was full of Royalists.

The Faringdon House you see today was mostly built in the 1780s by Sir Robert's descendant, Henry James Pye, George III's Poet Laureate, who seems to have made more money than most holders of that unremunerative office. He was, however, ridiculed by most of his contemporaries, especially by Byron, who wrote of him: 'Better to err with Pope that shine with Pye.' We do not know who wrote the nursery rhyme 'Sing a Song of Sixpence', but we do know that it was a punning parody of a now-forgotten 'Ode to Birds' by Pye. Let us be grateful that he had the good taste to employ John Wood of Bath to design his house. The result has been called 'a perfect example of an eighteenth-century gentleman's small country seat'. In order to see it, you have to go into the grounds: it lies in the middle of trees behind the church. When Sir Osbert Sitwell knew it in the 1930s, it belonged to the eccentric Lord Berners, composer, painter, writer and practical joker (he is Lord Merlin in Nancy Mitford's *The Pursuit of Love*). Sir Osbert described the house as

All Saints Church in Faringdon dates from the twelfth century and has many fine monuments and decorations

a 'spacious arcaded villa in the Palladian taste, its dove-grey outer walls covered in spring with magnolias the size of soup-plates', where fan-tailed pigeons dyed in various colours flew about the gardens. Berners once invited a horse to sit for its portrait in his drawing-room. The house is of stuccoed stone with a Tuscan porch and a fine entrance hall.

The grounds (open annually for the National Gardens Scheme) are said to be haunted by a headless ghost, that of Henry Pye's ancestor Hampden, whose head was blown off at sea when serving in the Royal Navy. The story goes that this was the result of a plot between the captain and Hampden Pye's stepmother, who wished her own son to inherit the family fortune. It is to haunt *her* that headless Hampden appears.

All Saints Church, one of the richest in the area, is nearby, at the top of the Market Place (Faringdon has always been an important market centre). You can see, on the low central tower, where the spire should be. This big cruciform church ranges from the twelfth to the nineteenth century, but most of it is thirteenth-century Transitional, such as the south door, with its wrought-iron dragon's head design (described by Pevsner as 'splendid agitated scrollwork'). The north door is Norman (probably about 1170), the font Perpendicular, about 200 years later. Notice also the beautiful carving on the nave capitals. Inside are monuments to two great local families, the Pyes and the Untons, who once lived at Wadley House, a mile east of the town. In the north transept is the kneeling figure of Dorothy, Lady Unton, in seventeenth-century alabaster, so alive that she seems to be breathing. Behind her is a white-marble wall monument to her husband Sir Henry, Queen Elizabeth I's ambassador to France, knighted for gallantry at the battle of Zutphen in 1586. The design of the monument incorporates an angel's head and a skull. The Pye Chapel is north of the chancel.

In the town, Church Street and Gloucester Street have several good Georgian houses. Westbrook House, in Gravel Walk, may

The Trout Inn lies opposite the ruins of Godstow nunnery

be as old as 1705, and the early eighteenth-century Friends' Meeting House in Lechlade Road is worth a glance. Notice, by the way, how many hipped roofs there are hereabouts (houses with sloping, not vertical ends). In the L-shaped Market Place the Crown Hotel may claim your attention in more ways than one: its front is Georgian, but parts of the courtyard behind date back to the fourteenth century, and there is an open Jacobean staircase. Opposite is the Bell, and nearby the imposing late seventeenth-century town hall on Tuscan columns.

North of the town is a National Trust area (over 260 acres) of meadow and woodland. East of it is Lord Berners' Folly with its octagonal, castellated and pinnacled top. It is not possible to visit it as it is now permanently walled up.

GODSTOW (*Oxfordshire*)

Meaning 'holy place of God'. It is 4 miles north-north-west of Oxford. The famous stone-built Trout Inn, its gardens and the prospect of seeing trout leaping, distracts attention from the main historical feature, Godstow Nunnery, whose ruins are opposite. The Trout was once the Nunnery's guesthouse. The Nunnery was built either in 1135, the first year of King Stephen's reign, or (as one early historian asserts) 'by Edithe ye Prioress in ye year 1138 and dedicated in honour of ye Virgin Mary and St John ye Baptist, by Alexander bishop of Lincoln in ye presence of King Stephen and his Queen.'

We are drawn straight into the story, part-history, part-legend, of Rosamund de Clifford, a young nun who attracted the attention of Henry II, Stephen's successor. John Aubrey's version of the story is that the King 'forced her to be his concubine' and built her a house or palace at Woodstock which had an underground labyrinth where the poor girl was installed (there is a pond at Blenheim called Rosamund's Well which may or may not be the site). Aubrey says she was poisoned by the jealous Queen Eleanor; other authors add that the Queen found her way through the maze by a clue or ball of thread, such as Theseus used when he slew the Minotaur. She died, by whatever means, in 1176 and was buried at the Nunnery (presumably as a penitent) and, Aubrey says, when her skeleton was dug up, her teeth were found to be of a wonderful whiteness. The Nunnery, of the Benedictine order, was endowed by Rosamund's father, Earl Walter de Clifford; the only historian of the time who dared to hint at her name, was Giraldus Cambrensis, who did so in a Latin pun (*in mundi verius rosa*), excusing Henry's conduct by saying he had had to imprison Queen Eleanor for fomenting revolt against him. Giraldus's Latin may have given rise to the traditional epitaph for Fair Rosamund: 'In this tomb lies the Rose of the World, the fair but not the pure.' Yet after her death the nuns treated her as a kind of saint, burning candles at her shrine. When, at the end of the eighteenth century, Godstow Lock was built (using prisoners from Oxford Jail), stone slabs from the graves of nuns were used to make a paved path to Wytham village nearby.

Some of the ruined Nunnery remains, but there is not much to see. The peacocks from the Trout strut about it, and it is used occasionally as a sheep or cattle pound. The wonder is that there is anything left of it at all. After the Dissolution in 1539, it was used as a house by Dr Owen, Henry VIII's physician. In the Civil War it became a strong-point and was burned down in 1645. Nothing of the twelfth century survives: what you see is mostly fifteenth-century, and the chapel is sixteenth-century.

The Trout is remembered by the pre-war generation of undergraduates as a sheltered hole-in-the-wall inn serving mild ale. Now it is almost part of Oxford suburbia, just off the Ring Road near two large motels, but it is still a popular pub. This area, **Wolvercote**, has been industrial since the seventeenth century when a water-powered papermill, at the instigation of John Fell, Bishop of Oxford, was set up to manufacture paper for the University Press, which, in a new concrete building, it still does today.

INGLESHAM, Upper and **Lower** (*Wiltshire*)
Derived from 'Ingin's ham'. This village is $2\frac{1}{2}$ miles south of Lechlade. It has a little church on the river bank, like Castle Eaton (you can just see it through the trees), but this church of St John the Baptist is special. Mostly thirteenth-century, it escaped the drastic restoration which marks the work of so many Victorian architects. It was very carefully handled in 1888–9 by the Society for the Protection of Ancient Buildings, under the supervision of William Morris the Pre-Raphaelite who really understood the Middle Ages. Despite its smallness, the church has aisles, but no tower. This, you feel, is what the parish church looked like at the time it was built. The pulpit is Elizabethan, the box pews Jacobean, with separate accommodation for the squire and the vicar. On one wall is an Anglo-Saxon sculpture of the Virgin and Child. Both north and south doorways are thirteenth-century. There is a pleasing roughness about the building; the floor is not quite even, and the roof

beams and old screens enhance this impression. There is a little stained glass in a few of the windows. In the churchyard, by way of contrast, there are carved Georgian tombstones.

There is a village cross in stone, 15 feet high, and a few mellowed stone houses nearby. The village's debt to William Morris is acknowledged by a commemorative brass at the church door which reads '. . . through the energy and with the help of William Morris who loved it.'

Inglesham was at one end of the old Thames and Severn Canal, which was opened in 1789, but never very successful, and finally closed in 1927. Traces of its course are visible at Cricklade and above Thames Head.

KELMSCOT (*Oxfordshire*)

Meaning 'Kenelm's cottage or sheepfold'. It is $2\frac{1}{2}$ miles east of Lechlade. Perversely, just because most people come here to look at the Manor House as a shrine of the Pre-Raphaelite movement, we shall look at the spread-out, grey-stone village first. That it was a prosperous farming centre around the beginning of the eighteenth century is clear from the several large square farmhouses – Lower House Farm, Manor Farm (with a seventeenth-century gabled and turreted dovecot, typical of this part of Oxfordshire), Bradshaws, and Home Farm. There is a characteristic Cotswold village hall (with a relief of William Morris, writer, artist, decorator and printer, carved by George Jack), and Philip Webb's memorial cottages to Morris, built in stone in 1902, six years after his death, and paid for by Morris's daughter Jane. Some cottages (another Cotswold touch) have fences made of big upright stones.

The small cruciform church of St George is very much the kind of country church that Morris and his disciples liked. Nave and chancel are Transitional-Norman (late twelfth-century) and the south door and font are both features of the original building. The transepts are perhaps a century younger. There are some wall-paintings and medieval glass, and some notable carved corbel heads. In the churchyard is a simple monument, decorated with carved oak and vine leaves, to Morris by his friend Philip Webb which has been compared by one authority to 'a Viking ridge tomb'. The village has two inns, the Plough and, down by the river on the site of an old lock, the Anchor. For some reason the name of the Manor is spelled Kelmscott, with two t's, the village with only one.

The lofty Elizabethan Manor House, of grey stone with gables and mullioned windows, is not easy to see as a whole until you are inside its high walls. Morris and Dante Gabriel Rossetti shared it for some years and made it into an expression of their ideas on beauty in general, interior decoration in particular, the concept of Christian socialism and the dignity of handcrafts as against mass production. For Rossetti the main attraction of the village (which bored him so much that he called it 'the doziest clump of old grey beehives') was Morris's wife Janey: his letters to her are locked in the British Museum and may not be published until 1989. It must have been an explosive ménage, with Rossetti complaining about everything and doping himself with chloral as a remedy for his insomnia.

The Manor dates back to about 1570. The north wing was added about a hundred years later by the Turner family of yeoman farmers who owned the house for many years. They succeeded another owner who is believed to have been one of the fifty-nine Roundheads who signed Charles I's death warrant. It has been called 'a most enjoyable small manor house' which 'hovers with homely informality over the flat river landscape', with a walled garden among pollard willows and elms which are spread more thinly now than in Morris's day. Morris, who lived here from 1871 until his death in 1896, describes the Manor at the end of *News from Nowhere*, that Utopian vision of a socialist commonwealth, and says: 'It has come to be to me the type of the pleasant places of the earth . . . As others love the race of man through their lovers or their children, so I love the earth through that small space of it.' The external feature

In the churchyard at Kelmscot is a monument to William Morris

which most pleased him was the roof with its graduated stone tiles: 'It gives me the same sort of pleasure in their orderly beauty as a fish's scale or a bird's feather.'

Inside the house are tapestries and wallpapers by Morris, furniture designed by Webb, and sketches by Rossetti of Janey and her two daughters, Mary (the serene one) and Jane (the wild one). When Mary (May) died she left the house to Oxford University as 'a home of rest for learned men'. But not enough learned men took advantage of it, finding it perhaps too 'dozy' as Rossetti had done. More fools they. The whole house was restored, no expense spared, in 1968 by the Society of Antiquaries. The Morris Society has striven to keep the house exactly as it was in Morris's time, and in the same year planted many new trees. It is open to the public on the first Wednesday in the month from April to September, but it is safest to make an appointment.

In 1878 Morris took another house beside the Thames, in Hammersmith Upper Mall and called it Kelmscott House (see Hammersmith). Two years later he acquired a biggish boat called the *Ark* and took Janey and the children up the river to the other Kelmscott. The *Ark* was propelled by four oars, but most of the rowing was done by Morris himself. From Kelmscott to Kelmscot is 130 miles.

KEMBLE (*Gloucestershire*)

This village is 4½ miles southwest of Cirencester, off the A429. Kemble Station is the nearest railhead to the source of the Thames in Trewsbury Mead, and is thus of importance to walkers. A peaceful village with a basically Early English church, the tower thirteenth-century but the rest rebuilt during the 1870s. The monuments inside include some eighteenth-century ones to a local family, the Coxes, and an effigy of a medieval knight in marble. Kemble House, built in stone, is a seventeenth-century manor. There are two more interesting houses at **Ewen** (1 mile east), the Georgian Ewen Manor, and the seventeenth-century Ewen House.

Ewen (compare Ewelme) means a source or spring (on an eighteenth-century map it is spelled Yeoing), and there are many rivals to the official Thames Head hereabouts. Ewen Mill (where Mill Farm now is) was one of the traditional Thames watermills of which nothing remains today (although Kemble Mill keeps its millstones used up to some eighty years ago).

Anyone who visits Thames Head by way of Kemble might be interested to see **Lyd Well**, about a mile down the valley, by an old wind-pump. Did the Romans bore this well, as local tradition asserts? It certainly looks more like the source of a great river than the mud of Trewsbury Mead. Lyd Well is seldom dry, and when it rains the water rushes out like a geyser. The water does eventually reach the Thames as one of its tributary streamlets; but we cannot claim a manmade torrent as a source.

The village pub at Ewen is the Wild Duck, at the crossroads. Its name is illustrated by a large clock above the door with pictures of wild ducks in flight (rather like Sir Peter Scott's). A solemn notice informs you that the inn's most celebrated customer, a Mr Cornelius Uzzle, used to do his bar parlour trick of eating twelve pounds of raw bacon at a sitting, passing the hat round for monetary contribution afterwards.

KEMPSFORD (*Gloucestershire*)

Possibly derived from 'Cynemaer's ford'. It is almost midway between Cricklade and Lechlade. The ford was an important one, both commercially and strategically, in medieval times. The village, on the Isis/Thames, is rich in history, occasionally mixed with legend. John of Gaunt had an estate here, and his presence is felt everywhere. The twelfth-century castle was demolished some five centuries later. There is an ancient connection between Kempsford and Leicester : the manor of Kempsford was acquired by Henry Plantagenet, Earl of Lancaster, who endowed a hospital at Leicester; his son Henry, a deeply religious man, on becoming Duke of Lancaster in 1350 gave the church of St Mary the Virgin at Kempsford (as a 'collegiate' church) to Leicester. The Duke's heiress was Blanche of Kempsford who became John of Gaunt's first wife in 1359. She was Geoffrey Chaucer's patroness, and his *Parlement of Foules* and *Book of the Duchess* were both dedicated to her; the latter as a lament after her death.

The church's fine central tower is always thought of as John of Gaunt's Tower: it may have been built as a memorial to Blanche when she died suddenly. It has Perpendicular windows below, and weather-cocks on its pinnacles. The vaulting has carved and painted heraldic devices. The chancel was extended by G. E. Street in the 1850s, and there is some Victorian stained glass. Puritan texts hang on the walls of the nave.

John of Gaunt had two more wives, Constance of Castile, on whose death he married his mistress of many years, Katherine Swynford. One of their sons, Bolingbroke, became King Henry IV. Legend plays a part in the story of Lady Maud, John's sister-in-law, who was staying in the original manor house beyond the church, down by the river. Maud was hiding another brother-in-law from his enemies in those troubled times; and her husband, returning unexpectedly and seeing them standing close together in conversation, misinterpreted the situation, attacked the man and pushed Maud into the river. She, being unable to swim, drowned. Her husband went into voluntary exile. The ghost of Lady Maud walks by the Thames at night, along the terrace known as Lady Maud's Walk (it is now part of the seventeenth-century vicarage's garden).

THE KEYNES — Ashton Keynes (*Wiltshire*), and Somerford Keynes (*Gloucestershire*)

The names appear to be fairly obviously derived — a *tun* where ash-trees grow and a ford only used in summer. Keynes is a landowner's name connected with Cahagnes in Normandy. The two villages are within a few miles of Cricklade, between it and Thames Head.

The memorable feature of **Ashton Keynes** is the little bridges across the Thames (here divided into several streams) each leading to a separate house: most of the houses are built of Cotswold stone. There is a local theory that this was once a trading town, when the river was more navigable; there also seems once to have been a monastery here. The village straggles a little, but you come upon attractive groups of farms and cottages. It is a village of four crosses where sermons used to be preached: one beside a shop, another near the White Hart Inn, another at the beginning of Church Walk, and one in the church-yard itself — this last has been converted into a war memorial. Holy Cross Church (twelfth-century) was remodelled by Butter-field in 1876: he enlarged the Norman chancel and redecorated it. The clerestory above the nave walls has an unusual arrangement of upright and sideways quatrefoils. The font is very tall. There is a monumental sculpture by Flaxman. The vestry has a twelfth-century wall in Saxon style, but does not suggest that there was a pre-Norman church here.

The bridges across the infant Thames at Ashton Keynes

At the end of Church Walk, by two fine stone houses, Ashton Mill and Brook House, the Thames begins to look more like a river. The seventeenth-century Manor House, still beside the water, stands beyond the main body of the village. The village is slightly at risk: gravel pits are bringing in too many lorries and new building does not always harmonize. There were once many elms here but recently they have died from disease.

Somerford Keynes is a little to the east of the river (still split into two main streams). Church and Manor stand together as they should. The church was founded in the seventh or eighth century, and the Saxon doorway in the north wall of the nave may be a survival of this. The Gothic tower is eighteenth-century. The Manor House is Tudor. The village, like many villages near the source of the Thames, has traces of old water-mills. Did the Isis once flow faster than it does now, that it could provide such water-power? Lower Mill at Somerford Keynes, not so long ago, was still grinding grain to feed the cattle on local farms.

LECHLADE (*Gloucestershire*)

Town or village? Guidebooks seem to disagree, but the fact that it has a Market Place, the way the buildings are grouped, and Lechlade's historical importance on the river (here often called Isis rather than Thames) as a commercial wharf centre for carrying stone (some of it for St Paul's Cathedral), coal and cheese by barge to London, should leave us in no doubt that it is a town. An observer of 1692 wrote: 'Here comes from Severn and Avon, handled at Tewsbury [Tewkesbury] where both these rivers do unite, and elsewhere, on horses and in carts and wagons by land, great weights of cheese, for hereabouts the boats' masters have warehouses to secure their goods . . .'

This was just a century before the Thames and Severn Canal was dug; and one of the boats' masters has left us an account of his cargoes in those days – to London, 'iron, copper, tin . . . brass, spelter, cannon, cheese, nails . . . and bomb shells'. From London, 'groceries, foreign timber . . . a few coals . . . raw hides for Tewkesbury and Worcester and gunpowder to Bristol and Liverpool'. Yet the Canal never lived up to the high hopes Lechlade and other Upper Thames towns held out for it. It was opened in 1789, its 30-mile length completed in less than seven years at a cost of £200,000. *The Gentleman's Magazine* reported that 'a boat with the union flag at her mast-head passed laden for the first time to St John's Bridge, below Lechlade, in the presence of great numbers of people, who answered a salute of twelve pieces of cannon from Buscot Park by loud huzzas. A dinner was given at five of the principal inns at Lechlade, and the day ended with a ringing of bells, a bonfire and a ball.'

Leland, in the sixteenth century, called it 'a praty old toune', and so it still is. You get marvellous little townscape views by just looking along its streets (I nearly used the word *picturesque*). The main street is wide, for this was once an important stage-coach stop on the way to Bristol and the West. Coaches came to the New Inn (redbrick, early eighteenth-century) in the Market Place from which roads lead out in three directions.

The octagonal spire of the church of St Lawrence dominates the riverscape for several miles. St Lawrence was a popular Spanish saint, and the old wool church was re-dedicated to him in honour of Katharine of Aragon, who once owned the Manor of Lechlade. The tower rises in three stages with pinnacled buttresses and castle-like parapets, decorated with splendid gargoyles. Inside, in a hollow above the east window of the Perpendicular chancel, is a statuette of the saint holding his gridiron. A third-century martyr, he was roasted alive on the gridiron, and is said to have shouted to his tormentors: 'I am done enough on this side — why don't you turn me over and eat?' The church, mainly fifteenth-century (it was begun about 1470 in Edward IV's reign), has an early sixteenth-century north porch. Inside, it is wonderfully light and spacious, nave and chancel (which run into each other) having many large windows. The chancel roof has about forty beautiful carvings of angels carrying articles used to torment Christ on the Cross, and some curious carved wooden bosses of men wrestling. In the middle of the nave hangs a brass candelabrum of 1730. The churchyard inspired a minor poem by Shelley in 1815: 'Here could I hope . . . that death did hide from human sight sweet secrets.'

Lechlade is full of interesting houses, many eighteenth-century and early nineteenth-century, some with odd door panels, as many as six and each one different (a fashion set by Richard Pace, a Regency architect hereabouts, who designed the Old Vicarage in 1805). Notice the high proportion of summer-houses and gazebos: these little look-out pavilions were once all the rage in this district. Lechlade has at least six: one is in the garden of an eighteenth-century brick house (with corner stones and an unusual porte-cochère) in Sherborne Street. Another — the most elaborate — is in Fairford Road at the gate of Butler's Court Farm, with sash windows and

Lechlade, a quiet town, is the head of navigation on the Thames and thrives on the trade the pleasure boats bring

chimney. It is believed to have been used as a shelter by passengers waiting for coaches.

Church House, just east of the church, is seventeenth-century. Morley House, on the northwest side of the Market Place, is a pleasing early eighteenth-century brick house. Burford Street (mostly eighteenth-century) is full of interesting things, such as Lime Tree Cottage, Ryton House, several Tudor dwellings and St Clothilde's Convent (formerly Lechlade Manor, *circa* 1872) which has been described as 'sort of Jacobean'.

NEWBRIDGE (*Oxfordshire*)

A village 9 miles northwest of Abingdon, on the A415 to Witney. Probably its 'newness' was because Radcot Bridge further up the river was older. Newbridge can be dated *circa* 1250, but there was much rebuilding in the fifteenth century. The stone came from Taynton quarries (near Burford, about 14 miles northwest) and was probably carried down the river Windrush by barge; and from Newbridge, Taynton stone was also carried downstream to Windsor for the building of St George's Chapel and to London for Wren's St Paul's Cathedral. John Leland, that accurate reporter, came here in Tudor times and described the country as 'fair champain ground, fruitful of corn . . . the ground there all about lieth in low meadows often overflown by rage of rain.' Apart from its two fine inns and their attractive riverside gardens, the place has not changed very much since the sixteenth century.

In a recent competition the Rose Revived has been voted the most beautifully named inn in Britain. Its history is relatively prosaic. It was once a hermitage; then an inn called the Chequers; then the Barge; then the Rose. A new landlord took over and called it the Crown. His successor, instead of calling it the Rose and Crown, as a less imaginative man might have done, gave it its present poetic and unforgettable name. On the right bank opposite is another inn, the Maybush, so close to the bridge as to be almost part of it.

Newbridge is in the parish of Standlake, an amorphous village with no special character and a good deal of development. However, it has some rewarding parts. St Giles' Church has much of the thirteenth and fourteenth centuries in it, and the west tower, octagonal with a spire too small, is odd. There seem to have been many additions in the thirteenth century, notably the transepts which originally had chapels attached. Notice the arch from aisle to north transept which is enlivened by corbels carved to represent women's heads. The church was restored in the 1880s, hence the angels about the roof, the carved Victorian woodwork and the ornate south door. The Rectory dates back to *circa* 1500, with a large wing added about 1660 with mullioned windows. The Manor House, half-timbered, is roughly the same date; and Gaunt House, $\frac{1}{2}$ mile away, was besieged in the Civil War.

OXFORD (*Oxfordshire*)

Derived from 'Oxen-ford'. How can I tell you about Oxford in less than a quarter of a million words? We must select a few of the best things and not try to see everything. Remember that Oxford is not just a university city: it has industry. Before young William Morris, afterwards Lord Nuffield, turned a bicycle shop, via a motorcycle factory, into a large part of what we now know as British Leyland, Oxford had only two major industries: printing and publishing at the Oxford University Press, and the manufacture of Frank Cooper's marmalade.

There is no city in the world like Oxford except Cambridge. One of the world's great centres of learning, Oxford has produced many leaders of British political, artistic, religious and scientific life. Prime Ministers of different parties began their careers here, from Pitt to Peel, Asquith to Attlee, Sir Harold Wilson to Mrs Margaret Thatcher. Many of them learned their Parliamentary manners at the famous Union Debating Society in St Michael's Street. Here Cardinal Wolsey, Sir Walter Raleigh, Sir Christopher Wren and Halley the astronomer all worked.

It was here that Florey developed penicillin, and several Nobel prize-winners (especially in the field of medicine) had their laboratories.

Oxford is Europe's oldest university except for the Sorbonne in Paris. We know that there was a fortified village here in the eighth and ninth centuries, built as a defence against the Danes, and by the Norman Conquest there seems to have been a centre of scholarship. The collegiate system began in the thirteenth century and the first chancellor was appointed in 1214.

We can explore the heart of Oxford by means of a perambulation starting at Carfax where the main north-south and east-west streets intersect. Everybody's favourites differ, but I want to include Christ Church College ('The House') and Cathedral; a walk down the whole length of High Street ('The High'); Magdalen College and Addison's Walk by the river Cherwell; New College, with its Chapel and Gardens; and Broad Street ('The Broad'). Anything else we have time for, such as libraries, museums and art galleries, will be a bonus. In warm weather, try to make time for hiring a punt just by Magdalen Bridge and poling up the Cherwell with its wonderful backwaters.

Assuming that your own boat is moored below Folly Bridge, and that you have only a day or two to spend here, you would be wise to call at the Tourist Information Centre in St Aldates, the street leading from Folly Bridge to Carfax, for help in planning your visit. Most Colleges open their quadrangles and chapels to visitors in the afternoons. Opening times are posted on college gates.

Christ Church College (in St Aldates) was founded in 1524 by Cardinal Wolsey who ruthlessly suppressed St Frideswide's Priory and other religious houses to pay for it. Tom Quad (264 × 261 feet) is the largest in Oxford, and Tom Tower (designed by Wren, 1682) contains Great Tom, a bell that tolls 101 times every night at 9.05 p.m. because there were originally

The river near Newbridge winds its way through low meadows

101 students who had to be in college by curfew time. The magnificent Hall contains a wonderful collection of portraits, and the staircase leading to it is by James Wyatt, with seventeenth-century fan tracery on the ceiling. The Cathedral (the smallest in England) is also the College Chapel: there are traces of Saxon work, but most of it is thirteenth-century. Among many fine features are some windows by Burne-Jones.

Walking east down High Street, we pass, on the left, *Brasenose College* (1509 with many seventeenth-century additions), *St Mary's Church*, and *All Souls College*, founded in 1437 in memory of the dead at the battle of Agincourt. All Souls is unique in that it has no undergraduates, only Fellows elected for their academic achievements. On the right, opposite St Mary's, is *Oriel College*, most of whose buildings are seventeenth-century and later, although it was endowed by Edward II in 1326; and *University College*, probably the oldest, endowed in 1249 by William, Archdeacon of Durham. On the right, Logic Lane leads to *Merton College*, founded in 1264, which has the oldest quadrangle (Mob Quad) and the oldest library in England (built 1371–9).

We turn left, by the *Queen's College* (the Queen was Philippa, wife of Edward III, but the buildings are mainly by Wren and Hawksmoor) into Queen's Lane. Please glance quickly at the friendly small quad of *St Edmund Hall* on your right, founded in memory of St Edmund of Abingdon, the first Oxford graduate to become Archbishop of Canterbury; and notice, next to it, St Peter in the East, dating back to Saxon times, now the Hall's library.

Queen's Lane becomes New College Lane, and the entrance to *New College* is on the right. It was founded in 1379 by William of Wykeham, Bishop of Winchester, who also founded Winchester College (his idea was to strengthen the ranks of the clergy after the Black Death). New College retains much of Wykeham's original building in the Cloister, the Chapel, the Hall, the Muniment Tower and the Kitchen. The Chapel, one of the largest in Oxford, was lavishly restored in 1877–81 by Sir Gilbert Scott, but much of the original building remains. Notice the stalls with their carved elbow-rests and misericords (fourteenth-century) and the great variety of stained glass. The gardens, enclosed by the old city wall, are deeply peaceful.

Continuing up New College Lane, we pass under the *Bridge of Sighs* connecting two parts of Hertford College and into Catte Street, with Wren's 1663 *Sheldonian Theatre* (where degrees are conferred) almost opposite and the *Bodleian Old Library* (containing more than three million books and 50,000 manuscripts) on the left, and the great dome of the *Radcliffe Camera* reading room (1737–49) beyond. Turning right and then left quickly, we come into Broad Street with *Exeter College* (1314) on the left and *Jesus College* (popular with Welshmen ever since Elizabeth I founded it in 1571) down Turl Street. On the right is *Trinity College* (1555), founded by Sir Thomas Pope whose alabaster tomb is in the chapel; and *Balliol College*, founded in the thirteenth century for 'sixteen poor scholars' by John de Baliol as a penance for kidnapping the Bishop of Durham. Its buildings are mostly Victorian. Opposite the west front in St Giles is *Martyrs' Memorial*, where Cranmer was burned at the stake in 1556.

Magdalen is a very large college with a stunning variety of architecture. Chapel, Hall, Cloisters, Deer Park and Addison's Walk – take your time, don't miss anything. Founded in 1458 by William of Waynflete (he was successively Master of Winchester, Provost of Eton, Bishop of Winchester and Lord Chancellor), its best-known feature is its dominating Bell Tower (1509), 144 feet high, from whose top the choir sing a traditional Latin hymn at 5 a.m. on May Day.

The Perpendicular chapel, badly damaged by the Puritans, was built in the 1470s and was restored around 1830 by L. Cottingham who also designed the stone screen and reredos.

Merton College Oxford – this college houses the oldest library in England

Christ Church College has the largest quad in Oxford University; it is called Tom Quad

The altarpiece of Christ bearing the Cross is by a Spanish artist *circa* 1650. In the Chapel is the tomb of Richard Patten of Waynflete, the founder's father; and in the ante-chapel (as in New College Chapel) the fifteenth-century stalls have grotesque carved animals on them.

The Hall has a magnificent Jacobean screen and an oriel window with portraits of Charles I and Queen Henrietta Maria. The Library contains some extremely valuable manuscripts and specimens of early printing.

Lincoln, Wadham, Worcester and St John's (both noted for their beautiful gardens), Pembroke, Corpus Christi, St Catherine's with its brand-new, rather frightening Danish building – these should not be offended that I have not mentioned them. They too have essential and historic wonders.

The *Ashmolean Museum of Art and Archaeology* (open daily) in Beaumont Street, the oldest museum in Britain, contains Greek, Roman, Egyptian, Mesopotamian and Ancient British antiquities, coins, paintings and curiosities such as Guy Fawkes' lantern and a jewel said to have belonged to Alfred the Great. The *Museum of Oxford* in St Aldates (open weekdays except Mondays) traces the city's history from Norman times to Lord Nuffield and his famous Bullnose Morris car. The *University Museum*, in Parks Road, specializes in natural history and is open daily (except Sundays). Near it, the *Pitts-River Museum* (open weekday afternoons) has an ethnological collection including artifacts found by Captain Cook. The riches of Oxford are endless. . . .

For panoramic views of the city, climb Carfax Tower (74 feet high, open daily in summer), or the University Church of St Mary the Virgin, High Street (88 feet high, open daily).

It is also possible, if you are so minded, to sail *underneath* Oxford (you should get permission from the City Engineer). The Trill Mill Stream begins near Oxford Castle and links the Castle Mill Stream of the Thames with the Thames itself, and returns by way of Christ Church Memorial Garden. Occasionally undergraduates try to navigate it. It is somewhat cleaner today than it was in the Middle Ages, when it was both a source of drinking water and a sewer. In the early 1920s the skeletons of a man and a girl were found in a boat on the stream; and twenty years before that, three boys explored it successfully in a canoe. One of them, then at Oxford High School, was the future Lawrence of Arabia.

RADCOT (*Oxfordshire*)

Meaning 'red cottage' or 'cottage thatched with reeds'. It is 3 miles north of Faringdon on the A4095. A Saxon charter says there was a stone bridge here in 958. Was it in the same place as the present (apparently fourteenth-century) bridge? The piers, however, may be some 200 years older. It was built of stone from Taynton quarries, like Newbridge, and is probably the oldest bridge on the Thames. It may have been built after a battle in 1387 when Robert de Vere, Earl of Oxford, in full retreat from Bolingbroke's army, found a bridge in ruins and was forced to ride his horse through the river ('leaping from the parapet' says one version) and swim to the opposite bank.

There seems to have been strife here in the Civil War too, if we assume that the earthworks known as the Garrison, just north of the bridge, are of the same date. Radcot was held for a time by Royalist forces based on Faringdon. Radcot House, nearby, is late seventeenth-century, with unusual oval attic windows and attractive gables. Mind how you go over the bridge: motorists tend to approach it too fast, and the roadway is only 12 feet wide. At the Swan Hotel, with its attractive riverside gardens, it is reputed that the coarse fishing here is very good.

SHIFFORD (*Oxfordshire*)

Meaning 'sheep ford'. Shifford is 6 miles east of Bampton via Cote — but access is on foot for the last bit — it is easier by water. There is almost nothing here except peace and quiet — the stone buildings of Shifford Farm, and the little chapel of St Mary which stands alone palely and loitering in the fields (built in 1863 on the site of a Georgian church). There must have been a town here a thousand years ago, if we may believe an Anglo-Saxon poem which says that Alfred the Great held a Parliament here. The poem is full of Saxon hero-worship:

There sat, at Siford, many thanes, many bishops and many learned men, proud earls and awful knights. There was Earl Aelfric, very learned in the law, and Alfred, England's herdsman, England's darling. He was King in England: he began to teach them, as we may hear, how they should live.

Shifford Lock is on a channel cut in 1896 to avoid a long bend to Duxford: here the original course of the river is still shallow enough to be forded by foot.

STANTON HARCOURT (*Oxfordshire*)

The name means 'enclosure on strong ground' or 'near stones'. It is 2 miles northwest of Bablockhythe. A village of thatched cottages and grey stone, with church, parsonage, and the remains of an historic manor house. The cruciform church of St Michael is a mixture of Early English and Perpendicular with a Norman sawtooth doorway in the porch. In the Harcourt Chapel and the south transept are several Harcourt family monuments, from that of Sir Robert, standard-bearer to Henry VII at Bosworth Field, with his wife Margaret, up to William the 3rd Earl Harcourt in 1830. The Harcourt Chapel was built *circa* 1470, and may be the work of William Orchard, the master mason of Magdalen College. On the east wall is a Victorian plaque tracing the family back to Bernard the Dane in 876. The stained glass in both chapel and chancel is mostly thirteenth-century. Two monuments have epitaphs by Alexander Pope, the poet and friend of the Harcourt family: one of them is to John Hewet and Sarah Drew who were 'both in one instant killed by lightning on the last day of

July 1718'. It happened in a haystack at harvest time, and Pope, much affected by this tale of rustic love, wrote a verse epitaph on them and sent it to his friend, Lady Mary Wortley Montagu, whose views on marriage were cynical. Foreseeing 'a beaten wife and cuckold swain', *her* verse ended: 'Now they are happy in their doom, For Pope hath wrote upon their tomb.'

Most of the Manor House, originally medieval, was demolished when the Harcourts, after six centuries here removed to Nuneham Courtenay. The 1st Earl Harcourt, having made the Grand Tour of Europe, found Stanton countryside not dramatic enough. But Pope's Tower and other features survive. The Tower (late fifteenth-century), formerly a chapel with a priest's lodging, was Pope's home for two summers while he finished translating the fifth book of Homer's *Iliad*. Pope inscribed, on a pane of glass measuring 6×2 inches, the words, 'In the year 1718 Alexander Pope finished here the fifth volume of Homer'. The glass is now at Nuneham Courtenay.

Next to Pope's Tower is the medieval Great Kitchen – the most complete of its kind in Britain. It has no chimney – the smoke escaped through shutters in the pyramid roof, which is surmounted by a weather-vane with a griffon (the Harcourt family emblem). Pope made fun of it, saying that the local country folk believed it was the scene of an annual Witches' Sabbath. The Manor gardens are very rewarding; they are open regularly.

The village has several ponds, which give pleasing reflections of buildings. The seventeenth-century Parsonage has medieval fishponds beside it: it is a fine, solid stone house built about 1675 and, in all essentials, unaltered.

North of the church is Wesley's Cottage, where John and Charles Wesley and their sister Kezin used to stay when they came to visit their friend the vicar. The Devil's Quoits, three prehistoric stones near the village (the biggest is 9 feet high and 6 feet wide), are of doubtful origin: were they put there to commemorate the battle of Bampton, which local lore says took place between Saxons and Britons in AD 614? Or are they just ancient boundary stones? Or the remains of a Druids' circle? Near the village is the secret wartime airfield from which Churchill flew to Yalta in 1945.

WOODSTOCK (*Oxfordshire*)

The name means a 'place in the woods'. Woodstock is 8 miles north of Oxford. The 'woods' were Wychwood Forest, of which this was once a part. It was a 'royal demesne' before the Norman Conquest and is mentioned as such in Domesday Book. Henry I built a palace-cum-hunting lodge here, and also a zoo with lions, camels and a favourite porcupine. Henry II held a council here in 1163, and came here to enjoy both hunting and Fair Rosamund (*see* Godstow). Edward, the Black Prince (sometimes called Edward of Woodstock), was born here in 1331. Woodstock Manor or Palace was one of the several places where Elizabeth I was imprisoned during the reign of her sister Mary; she was here for six months in 1554. This favourite Royal residence (which stood a little to the north of the bridge across the lake in Blenheim Park) was badly damaged in the Civil War, and the manor was eventually presented to the victorious Duke of Marlborough (*see* Blenheim).

We do not know clearly what the old Palace looked like, but all reports say it was magnificent, with a 'spacious church-like hall', a circular chapel, and a 'great cloister' with gardens in the middle. The buildings were much enlarged by Henry VII; and yet by the time Elizabeth was imprisoned here they had fallen into disrepair, so that she occupied only the gatehouse. The Manor's destruction is described in Scott's *Woodstock* (1826), set in the Civil War: it then belonged to the Cavalier Sir Henry Lee, Ranger of Woodstock Forest, whose daughter fell in love with a Roundhead.

The resident lock-keeper at Shifford Lock. The lock is very isolated and lonely

Today, Woodstock is a mellow country town with still much of the eighteenth century in it, despite twentieth-century encroachment. The cottage industry of hand-stitched glove-making, 400 years old, survives. Only two houses show the influence of Vanbrugh's Blenheim — Hope House (early eighteenth-century) in Hensington Road and the Rectory, seventeenth-century but altered in Georgian times in a way Pevsner finds 'elephantine'.

In High Street and Market Place are numerous seventeenth-century and eighteenth-century houses and shop-fronts, some with bow-windows. Glorious old inns abound: the Star (with eighteenth-century façade, and seventeenth-century back), and, opposite, the justly famous Bear Hotel, which likes to trace its origins back to 1237, but most of what we see is a mixture of sixteenth to eighteenth centuries. Notice the fine carved stone fireplace in the bar. The town hall, by Sir William Chambers (1766), was commissioned by the 4th Duke of Marlborough: originally a council chamber on arches (the underpart may have been used as a market) the arches were enclosed in 1898. In Park Street are the post office (in a seventeenth-century house), Fletcher's House (sixteenth-century, now a museum) and Chaucer's House which is probably on the site of a fourteenth-century house where the poet and his son used to stay when visiting Woodstock. Three more old hostelries, the Feathers Hotel, the Marlborough (in Oxford Road) and the Pyed Bull are all eighteenth-century. Old Woodstock (also on the Oxford Road) isn't all that old: most of the cottages are Victorian.

The church of St Mary Magdalene has only been Woodstock's parish church since the eighteenth century. Its predecessor was St Martin's at Bladon. The oldest part is the Norman south doorway with zigzag decorations. The east window is thirteenth-century, the octagonal font only a little later. The west porch, west window and inner doorway all belong to the fifteenth century. The rest is mostly Victorian, from a major restoration in 1878. The classical tower (1785) with parapet and pinnacles contains bells which you are sure to notice before you have been long in the town: they have a different peal for each day of the week.

WYTHAM (*Oxfordshire*)

Meaning 'homestead by the bend'. This village is 3 miles west-northwest of Oxford off the A34. The 'bend' is the 8-mile meander — practically a north–south U-turn — between Pinkhill Lock and Folly Bridge, Oxford; so that Wytham is on a sort of peninsula about $3\frac{1}{2}$ miles across. Light craft such as canoes can cut out three locks (but they will lose Godstow and Port Meadow) by using Seacourt Stream, which branches off to the right by Hagley Pool, just above King's Lock, and rejoins the river a little before Folly Bridge. In the last years of the eighteenth century, when the new canals were a real threat to river traffic, a Government report suggested that the 'Wytham stream' (i.e. the Seacourt) should be the main navigation channel. 'Seacourt' was the name of a lost village about midway between Wytham and Botley on the hillside where Marley Wood meets Wytham Park. The stream runs by Wytham's old mill-house and the University Field Station.

Wytham, which seems to have had the same name since 957, the earliest written record we have of it, is a village of limestone cottages, some with thatched roofs, others with stone tiles. One or two new houses have been built with the same materials so as to harmonize, and it is not easy to guess the age of any building. Even the dovecot at the White Hart Inn is of a piece. The church was rebuilt in 1814 with materials taken from Cumnor Place (*see* Cumnor). There is some seventeenth-century Flemish stained glass in the east window, all in blues and yellows. Notice too the grotesque corbels of bagpipe-players. There are brasses (on a tombstone in front of the altar) to Robert de Wightam (he is shown in armour, for he fought in the Hundred Years' War and died in 1406) and his wife Juliana.

The so-called Wytham Abbey, once the seat of the Earls of Abingdon, which still has Tudor gatehouses and hall, was perhaps never an abbey at all, though there may have been an ancient nunnery on the site. The sixteenth-century house was built by the Harcourts (a branch of the Stanton Harcourt family) and much altered by the 5th Earl of Abingdon, that user of other people's rubble: this time, instead of Cumnor Place, he used Rycote Park, near Thame. But the doorway by which you enter the churchyard (it has a Perpendicular arch), though next to the Abbey gates, came from Cumnor.

Wytham Woods were bequeathed to Oxford University and used by Sir Charles Elton, father of ecology in the twentieth century, for his studies of animals and his subsequent writing of *Pattern of Animal Communities* (1966).

YARNTON (*Oxfordshire*)
It is 5½ miles northwest of Oxford off the A34. The church and the Manor House are the two chief features of this pleasant stone-built village; and both owe much to Sir Thomas Spencer in the early seventeenth century. He built the Manor, which was (like so many fine houses along the Thames Valley) badly damaged in the Civil War. It was originally one of the largest Jacobean houses in England, but the Spencers could not afford to rebuild it, and it was sold to a farmer who demolished two of the three wings. It continued as a farm until 1897, when the new owner had it restored by Thomas Garner, who also laid out the gardens in a very formal style. There is still much of the seventeenth century inside the house (unfortunately not open to the public).

The church of St Bartholomew, originally thirteenth-century, was enlarged and restored between 1611 and 1616 by Sir Thomas Spencer, who added the Spencer Chapel and the south porch, also the four-stage southwest tower. The church is full of Spencer tombs and monuments. The stained glass, very plentiful, is English and also there is much Flemish, collected by one Alderman Fletcher, and presented, with other gifts, to the church in the early 1800s. In the Spencer Chapel is Oxfordshire's largest collection of seventeenth-century armorial glass, showing angels holding shields of the Spencers and related families.

Byways, an Edwardian small house, designed by C. R. Ashbee in 1907, provides Yarnton's only literary association. In about 1920 it belonged to Agnes Evans, friend of A. E. Coppard, author of *Adam and Eve and Pinch Me*, a collection of short stories, one of which is set in Yarnton. He gave her an acacia tree for her new garden, and commemorated it in a poem, 'The Sapling'.

CHAPTER THREE

Upper Thames

Below Folly Bridge, the Isis does not appear quite as it did – and how I betray my age as I use this phrase – before World War II. Where are the old college barges that excited undergraduates used to jump off, fully clothed, into the water in Eights Week? Instead, there are more practical boathouses. We used to invite our families to tea on the college barge while watching the races. The barges had a kind of mad beauty: some of them had once belonged to London City Livery companies, dating back to the days when the Lord Mayor's Procession took place on the river. They had windowed prows like Nelson's *Victory*, but being made chiefly of wood, they could not last forever. One or two of them are being restored by the Oxford College Barge Preservation Trust. Others have been used as houseboats elsewhere: yet others have been destroyed. I miss them.

Head of the River means not Thames Head, but the winning crew in Summer Eights Week, the boat races which begin above Iffley Lock. On the south side of the bridge is the headquarters of Salter's, who run passenger launches up and down the river and make light craft for all kinds of river users. On our left are Christ Church Meadows, at whose banks the barges used to be; and as they end, Oxford's second and very different river, the Cherwell, joins the Isis in two streams. The Cherwell (which, like the Isis, has given its name to an undergraduate magazine) does not accommodate motor-launches. It is essentially for punts and canoes and girls on warm summer afternoons, and you hire your light craft at Magdalen Bridge. You can take punts upstream for about 7 miles to Islip, and canoes about 20 miles, as far as Aynho. The Cherwell rises in the borderland of Northamptonshire and Warwickshire, not far from Daventry. It links up with the Oxford Canal and so with the Avon and the Midlands, Wales and the Humber Canals. Soon after it leaves Magdalen Grove, the Cherwell flows past Parson's Pleasure, the famous nude bathing place where women are asked to walk round the screening arrangements while men only push their boats up the rollers. One's memories are of very old dons in jock straps . . .

Opposite the mouth of the Cherwell, on the right, is the University Boat House. Soon the river bends and narrows: this is the Gut, where much of the bumping in bumping races happens. Just before we go under Donnington Bridge (a structure of no great interest), glance about to see if you can find any of the old college barges being repaired in an inlet. We are now within $\frac{1}{2}$ mile of Iffley, and it is rewarding to look back occasionally for a fair view of the University.

A few yards before you enter Iffley Lock you may notice a big mooring ring at the side: this is the starting place of the boat races which end by Folly Bridge. Iffley Lock was one of the first pound locks (called turnpikes at the time) built by the Oxford-Burcot Commissioners in the seventeenth century at the command of the first two Stuart kings. After the lock we pass under the Isis road bridge; ahead is an old railway bridge, and immediately before it Hinksey Stream (linking up with Seacourt Stream and Hagley Pool, which we saw on the other side of Oxford a few hundred yards above King's Lock) joins the river from the right.

Past Kennington Island the river is rather featureless, except for Bagley Wood rising away on our right, until we come to Sandford Lock, with its thundering weir and the well-known chimney of its papermill. The weir-pool is notorious for drownings, and you are warned by a stone column that five undergraduates, all, strangely, of Christ Church, lost their lives here in 1843, 1872 and 1921. The last two were Michael Llewelyn

Davies, whose guardian was Sir James Barrie, who had written the story of *Peter Pan* for him and his brother, and Michael's friend, Rupert Buxton.

Just under 2 miles further on, Radley College boathouse comes up on the right. Radley rivals Eton as a rowing school, and you will probably see one of its crews training. You can't see the College, or anything much on this side, because the river bank is so high. So look at the water, which has suddenly turned dark blue. Why? Not because it is near Oxford, where the river is greenish brown. Is it some quirk of geology hereabouts? I do not know.

On the left (east) bank a deer park opens up, and Nuneham House (which was built by the Courtenay family in the eighteenth century but now belongs to the University) can be seen — intermittently obscured by trees — at the top of a gentle hill of turf, set in an estate and village of 1,200 acres. The park gives way to Lock Wood, the trees coming down to the water's edge. We are now on a relentless curve to the right, and after passing under another railway bridge we are less than $\frac{1}{2}$ mile from Abingdon. Just before Abingdon Lock, a channel branches off to the left — we shall meet the other end of it at Culham Bridge 2 miles on. This is known as Swift Ditch, and is believed to have been the original course of the river before the monks of Abingdon Abbey, in the tenth and eleventh centuries, dug and deepened the channel that now goes through Abingdon town. But Swift Ditch was in use until 1790, when the present Abingdon Lock was built. Though overgrown, it can still be explored by canoe. The part of Abingdon between Swift Ditch and the main river is called Andersey Island.

The fairest view in Abingdon — and perhaps it is the best country-town-scape of the whole Thames — is the sight of St Helen's Church spire behind the tall chimneys of the early eighteenth-century almshouses seen across the water from the opposite bank. The bridge, altered in the 1920s, has foundations from the fifteenth century and must have been more handsome

once than it is now. Soon afterwards, the river Ock joins the Thames on the right: it is marked by an iron bridge, a monument to the old Wiltshire and Berkshire Canal which used to enter the river 100 yards further down. The Ock, a shallow stream which knows no town before it arrives in Abingdon, is said to be rich in crayfish. Unfortunately it is not navigable: a pity, because to canoe up it would be a wonderful way to see the Vale of the White Horse.

We are now in Culham Reach, where the river broadens out and is full of dinghy-sailors. If we are in a launch, we remember our river manners and the rule that power gives way to sail. By Culham Bridge, on the left, Swift Ditch re-enters the mainstream. The bridge, which gives us some idea of what Abingdon Bridge once looked like, was built in 1415 by the Guild of the Holy Cross.

About $\frac{1}{4}$ mile above Culham Lock, a stream goes off to the right: this, like Swift Ditch, is the old course of the river, and pours itself over roaring weirs into Sutton Pools. I am going to ask you to make a detour soon, but not here. This is your chance to see a wonderland — the cool peace of Sutton Pool and the ancient beauty of Sutton Courtenay: water deep enough for launches, fringed everywhere with weeping willows. All this is not to be missed. After Culham Lock a backwater goes off immediately to the right, and this is the way to reach the village. Let us give thanks to the grasping medieval miller who once had a mill here, and charged such high tolls to river-users that they bypassed him with the Cut that now takes us through Culham Lock. Thus was created one of the most beautiful backwaters on the Thames.

Under a railway bridge — not a disused one this time for it carries the main line to Oxford — and Appleford village is now on the right: you can just see the church spire among the trees. (That railway bridge, by the way, can be a hazard to tall sailing craft — it is only 13 feet above the water.) This is a good stretch for both sailing and fishing, and you will probably see one of

the characteristic sights of the Upper and Middle Thames – rapt little boys in the early morning, casting very professionally, and very old men with absolutely stationary rods, sitting half asleep in the shelter of vast umbrellas.

Clifton Cut, another example of corner-snipping on a meandering river which has created an artificial island between it and the old channel, brings us to Clifton Lock. Scenically, the three miles between Culham and Clifton Locks are fairly flat and dull, so for what we are about to receive let us be truly thankful.

I have a special affection for Clifton Hampden. It has been criticized as being 'ruined by caravans'. I have not found it so. The caravans are there indeed, but spaced out discreetly and sheltered by trees. When Jerome K. Jerome visited the Barley Mow Inn here in the 1870s it was a thatched fourteenth-century cottage clearly visible from the river. Today it is separated from the water by a tree-fringed meadow 50 yards long, but do not let that deter you from its excellent hospitality. The church of St Michael and All Angels dominates the picture from a steep little cliff, and faces Sir George Gilbert Scott's graceful (1864) bridge across the river, in mellowed red brick with Gothic arches. But why did he make it so narrow? There is room for only one traffic-lane controlled by stop-go lights.

Clifton Lock is probably the best place to branch off if you want to visit Long Wittenham. Take the channel on the east side of Clifton Lock: it is navigable for small cruisers as far as the Plough Inn, and the backwater is most attractive.

The river, which is flowing due north, having curved steeply from Appleford, now begins to curve, serpent-like in the opposite direction, so that after $2\frac{3}{4}$ miles, when it reaches Day's Lock, it will be flowing due south. The village of Burcot, on the left, apart from its historical importance in the navigation of the river, is pleasant if unremarkable: some of its houses and gardens come down to the water's edge, but you cannot moor here.

Sutton Pool is a pretty backwater; here the old course of the river falls over several weirs into the pool

By now you will have had your first sight of Sinodun Hill, a landmark for many miles around – twin mounds which were made into prehistoric earthworks, whether for religious or military purposes is uncertain. These mounds are also known as Wittenham Clumps because of the trees on top, and the locals have coarser expressions for them, such as Mother Dunch's Buttocks – Mother Dunch was the wife of an unpopular local squire whose family had been associated with Little Wittenham since before the Civil War: the Dunches were related by marriage to Oliver Cromwell. What is indisputable is that it is well worth the climb to the top of Sinodun for a splendid view of the winding Thames, with Little Wittenham Wood in the foreground.

Day's Lock, the main gauging station for measuring the flow of water in the upper river, was known as Dorchester or Wittenham Lock until about 150 years ago. Dorchester is on the Thame, not the Thames. The Thame, which joins the Thames-

Wittenham Clumps on Sinodun Hill, near Day's Lock; once a commanding Iron Age hill-fort

Isis about ½ mile below the lock, and rises near Aylesbury about 25 miles away, is shallow and cannot safely be navigated by motor-launches, though canoes can penetrate several miles upstream. The Thames now twists and turns a good deal, and gives you different views of Sinodun – now you see it, now you don't. Sometimes you think you are going backwards, which is as well, because the river is dullish until, about a mile above Shillingford, the trees grow thicker, and the banks are sprinkled with desirable riverside houses as we approach Shillingford Bridge, one of the finest on the whole river. Built in 1826, there seems to be only one word for its well-proportioned three arches in brick and stone – 'noble'. The Shillingford Bridge Hotel on the right, almost on the bridge, is handsome but for my taste a little over-sophisticated, with its Hollywood-style swimming-pool amid turf as fine as a putting-green. Behind it rise thickly wooded slopes and a line of Lombardy poplars, a beautiful setting for what I always think of as a honeymoon or romantic-weekend hotel. There used to be a dragon's head prow of an Oxford college barge displayed here – perhaps there still is, but on my last visit I could not find it. Hotel, bridge, woods – that's all there is, but it has magic.

The next mile is less interesting to look at, but it has its compensations. On the left side the riverbank rises sharply, pitted with holes where sand martins' nests either are or have been. On the right, the land becomes flatter, giving us our last glimpse of Sinodun, and soon there are willows and reeds and all the waterfowl the river provides.

Benson Lock, like most locks below Godstow, is fully mechanized. The village of Benson was important in the eighteenth century as a stopping place for the London–Oxford coach, which is why it has three large inns, the Castle (with its original wrought-iron sign), the White Hart and the Crown. Around Benson Lock and cruiser station are all the amenities the river-traveller could possibly want; but there is a still more important reason for going ashore here: 2½ miles away – and you may have to walk it unless you have fold-up bicycles on board – is Ewelme, the most complete fifteenth-century village in England and not to be missed.

Benson merges into Preston Crowmarsh, the village on our left, as the river turns due south and stops wriggling for the next 3 miles. Indeed, there are no locks between Benson and Cleeve, giving a clear stretch of 6½ miles, the longest on the whole river. This makes it a useful training stretch for Oxford and other crews, especially by Wallingford, which lies on the right bank. On the opposite side is the village of Crowmarsh Gifford, which is worth a short walk to see the small Norman church of St Mary Magdalene. If I call Wallingford a sleepy town, I mean it no harm: it is certainly busy enough, but it has a deep peace about it which to the city-dweller is enviable. Here, you think, people know what really matters, like the working of the land.

Wallingford Bridge, which has seventeen arches, is a study in architectural history. Six of the stone arches cross the river; the other eleven carry the road over a flood-plain. You will notice that the bridge on the downstream side has pointed arches, with ribs underneath (we have seen those ribs before, at Newbridge and Radcot), while on the other side the arches are rounded and smooth. This is because the bridge was widened in the early years of the nineteenth century, in a different style based on different engineering principles. It does not make the bridge any less noble. There is a great deal of the eighteenth century in Wallingford, and some of it is to be seen after we have negotiated the bridge, as soundly proportioned Georgian houses appear, with gardens reaching down to the water.

We are now near the site of Chalmore Hole Lock, removed exactly a century ago. Why did anybody bother to build it in 1838, since the fall of water was only 18 inches? Just greed for lock fees? Readers of *Three Men in a Boat* will remember the narrator's panicky confusion as he rowed down the river trying to find it, not knowing that it had been removed since his last river trip.

The river again becomes rather featureless for a mile or two, until, on the left, Mongewell Park comes up. The small Norman church of St John Baptist, now mostly ruined, stands by the river in a romantic setting. The original Mongewell House, which was Georgian, was replaced in the 1890s by a late seventeenth-century-style house. This, in 1953, became the nucleus of Carmel College, a group of buildings making up a theological school and comprising a synagogue, classrooms, amphitheatre, and an exhibition hall — a kind of miniature university set in attractive parkland. Opposite, an almost imperceptible stream, Bradford Brook, joins the Thames. Just before it, on the right, you may be able to see traces of an archeological mystery: this is the line of Grim's Ditch or Dyke. Grim is the Devil, and his dyke, which stretches for 50 miles towards Henley and into Buckinghamshire, may have been a Roman *vallum*, or a Saxon boundary of the seventh century, between Wessex and Mercia — nobody knows.

After Mongewell, still on the left bank, comes North Stoke, which you can barely see for the trees. The river now veers slightly to the right in a southwesterly direction, and soon the grim Fairmile Mental Hospital comes into view on the right-hand side. Beyond it, well away from the river, is the village of Cholsey. It is a long time since we saw a well-designed railway bridge, and now, beyond three islets, we have it: Brunel's brick viaduct at Moulsford, comparable (except in size of span) to his great bridge at Maidenhead.

The river straightens out and begins to turn south again as we approach Moulsford proper, passing its much-restored Norman church beside the river. A little further on is one of the river's most celebrated inns, the Beetle and Wedge ('beetle' comes from an Old English word meaning a heavy mallet). This ancient inn is now more of a modern hotel, and you will be glad of it. If you have been towpath-walking for the last few miles (say, from Benson downstream) you will be pretty tired and probably harassed. Not only is there the usual lack of ferries, and no other way of crossing the river since Wallingford, but the towpath itself is often in poor condition because of the eroded river bank; to get from Benson to Wallingford on foot, it is best to cross over Wallingford Bridge, turn right through Crowmarsh Gifford, and so, through North and South Stoke, to Goring. If you choose the other bank, you will have to turn away from the river at Cholsey, return to it at the Beetle and Wedge and stick by the river until you come to Streatley, where you can cross the river by Goring Bridge. All this is explained in the invaluable booklet *The Thames Walk*, published by The Ramblers' Association. My snap judgment is that you are far better off in a boat.

Before the exasperating rearrangement of county boundaries it was easy and convenient to think of the left bank (going downstream) as Oxfordshire (until you get to Reading) and the right bank as Berkshire. This is still possible about $\frac{1}{2}$ mile below the Beetle and Wedge, where the county boundary comes down to the river on the right side, which we can now, for many miles, call Berkshire.

If the river has seemed to be undramatic for the last stretches let us prepare ourselves for something really grand. Two lines of chalk hills (or should they be regarded as one?) are separated, indeed cut through, by the Thames, giving us the Berkshire Downs to the right and the Chilterns to the left. This is, of course, the Goring Gap. The first outpost of Goring (or perhaps the last outpost of South Stoke), on what we may now call the Oxfordshire bank again, is another famous riverside pub, the Olde Leatherne Bottel, attractively covered with russet tiles and creeper. You may, of course, wish to sample the medicinal waters of the Goring Spring which bubbles up here — a seventeenth-century authority said they are good for corns, ulcers and sore eyes — but it is more probable that you will by now be needing something stronger.

At Cleeve we enter the Gap, as the Berkshire Downs come into view. Cleeve Lock, built in 1788, claims to have the oldest lock-keeper's cottage on the river. It looks more Victorian than Georgian, with its tall chimneys and pointed windows, and has great charm. Cleeve Mill, on a backwater, reminds us of why so many weirs and locks were originally built. Between here and Goring Lock is only $\frac{5}{8}$ mile: as Benson to Cleeve was the longest distance between two locks (a great advantage to the Oxford University Boat Club) so Cleeve to Goring is the shortest. But let us not hurry: this little stretch of river is divided into swift streams and numerous backwaters by a chain of small islands (you will need a light boat for some of the shallower waters). All are fringed and sheltered by the trees – mostly willows – which are the making of the character of the Middle and Upper Thames.

The Gap is looming around us, chalk hills showing flecks of white where there are chalkpits, beech woods on top, chestnuts and maples too; and soon the roaring of the weir at Goring Lock can be heard. This lock, like Boulter's, has three pairs of gates instead of two to enable more boats to sail up and down the river in peak season. Just before we enter it, the twin townships of Goring and Streatley face each other across the water, linked by a peculiarly attractive long bridge which takes you across swiftly running streams. Goring, with its chunky church tower, is on the left – rather over-developed with housing but still pleasant to look upon. Streatley, on the right, also has a chunky church. Much more soothing with its Georgian houses, Streatley greets the river-traveller with the famous and tempting sight of the terrace of the Swan Hotel. All around, the old Thames potion of water, willows, distant Lombardy poplars, moored boats and glinting reflections works its magic. Resist it if you can.

From Goring onwards, as the effect of the Gap recedes, the smaller pictures of the riverscape come thick and fast. Between here and Mapledurham the river and its surroundings are beautiful. Without actually using the word *picturesque* – and I am not sure whether his choice of words is a leg-pull – Robert

Gibbings, writing in 1939, said that this middle section of the river was crowded with views that 'might have dropped from gold frames at the Royal Academy'.

The river bends to the left, turns due east for about $\frac{1}{2}$ mile (during which it passes under another handsome Brunel railway viaduct) and then, by Hart's Lock Wood, which comes down to the water on the Oxfordshire bank, straightens out into a southerly direction. Several generations of the Hart family served the river, and you can see, by a little bunch of islets opposite the grounds of the Child Beale Wildlife Trust at Lower Basildon, where Hart's Lock used to be. (There was also a Hart's Weir, at Eaton Bridge just above Kelmscot, kept by the same family.) The last traces of Hart's Lock were removed in 1910.

On the right bank, $\frac{1}{2}$ mile away in the woods, you should be able to catch a glimpse of the Palladian mansion of Basildon Park, built in 1776 by John Carr of York, who also designed Harewood House, redecorated Boodle's Club in London, and laid out part of Cheltenham. Basildon Church and vicarage can be seen from the river, but most of the village is farther inland. After Hart's Lock Wood, on the left bank, the grounds of Coombe Park come down to the water. Only one wing of the eighteenth-century mansion, Coombe Lodge, remains. The river flows due east again as it approaches the villages (or are they towns?) of Whitchurch and Pangbourne, twinned like Goring and Streatley. Being on opposite sides of the river, they are united by a bridge, but with a difference – it is one of the two surviving toll-bridges on the Thames (the other is Swinford Bridge, by Eynsham). Built of iron in the 1880s, it must be one of the last of its kind. Not very interesting to look at, it is a good place for an attractive view of Whitchurch Lock.

As Streatley is prettier than Goring, so Whitchurch surpasses Pangbourne. Together they offer the best of the typical

The Thames at Streatley where the bridge over the river unites it with Goring

Middle Thames riverscape, with perhaps rather too many excessively neat villa-gardens coming down to the water's edge. We are in fairly deep commuter-country. We are also in very deep 'Mr Toad' country, for Kenneth Grahame lived at Pangbourne for many years, and river-travellers can amuse themselves by studying the stately homes they see and trying to guess which of them inspired Toad Hall.

The shallow little river Pang joins the Thames by Whitchurch Lock, after an unadventurous journey through Berkshire fields, farms and woods, passing within sight of Bradfield College. It affords dry fly-fishing and is said to be full of trout.

Before we leave Pangbourne, let us remember that it was here that the Three Men In A Boat, cold and tired after two solid days of rain, abandoned ship, took a fast train to London and, after a good dinner in Soho, cheered themselves up at the Alhambra Music Hall.

Could this be Toad Hall, coming up on the left 1½ miles below Whitchurch? It is Hardwick House, well back from the river among trees on a hill — a mainly Tudor brick mansion with gables and mullioned windows where Queen Elizabeth I undoubtedly slept. Opposite it is a small island where many river-users picnic. The river, still moving east, begins to turn south above Mapledurham Lock, after which there are divided streams and islets.

There really are maples at Mapledurham. I shall not call the house, the church and the weatherboarded mill picturesque, but like Shillingford Bridge, they are the subjects of many paintings. If you wish to photograph the mill, you are advised to go round the left side of the island and take it from the backwater. This tiny village, far from any main road, isolated from the houses on the opposite bank because you cannot walk across the lock, seems invulnerable. The village was part of the setting for the television series of *The Forsyte Saga*; to Soames Forsyte, whose house was named The Shelter, this village represented England and all that it means.

The railway that followed the Thames along the right bank from Basildon to Pangbourne, and left it to cut a 2-mile corner off a bend in the river, now returns on top of a high embankment where Tilehurst Station perches as if it might fall into the water. The bungalows and moored boats become thicker, and there are not unattractive municipal gardens on either side, with a long riverside promenade before the white arches of Caversham Bridge appear. Caversham rises up a hill on the left, with Edwardian-type villas amid trees. Opposite is Reading, nowadays with much concrete; but the industrial city is not properly on the Thames. Biscuits, seeds and Oscar Wilde's jail — we shall hope to show you that there is more to Reading than this. Through Caversham Lock and downstream for a few hundred yards, and the Thames is joined on the right by the Kennet, that famous trout stream which is navigable by canoe for about 30 miles, as far as Hungerford, and is inextricably linked to the Kennet and Avon Canal. Motor cruisers can go up the canal as far as Aldermaston Wharf — but by 1986 it will be navigable through to Newbury.

I said, near the beginning of this book, that fully to enjoy the Thames you must be a connoisseur of gasworks. It is a gasworks that leads us to the unexpected pleasure of Blake's Lock on the Kennet, where, amid oldish houses and pubs with names like the Jolly Anglers, the gasholders actually contribute to the river scene.

Mapledurham House, built in 1588–1606 by the Catholic Blount family, has many relics of religious persecution

Oxford to Reading - 38 river miles

ABINGDON (*Oxfordshire*)

From 'Aebbe's dun or hill'. The wisest thing Abingdon ever did was to refuse to allow the Great Western Railway from London to Oxford to pass directly through the town, which might otherwise have grown as big and industrial as Reading. Abingdon has been a prosperous market town for at least 900 years. Its Monday market has existed since before 1086, and the Fairs of St Mary, St Edmund and St Mark were known all over England in their day. So it makes sense to begin our tour of the town in the Market Place (now tree-lined and pedestrianized). The County Hall, where you will find the Information Centre, reminds us by its name that Abingdon was once the county town of Berkshire (until 1974). The Hall was built (1678–82) by Christopher Kempster of Burford, one of Wren's masons who worked on St Paul's Cathedral. Its cellars were used as warehouses, the ground floor as a market, and the first floor as a court-room (now a small museum, open afternoons).

To the east of County Hall is the twelfth-century St Nicholas Church. Inside it is the tomb of John and Jane Blacknall (1684), on which, by the terms of John's will, loaves of bread are placed every month for the poor. Next to the church is Abbey Close and Gateway (1460). The Abbey, of which only parts survived the 1538 Dissolution, was once among the richest in Britain. The Abbey Buildings, at the end of Thames Street, are open daily in the afternoon, but closed on Monday from October to March. You enter by the old Granary, used as a 'house of correction' until about 1800. The Checker (counting house) is a thirteenth-century building, and the Long Gallery, with its magnificent oak-beamed roof, is the *pièce de résistance*.

The Thames flows past St Helen's Church, Abingdon, an important riverside town for nine centuries

Before the Abbey Gateway is the Guildhall, where there is an exhibition of paintings, the Corporation plate and a large collection of eighteenth-century pewter. The old buildings round Roysse Court include the original rooms of John Roysse's grammar school (1563) and of St John's Hospital for 'strangers, travellers and the poor'. Near Roysse Court, too, is a fine old coaching inn, the Crown and Thistle (*circa* 1605): its name means the union of England and Scotland under James I.

Bridge Street, leading southwest from Market Place towards the river and Nag's Head Island, takes you also to the Old Gaol, built 1805–11 by French prisoners during the Napoleonic Wars. It became a corn-store for nearly a century until 1974, when it was converted into an impressive arts and leisure centre, open daily (except Bank Holidays). Here you can swim, roller-skate and play badminton. There is a bar, a cafeteria and a pleasant garden by the river. The Upper Reaches Hotel nearby is on the site of the tenth-century Abbey watermill. You can see the mill inside the hotel: it was grinding corn until 1967.

East St Helen Street contains many old houses, such as Twickenham House, built in the eighteenth century by the Tomkins family who made their money in malt, and No. 28, where William III stayed in 1688. The street leads to St Helen's Church, wider (108 feet) than it is long: one of the few churches in the country with five aisles. The tower and spire have flying buttresses and (in Masefield's words) are 'gleaming with swinging windcocks on their perches'. The church dates from the thirteenth century and was greatly extended during Abingdon's wealth as a wool town. Over one aisle is a unique painted roof panel (1390) of the Tree of Jesse. There are more roof paintings of kings, prophets, Christ crucified and the Annunciation. Among many monuments, a 200-year-old candelabra,

The ancient town of Abingdon has much architecture of interest. In Market Square are St Nicholas Church and Abbey Gate

the tomb of John Roysse, a seventeenth-century pulpit and a forest of pillars, you may be able to find the tablet that fascinated Jerome K. Jerome. It is dedicated to a Mr W. Lee who 'had in his lifetime issue from his loins two hundred but three'.

Never was a town so well provided with handsome almshouses. They enclose the triangular churchyard. The Long Alley Almshouses were built in 1446 and are still in use, administered by Christ's Hospital: you can visit them by arrangement with the Matron. Twitty's and Brick Alley Almshouses are dated 1707 and 1718 respectively. Abingdon is also rich in parks and gardens and facilities for children. Beyond Abbey Close and the mill-stream are an open-air swimming pool, tennis courts and a nine-hole pitch-and-putt golf course. In the Abbey Grounds are a slide, swings and an 'iron horse'. From Nag's Head Island you can hire boats, and the gardens at the end are a good place to relax and watch the river-life.

BASILDON (*Berkshire*)

From 'Bessel's Valley'. Basildon is on the A417, midway between Streatley and Pangbourne and it is well worth visiting for two main attractions: Basildon Park, a National Trust property, and the Childe Beale Wildlife Trust, both within easy reach of the river. Basildon Park (open Wednesday–Sunday afternoons, April–October) is a classical eighteenth-century house built by John Carr of York for Sir Francis Sykes in 1776, in a beautiful setting of hilly parkland overlooking the Thames Valley. In it are an unusual octagon room, much fine plasterwork, an outstanding collection of pictures and furniture, an unexpected Anglo-Indian room, and a Shell Room housing a large collection of land and sea shells (some of them used to decorate the walls). The house owes much to Lord Iliffe, who bought it in 1952 and restored it.

Basildon Church, originally thirteenth-century but much restored in Victorian times, has a monument to Sir Francis Sykes by Flaxman; and also a tablet to the village's most valuable son, 'Jethro Tull, Pioneer of Mechanized Agriculture, Author of Horse-hoeing Husbandry. Baptized in this Church 30th March 1674, buried here 9th March 1740'. Tull's ideas were ridiculed during his lifetime, though they were put into practice by the end of the eighteenth century.

The Childe Beale Wildlife Trust has pleasant grounds by the river, with lakes and a large collection of birds in natural outdoor surroundings. Here you will find peacocks, Highland cattle and various breeds of sheep: a good place to take children, it is open in summer from Easter until September. There is also a collection of statuary. A local industry of osier-farming used to flourish here, but is now extinct.

BENSON (*Oxfordshire*)

Meaning '*tun* of the Bensingas'. Benson is on the A423, 2 miles north of Wallingford. It was still often called Bensington in the early 1920s. It has three big coaching inns. The Castle Inn, at the crossroads, is Georgian (this part of the village shows you what it looked like around 1750) and its wrought-iron sign, scrolled with a pineapple design, must have been familiar to coach travellers. The White Hart nearby is Regency, and the Crowns in High Street is dated 1709.

St Helen's Church, in flint and stone, is largely Victorian but retains its Georgian tower. Inside, nave, aisles and arcades show traces of their thirteenth- and fourteenth-century origins, and there is a Norman window in the south aisle. Tradition has it that Bensington was the site of a decisive battle between Offa of Mercia and Wessex. Offa won, but the effort weakened him so much that Mercian power declined thereafter.

Benson also has a Veteran Cycle Museum. It is privately owned but can be visited by appointment (telephone Wallingford 38414).

For the cruiser, Benson is the place to alight if you want to visit Ewelme (see entry), 2 miles away. If you take the Ewelme Road, Fifield Manor (1 mile northeast), a mixture of late eighteenth-century and Victorian design, with its big eighteenth-century barn, is worth a glance.

CHOLSEY (*Oxfordshire*)

From 'Ceol's Island'. It is 2 miles south of Wallingford on the A329 riverside road to Reading. On the river here is Fairmile Mental Hospital and behind it Cholsey, which while not unmissable, has one or two points of interest if you happen to find yourself there. Cholsey shares a railway station with Moulsford, and it is the nearest railhead for Wallingford. If it has little to look at, it has plenty of historical associations. King Ethelred II (not Unready so much as Redeless) founded an abbey here in 986, possibly to earn remission for the murder of his brother Edward. While it suffered the usual fate of monasteries attacked by the Danes and later by Henry VIII, and no trace remains, it is interesting to speculate whether St Mary's Church began as the abbey church. Its central tower (the church is cruciform)

may be Saxon in origin: experts think that the stone quoins are evidence of this. The rest is mostly Norman, with thirteenth- and fourteenth-century additions; and the earliest monument is a brass to a vicar, John Mere, who died in 1471.

The abbey, like that of Abingdon, must have been very prosperous indeed: those monks knew a thing or two about farming. The barn of Great Coxwell, Oxfordshire, is generally regarded as the largest surviving tithe barn in the county but Cholsey Abbey, latterly belonging to Reading Abbey, had one twice as big, built probably in the late twelfth century: it was 303 feet long, 62 feet high and 54 feet wide, and its roof was supported by thirty-four pillars each 4 yards in circumference. We may mourn its loss: it was demolished in 1815.

CLIFTON HAMPDEN (*Oxfordshire*)

Meaning '*tun* on a slope or on brink of river'. On the A415, 4 miles east of Abingdon, it is strikingly situated on a bend of the river. This lovely village is full of sixteenth- and seventeenth-century cottages, many with thatched roofs which remind Pevsner of tea-cosies. The hand of the Victorian architect Sir George Gilbert Scott the Elder may be seen in the Norman-style bridge which he rebuilt in 1864 to replace a ferry; in the church of St Michael and All Angels, which he twice restored (1844 and 1866); perhaps in the carved wooden lych-gate; certainly in the gabled Manor House with mullion windows which he built as a vicarage in 1843–6; and also in the local school.

The Barley Mow inn, on the right side of the bridge, is the one mentioned in *Three Men in a Boat* (but Jerome did not write any of the book here). He calls it, 'the quaintest most old-world inn up the river . . . its low-pitched gables and thatched roof and latticed windows give it quite a storybook appearance, while inside it is still more once-upon-a-timeyfied.' (When he is sentimental, Jerome can be awful.) Being 6 feet 2 inches tall, I found it the 'head-bangingest' pub on the Thames. It is of cruck construction, a very early kind of timber frame and a typical

method of building in the south in the Middle Ages (there are also cruck-framed cottages at Long Wittenham). The inn was damaged by fire in 1975 but seemed in excellent condition when I was there in September 1982.

John Masefield and his wife, Constance, lived for nearly thirty years in an Edwardian riverside house called Burcote Brook. Here he owned 15 acres of woods, tall trees, a rookery, willows, a boathouse, kingfishers and nightingales. He wrote to his friend H. W. Nevinson, 'We look out onto the river and on Wittenham Clumps, and the new Suffragan Bishop of Dorchester will be within a mile to snatch us from the gulfs of Erastianism, Aryanism and Socinianism, ever lying in wait to devour.'

The church, perched on a cliff-side, is reached by five flights of steps and at the top you are rewarded with a view. Little remains of the original medieval church except the stonework in the south wall and east end, a twelfth-century arcade, thirteenth-century lancet window, and (in the north wall) a twelfth-century relief of a boar hunt. Here you will find a memorial to a local character, Sergeant William Dyke, who fired the first shot at the battle of Waterloo. He fired it *accidentally*. Suppose he hadn't – would the battle have been even more of a 'damned close-run thing' than Wellington said it was? Poor Dyke was court-martialled, but was later pardoned by the Duke himself when on a visit to Nuneham Courtenay.

CROWMARSH GIFFORD (*Oxfordshire*)

Meaning 'marsh with crows'. It is opposite Wallingford on the river. Anywhere called Gifford is likely to have been owned by Walter Gifard (said to have been standard-bearer to William of Normandy) in the eleventh century. Gifard was a Norman nickname meaning bloated. No outstanding attractions in this village, but it does have a nice little Norman church (St Mary Magdalene) which you reach after $\frac{1}{4}$ mile's walk from the river.

Clifton Hampden Church stands on a cliff above the river overlooking Sir George Gilbert Scott's fine brick bridge

Its large oak vestry door is full of Roundhead bullet holes. Founded early in the twelfth century, with a north transept added a little later, it retains a lot of the original church — nave, chancel, decorated doorways, and a certain amount of tasteful Norman-style decoration added in a Victorian restoration.

Howberry Park, whose grounds come down to the river just above Wallingford Bridge, was originally a mansion which is accepted by some authorities as an eighteenth-century house on the site of an Elizabethan manor, but is dismissed by Pevsner as mid-nineteenth-century 'Jacobethan'. We shall not have much opportunity of finding out the truth, for it is now the nucleus of the laboratories of the Institute of Hydrology.

CULHAM (*Oxfordshire*)

From 'Cula's ham'. It is on the A415, 2 miles southeast of Abingdon. Church, pub, green and cottages make a pleasant

One of Culham's fine houses facing the village green

village group. The Manor House was rebuilt in the early 1600s by Thomas Bury (his initials appear on the porch). The west wing is part of the original fifteenth-century building which was a grange of Abingdon Abbey. Some half-timbering dates from this time, but most of the house is built of Cotswold stone with mullioned windows. The house as a whole is L-shaped, one wing having been demolished after the Civil War. In the gardens is a seventeenth-century sundial on a medieval column, a large gabled brick-and-stone dovecot (1685) with 4,000 nesting places, and a good deal of topiary.

Culham House, in blue and red brick is Georgian; so is the Old Vicarage. Culham College (1852) was founded by Bishop Wilberforce ('Soapy Sam') as a teacher's training college. Culham Bridge (the old one, not the modern concrete one which bears the brunt of the traffic) is a companion to Abingdon Bridge, built in 1416 by the Guild or Fraternity of the Holy Cross: it has five pointed arches of different sizes.

DIDCOT (*Oxfordshire*)

Meaning 'Duda's cot'. It is 3 miles south of Long Wittenham. 'Didcot?' I hear you say. 'Nobody ever goes to Didcot except to change trains.' Oh, but they do, especially if they are railway buffs who want somewhere to take the children on a wet Sunday. The Didcot Railway Centre (open Easter to October) has a comprehensive collection of Great Western Railway (GWR) locomotives (many of them steam) and rolling stock.

Didcot's power station, with its six vast cooling towers, is visible for miles around: it draws its water from, and returns it to, the Thames. Despite this and the impact 140 years ago of the railway industry, there is still a village here, with one or two thatched cottages.

DORCHESTER (*Oxfordshire*)

From 'bright place' which became a Roman station. It is 9 miles southeast of Oxford on the A423. Town or village? The volume

The gabled George Hotel, Dorchester, is sixteenth-century and lies opposite the Abbey gates

of traffic on the main Oxford–Henley road makes it seem like a town. But Dorchester's historical importance is very much greater than its size. It is one of many places which can claim that, had history been only a little different, it might have become capital of England.

Between the Thames and the town (which is really on the river Thame) are fields with double earthworks from the Iron Age known as the Dyke Hills: this, it seems, is where the first people of Dorchester lived. The Romans took advantage of the strategic position of the river-crossing on the road from Silchester in the south to 'Alchester', an encampment near Bicester. Fragments of tessellated pavements, coins and other Roman relics found here can now be seen in the Ashmolean

St Mary's Church, Ewelme. The author Jerome K. Jerome's ashes are buried in the churchyard

Museum in Oxford. The Romans called this town Durocina, and traces of its ramparts are still visible.

By the fifth century AD the Saxons had moved in, and by 634 Dorchester was ready to become a missionary centre for most of southern and part of midland England. In that year St Birinus was given, by his most powerful convert King Cynegils of Wessex, a 'see' equivalent to the modern dioceses of Winchester, Salisbury, Guildford, Hereford, Worcester, Bath and Wells, and more besides. But after the Norman Conquest the bishopric was transferred to Lincoln, and the cathedral in 1170 became an Augustinian abbey. Most of it was destroyed in the Dissolution of the Monasteries in 1536, but the abbey church was saved for the town by a rich merchant named Richard Beauforest. It is one of the great ecclesiastical buildings of southern England. Birinus, who came from Milan and brought Christianity beyond the territory of Augustine, has his shrine here, in the south choir – a modern (1964) reconstruction from fourteenth-century fragments.

The choir, especially its fourteenth-century extension to the east, is the glory of the church. Tracery and figure sculpture are used without restraint, with a huge east window and lines of figures portraying scenes from the life of Christ. The great north window, the famous Jesse Window, is an extraordinary design with intricate carving: stone and stained glass mingle to form a genealogical tree growing out of Jesse's body, with branches showing the ancestors of Jesus, the angel Gabriel and the Three Wise Men. Among many treasures (you need a whole day to see this church) are a twelfth-century lead font which survived the Reformation; paintings and wall-paintings; the medieval glass of the east window; and monuments galore, including a very lifelike effigy (in the south choir aisle) of a thirteenth-century knight drawing his sword angrily, and (a gem for the collector of odd epitaphs) a black tablet, in the south aisle, to a Mrs Sarah Fletcher who died in 1799, 'a martyr to excessive sensibility'.

The rest of the town is a feast for the architectural eye and anyone with a feeling for history. There are several old coaching inns – among them the sixteenth-century George Inn, with an arched carriageway leading to the courtyard, and the White Hart (dated 1691). The Old Schoolhouse, originally the abbey gatehouse, is now a museum containing relics of the priory which was demolished at the Dissolution. Two culs-de-sac are worth examining: Rotten Row, off High Street, has seventeenth-century half-timbered brick cottages, and Malthouse Lane has some thatched cottages of roughly the same age. Beyond the bridge (over the Thame, not the Thames, and built in 1815) is the village of **Overy** with yet more thatched cottages. One of them, Molly Mop's Cottage (1701), has thatch with flint and brick arranged in patterns like a cake.

EWELME (*Oxfordshire*)

From the Old English *aewielm* meaning 'spring or source'. It is on the B4009, 2 miles east of Benson. Watercress, which is grown here, needs very pure water, and that is provided by the spring (rising near the church) which gives this village its name. If you want to know what England looked like in the fifteenth century, look around you – in brick and flint, school, almshouses, church, all are of the 1430s and '40s. From the spring the village rises in a steep slope amid orchards.

The Manor House (Georgian) contains fragments of a Royal Palace, once the home of the Chaucer family, enlarged by the poet's granddaughter Alice after her marriage to William de la Pole, Earl (afterwards Duke) of Suffolk. During the sixteenth century it was used as a country retreat by Henry VIII and Elizabeth I. There is a local tradition that Henry VIII brought Catherine Howard here for their honeymoon. The

OPPOSITE Dorchester Abbey Church is 200 feet long and has a fine window representing the Tree of Jesse
OVERLEAF The Thames flows through Goring and on towards Henley along a stretch of countryside of outstanding natural beauty

Tudor connection is remembered in Queen Elizabeth's Walk and King's Pool: I should like to believe the story that Anne Boleyn pushed her monarch into it.

The almshouses can be dated to 1437, when Henry VI licensed the de la Poles, Yorkshire merchants who had come up in the world, to build the first of them for thirteen distressed men – they were cared for by two priests who required them to go to church five times a day. The houses are arranged round a cobbled courtyard like a cloister, sheltered by a tiled (formerly thatched) roof. They originally had only two rooms each, one up, one down, and are built of brick, timber and stone. As this is one of the earliest examples of brick being used for building in Oxfordshire, architectural scholars think the builders may have been Flemings brought from East Anglia. The almshouses, now modernized, are still in use. By one of those baffling ancient traditions, their Master is the Regius Professor of Medicine at Oxford.

The Suffolk connection is seen in St Mary's Church rebuilt by the de la Poles (at about the same time as the almshouses) on the site of a fourteenth-century church (whose tower survives). It is in excellent condition: for once we do not have to curse the Roundheads for damaging it, for when the Civil War came to Ewelme, the local commander, Colonel Francis Martyn, protected it and all its furnishings. In the richly-ornamented Chapel of St John is the tomb of Alice, Duchess of Suffolk (who died in 1475) with an alabaster effigy supported and surrounded by angels. Colonel Martyn is buried here, and there are many brasses, notably to Thomas Chaucer (the poet's son who married Ewelme's heiress) and his wife Matilda Burghersh. The font has an extraordinary carved wooden cover ($10\frac{1}{2}$ feet high!) – there is only one other like it, at Ufford in Suffolk.

OPPOSITE Whitchurch Village is grouped around its stone church. A toll bridge over the Thames links it with Pangbourne
PREVIOUS PAGE Cliveden House, built in 1850, became the home of Nancy Astor, the first woman Member of Parliament

The school (founded 1437), next to the almshouses, is linked to a mainly Georgian master's house which has some fifteenth-century brickwork. Originally a grammar school, it is one of the oldest schools still in use. The Old Rectory and Ford's Farmhouse are among many old houses in the village.

Jerome K. Jerome is buried in the churchyard. After the success of *Three Men in a Boat* (1887) he bought Gould's Grove, a farmhouse about $1\frac{1}{2}$ miles outside Ewelme. Here he had a summer-house called The Nook, sheltered by a yew hedge, where much of his writing was done.

GORING (*Oxfordshire*)
From 'Gara's people'. It is 9 miles northwest of Reading, near the junction of the A329 and the B4009. Goring is to Streatley as Gilbert is to Sullivan. On our down-river journey this is the point at which we leave a largely agricultural valley for what has been called 'sophisticated Thames'. We do so in the V-shaped ravine between the Chilterns and Berkshire Downs, where wooded slopes come down to the water – here very wide. Goring grew rapidly in Edwardian times, with luxury villas and balconied boathouses. Let us not condemn it for being commuter country. Stand on that long wooden bridge linking Goring with Streatley and be thankful for so much beauty.

The church of St Thomas of Canterbury (early twelfth-century) once had an Augustinian priory attached to it. It did not survive the Dissolution, but traces of its foundations have been discovered in an excavation in 1892, and some of its medieval tiles may be seen in the vestry of the church. The tower has four stages, the bell-stage being Perpendicular. The bells are famous: one is 600 years old. The font, tub-shaped, is as old as the church. A number of monuments and brasses span four centuries from 1401 onwards.

The village has several buildings worth more than a glance – two almshouses dated 1786 near the church, a seventeenth-century vicarage with tiled gables in Manor Road, and, in

Station Road, the Miller of Mansfield Hotel, mainly Georgian, with a seventeenth-century wing of flint and brick relieved by small Gothic windows. How did this inn get its name, and is there a connection with Mansfield in Nottinghamshire? Legend has it that King Henry III, hunting near Mansfield, called incognito at John Cockle's mill and asked for food and drink. The hospitable miller gave his unknown visitor venison and ale. After a hearty meal the king revealed who he was: the forest belonged to him, and the miller must have been poaching his deer. The miller, terrified, begged for mercy. The grateful king forgave him, and gave him land in Goring on condition that he should never refuse hospitality to any weary traveller.

In the seventeenth century Goring held an annual feast, an occasion of alcoholic merriment. The only way of crossing the river then was by ferry. After the Feast in 1674 sixty people from Streatley (far too many for one ferry-load) crowded into the boat which went out of control, plunged over the weir, and drowned them all.

HARDWICK HOUSE, Whitchurch (*Oxfordshire*)

It is 2 miles east of the village. Sometimes called Hardwick Court, and not to be confused with the more famous Hardwick Hall in Derbyshire. It is clearly visible in the trees on your left about $\frac{3}{4}$ mile above Mapledurham Lock, and its lawns come down to the water. Both Hardwick and Mapledurham House can claim that Queen Elizabeth I stayed there more than once. Hardwick, another casualty of the Civil War, was built in early Tudor times (probably on the site of an older house) by Richard Lybbe, who bought the lordship of the manor from the Hardwick family in 1526. It is F-shaped and pleasantly irregular with gables, two storeys high with attics, and mullioned windows with transoms across them. In the seventeenth century (probably about 1672) a new wing was added to repair the war damage, in much the same style as the original brick house, but with cleaner lines. The chimneys are different too — straight up

instead of the earlier diamond-shaped ones. The entrances are in the middle of the main block, which was glorified in Queen Anne's time with a pointed dome on top.

Inside, one room on the first floor is excessively rich in late sixteenth-century decoration — plaster portraits of famous people on the ceiling, pilasters, arabesques, friezes, the lot — more amusing than beautiful. It seems that Charles I, while a prisoner at Caversham in 1647, was allowed to come here to play bowls. The Lybbes lived here until about 1890, when the manor was sold to Sir Charles Day Rose, M.P.: his emblem, a rose, can be seen about the estate on walls and gates. Long before Wimbledon and modern lawn tennis developed internationally, Sir Charles built two courts here for real or Royal tennis.

IFFLEY (*Oxfordshire*)

Probably meaning 'plovers' glade', It is 2 miles southeast of Oxford. Suburb of Oxford, maybe, and connected to it by Iffley Road, traditionally full of undergraduates' lodgings: would that every suburb had something as wonderful as St Mary's, one of the best-preserved small Norman churches in England. You really need several hours to look at it properly. Built about 1170, probably by the St Rémy family, it is exuberantly rich in decoration, and windows and doors are deeply recessed to allow plenty of it, either representational sculpture or zigzag and other patterns. Central tower, chancel and nave (no aisles) are almost as they were in the twelfth century. The church was sympathetically restored in mid-Victorian times and the rose-window of the west front, with its zigzag mouldings, is by J.C. Buckler (1856), true to the original style.

Both west and south doors are richly carved, the latter especially — rosettes, quatrefoils, grotesque animals, Bible stories, sawtooth and yet more zigzag. The three-stage tower, with its curiously graceful buttresses, is well proportioned: inside, its arches are decorated. The late twelfth-century font, 'big enough to baptize by total immersion', says one observer, is made of black slate. There is much fifteenth-century stained glass, which includes the shield of John de la Pole, Duke of Suffolk (*see* Ewelme).

The stone-built thirteenth-century Rectory, the 1838 thatched school (a converted barn), and the nearby Dame School (marked 'Miss Sarah Nowell's School 1822') are among several other interesting houses. Mill Lane, to the right of the church, leads to Iffley Lock. The last house on the right is Grist Cottage, part of a thirteenth-century mill which was burned in 1908. All that remains of it is a millstone with a plaque in the grass at the end of the lane.

MAPLEDURHAM (*Oxfordshire*)

From 'maple ham and stream'. It is off the B479–B4526 between Caversham and Goring. A strangely cut-off village, seemingly of another age, which some have called feudal. Not easy to get to, its remoteness may have something to do with lack of amenities like shops and pubs and its freedom from development. No matter: be content with the House, church, watermill and other buildings in a beautiful leafy setting. The approach contains a row of six almshouses dated 1613 which have been converted into two cottages. Near it is White House, of uncertain date: it used to be a pub, the King's Arms, and before that it was known as the Priest's House.

Mapledurham House is a brick Tudor manor built about the time of the Armada by the Blount family, one of whom still lives there. From some angles it looks a pleasant jumble of gables and too-tall chimneys until you see the façade. In the Civil War Sir Charles Blount was a Royalist but he somehow managed to defend his home which suffered less damage than Hardwick. Mapledurham (open to visitors at weekends from Easter until the end of September) has some finely decorated rooms and an eighteenth-century chapel. The Blounts were Roman Catholics, and a priest-hole and a secret passage survive as evidence of persecution. Alexander Pope was friendly with Teresa and Martha Blount; he was for some time in love with Martha, and wrote verses for both girls. The house is approached (from the Caversham direction) by an avenue of limes. There used to be elms, which caused a local superstition that an elm falls whenever a Blount dies. Dutch elm disease has made nonsense of this.

St Margaret's Church (mainly fourteenth- and fifteenth-century on the site of an earlier building) has some fifteenth-century stained glass in the chancel east window depicting the lives of various saints; monuments to members of the Blount family (and also the Rose family of Hardwick); the tomb of Sir Richard Blount (d.1628) and his wife Cicely; an impressive brass to Sir Robert Bardolf (d.1395); and a separate Roman Catholic chapel (the south aisle) for the Blount family. The clock was given to the parish in 1832 by William IV because his natural son by Mrs Jordan, the Reverend Lord Augustus Fitz-Clarence, was vicar (1829–54) and built the vicarage. Many in Mapledurham attended Eton College because Henry VI made it patron of the living.

The old corn mill by the river, the oldest still working on the Thames, was adapted early in the twentieth century to pump water for the estate reservoirs and also to drive a dynamo for a private electricity supply. It may be inspected at the same time as the House. If you haven't got your own river transport, you can get to Mapledurham in the launch *Caversham Lady* which leaves Caversham Bridge on days when House and Mill are open.

MOULSFORD (*Oxfordshire*)

Meaning 'Mul's ford'. It is $2\frac{1}{2}$ miles north of Streatley on the A329. The village is only just inside Oxfordshire, for less than 1 mile downstream the county boundary restores us to Berkshire on the right bank. Moulsford is not a 'must', but if you happen to find yourself here there is plenty to interest anyone

who likes old cottages, some of them timbered. The Beetle and Wedge Hotel, old in origin but much modernized, is an obvious attraction. Moulsford Manor is a training school for nurses. Nearby, and close to the river, is the tiny fourteenth-century church of St John the Baptist, which underwent restoration by Sir Gilbert Scott: from the river you can see its shingled spire rising above the weeping willow. There used to be a ferry here, run by the landlord of the Beetle and Wedge, who charged six (old) pence to cross the river.

NUNEHAM COURTENAY (*Oxfordshire*)

From 'new ham'. It is 5 miles south of Oxford on the A423 road to Henley. What you see from the river is very different from what you see on the road, where pairs of identical eighteenth-century cottages line both sides. This was due to Simon, 1st Earl of Harcourt, who found that the old village was in the way of the landscaped gardens he planned with Capability Brown. The gardens were to contain Nuneham Park, his grand new house with a distant view of Oxford, to which he moved when he grew tired of Stanton Harcourt. This high-handed action, attacked by Oliver Goldsmith in *The Deserted Village* (1770), 'the man of wealth and pride/Takes up a space that many poor supplied', was fairly common in the eighteenth century, and not all landlords built new houses for the evicted. Goldsmith also mentions an old widow (her name was Barbara Wyatt) who alone was allowed to end her days in her clay hovel. There is a memorial to her on the terrace of the Park. Looked at in another way, Nuneham Courtenay is a 'model village'.

The gardens, described by Horace Walpole as 'the most beautiful in the world', were almost ruined by Army occupation in World War II. They were seen at their best by the 2nd Earl's distinguished guests, who included George III and Queen Charlotte, J.-J. Rousseau, who planted foreign wild flowers in

Mapledurham Mill is the oldest on the river and ground corn until earlier this century

Nuneham Courtenay, a classic model village, was built by Lord Harcourt

the grounds (especially periwinkle), and Fanny Burney. The house, which started as a smallish Palladian villa designed by one Stiff Leadbetter, was altered continually while it was being built, to make it grander: both Carr of York and Robert Adam were called in to help. Henry Holland and others all had a go at improving the interior. Nuneham Park now belongs to Oxford University, from whom permission to visit it should be obtained. Prominent on a hill is part of the Jacobean Carfax Conduit, used as a focal decoration instead of a temple or Gothic ruin: it was removed from Oxford in the 1780s because it obstructed a pavement.

All Saints' Church (on a hill in the Park) was designed by the 1st Earl himself, assisted by 'Athenian' Stuart who had studied ancient Greek and Roman architecture. It has a dome like a temple, and is placed for landscape effect. Inside, there is much nineteenth-century embellishment and many Harcourt family monuments. A second All Saints' Church was built in the village in 1872–4 (in thirteenth-century style) so that the villagers should not have to toil all the way up the hill to worship.

Between Nuneham Park and the railway bridge above Abingdon is Lock Wood, which marks the site of an old flash weir. Here, in the 1860s the Reverend Charles Dodgson, lecturer in mathematics, brought the three young daughters of the Dean of Christ Church on whole-day excursions, picnicking in Nuneham Woods while as Lewis Carroll, he told them the adventures of *Alice* (named after the middle daughter) *in Wonderland*. Nuneham, like Port Meadow and Godstow, must take some credit for the book; although the Thames is never mentioned in it.

PANGBOURNE (*Berkshire*)

Meaning 'stream of Paega's people'. It is 6 miles west-northwest of Reading on the A329. Almost the first thing you notice, at the north end of the main street, is a sign in memory of Kenneth Grahame; he shares it, curiously, with Pangbourne's other hero, King Berhtulf of Mercia who in the ninth century gave the village its charter. If you ask the present owner nicely, you can look inside Church Cottage, where Grahame lived from 1924 till his death in 1932. (He was buried, not beside the Thames, but in St Cross churchyard near the Cherwell in Oxford, in the same grave as his son Alastair, who had been killed by a train at the age of twenty.) The house and garden are sheltered from traffic: the old village round-house or lock-up is now a tool-shed. Our concept of Mr Toad and the whole riverscape of *The Wind in the Willows* owes a great deal to the illustrator, E. H. Shepard, who came here often to study his subject.

The church of St James the Less has an eighteenth-century tower: the rest of it was much remodelled in the mid-nineteenth century. The pulpit is Jacobean, and there are one or two notable monuments. One shows Sir John Davis (1625) in armour: he was knighted for deeds of valour when fighting against Spain in Elizabeth I's reign. He is shown amid his family;

they include a daughter-in-law who was the sister of Sir John Suckling, poet, courtier and adventurer (he fled into exile after being concerned in the attempt to rescue the Earl of Strafford from the Tower of London).

Pangbourne has many contrasts: showy Victorian villas along Shooter's Hill Road, but attractive seventeenth- and eighteenth-century houses elsewhere. Bere Court, once a dependency of Reading Abbey, is Georgian. The Nautical College (1917) looks down on the scene from its 350-foot hill. Probably you will come ashore at Pangbourne for its shops and pubs, and to follow the example of Jerome and his friends by visiting the Swan Hotel, one of the several riverside hostelries. As always, the river, the weirs and the trees are the thing. No: Pangbourne should not be dismissed as a commuter town. It is linked to Whitchurch, on the Oxfordshire bank, (*see* entry) by an iron toll-bridge of Victorian vintage: at the time of writing it costs 5p to take a car across.

READING (*Berkshire*)

From 'Reada's people'. About twenty-five years ago Reading, the most populous town on the Thames next to London, began to transform its image and pull its important cultural heritage together. Much redevelopment has greatly altered its physical character. Its industries include brewing, insurance, electronics, and foodstuffs. It has new shopping and civic centres, and several excellent museums reflecting the life and history of the surrounding country.

Although today Reading is not truly 'riverside' except at Caversham, its position gave it strategic importance in medieval times. It suffered from the Danes in the ninth century and was burned by Sweyn in 1006. By the time of the Domesday survey there were only thirty houses here. In 1121 Henry I founded an abbey here for 100 monks; he was buried in Reading. The abbey was consecrated by Thomas à Becket in the reign of King Henry II. One of its monks, John de Fornsete, composed

'Summer is icumen in'. There is a story that the abbey was founded to contain a holy relic, the hand of the Apostle James; and indeed the bones of a human hand were discovered in the ruins of the abbey in 1786 and eventually found their way to St Peter's Church, Marlow. The last abbot, Hugh Faringdon, and two of his monks were hanged, drawn and quartered in 1539 for resisting the Dissolution. Henry VIII built a Palace here of which very little survives.

There are enough of the abbey remains for us to get some idea of what it looked like — part of the chapter house, the thirteenth-century gatehouse (now a museum), a wall of the dormitory, a fragment of the refectory. They were built massively of flint and rubble, at the end of Forbury Street. The parish church of St Lawrence, at the top of Market Place, was also founded by Henry I and rebuilt in the thirteenth and fifteenth centuries (Perpendicular). It contains several brasses and a monument to John Blagrave the mathematician (d.1611). It used to have some stained glass but it was all shattered by bombs in World War II. Blagrave has a street named after him (the nineteenth-century Gothic town hall is in it). Greyfriars Church, which in its time has served as guildhall, workhouse and prison, was founded by Franciscans in 1285.

Reading has about 500 acres of open spaces and parks, among them Forbury Gardens (where there is a pompous lion monument in memory of the nineteenth-century Afghan Wars) and the 120-acre Prospect Park, rich in trees, on Bath Road. London Street has a few Georgian buildings, and some older. The nineteenth-century Royal Berkshire Hospital cannot fail to catch your eye, and among many new buildings is The Hexagon, by the Butts Shopping Centre, where plays and concerts are performed and exhibitions mounted.

The University, opened in 1892 and affiliated to Oxford, became independent in 1926 and has grown strikingly since. Much of it has moved to Whiteknights, which provided 300 acres of parkland as a campus setting. It now has 6,000 students and twelve residential halls. Its researches into agriculture; horticulture and dairying are of especial importance: the National Institute for Research in Dairying is part of the university. The Museum of English Rural Life at Whiteknights (open daily except Mondays) was founded by the University in 1951: it contains a splendid collection of mainly nineteenth- and early twentieth-century rural life, and of agriculture and other related industries. The university also runs the Cole Museum of Zoology and the Ure Museum of Greek Archeology.

The main municipal buildings in Blagrave Street contain the public library, an art gallery and the excellent Reading Museum. Its most important exhibits are from Silchester (10 miles south-west), which as Calleva Atrebatum was capital of the area in Roman times. Here are model reconstructions of what the Roman city looked like, its houses and temples and forum; and a rich collection of everyday objects which have convinced one local historian that the 'savage Germanic tribes' who destroyed it all were a thousand years behind it in civilization.

North of the Thames, **Caversham**, in its odd little enclave of Berkshire, sprang up mostly in the nineteenth century, though it has Caversham Park, remains of an eighteenth-century mansion which now houses the BBC Monitoring Station. Near-by is Queen Anne's, a leading girl's public school (the girls all wear stylish red-lined cloaks).

Literary associations? Jane Austen and her sister Cassandra attended Mme Latournelle's Abbey School (originally in the abbey gateway) in 1785–7; so later did Mary Russell Mitford, who afterwards lived at Three Mile Cross, just south of Reading, in a cottage now called The Mitford. Here she wrote *Our Village* (1824–32).

SANDFORD-ON-THAMES (*Oxfordshire*)

Meaning 'sandy ford'. Situated 4 miles south of Oxford on the A423. Despite the chimney of the papermill and the village's mournful reputation for bathing fatalities, it is worth more than a glance. St Andrew's Church (eighteenth-century) still shows some Norman features in the nave and chancel, and in the window in the south chancel wall. There were several alterations and additions in Victorian times, including a Norman-style west tower; but the porch was built in 1652 by Lady Eliza Isham, who is gratefully acknowledged by a tablet: '*Porticus Patronae*, Thankes to thy Charitie, religiose Dame,/ Wych found mee old and made mee new againe.'.

Temple Farm shows traces of a thirteenth-century building, a Community of Knights Templar, and part of their chapel in a barn. Similarly, Minchery Farm, on the way to adjoining **Littlemore**, has remains of a twelfth-century Benedictine nunnery. Littlemore's church of St Mary and St Nicholas was built in 1835 for a religious community planned here by J.H. (Cardinal) Newman, leader of the Tractarian Movement and author of the hymn 'Lead kindly light', before his conversion to Rome. It is a severe design, and the church tower, which was to have had a spire, was never completed. The screen, with crucifix and figures, was carved at Oberammergau and presented to the church in 1901. Newman also planned to build a monastery here: beside the church is a row of cottages which he converted into a retreat. It was here too that Froude, Pusey and other figures of the Oxford Movement came to stay.

SHILLINGFORD (*Oxfordshire*)

Probably meaning 'ford of the Scillingas'. It is 2 miles southeast of Dorchester on the A329. For such a very small village, the population is extremely well supplied with inns – the Kingfisher and the Old Bell on the A423 Oxford–Henley road, and the luxurious Shillingford Bridge Hotel by the river on the A329 to Wallingford. You come here to see the bridge and enjoy a riverscape that no other river can provide; yet there are also one or two other things to look at. Such as two eighteenth-century residences, both with five bays: Shillingford Farmhouse (grey and red brick) and Riverside House. There used to be a ferry a

couple of miles upstream with the curious name of Keen Edge, which scholarly guesswork assumes was a corruption of Cane Hedge, referring to the osier beds along the banks of this stretch of the Thames.

Shillingford's only literary figure was (for a short while) W. B. Yeats, for whom 'a terrible beauty' had been born in the violent struggle for Irish Home Rule. Letting his house in Oxford for the summer, he brought his wife and child to Minchen's Cottage, on the road to Warborough, north of the village. Here he wrote part of *Meditations in Time of Civil War*.

THE STOKES, North and South (*Oxfordshire*)

From the Old English *stoc* meaning 'place or cattle farm'. It is $2\frac{1}{4}$ and $3\frac{1}{4}$ miles south of Wallingford on the B4009. There is also a 'grey' area between them known as **Littlestoke**. These villages are not quite the rustic paradise described in a book of 1892 which I chanced upon recently – '. . . you meet in them the farmer-men in their smocks, and their brown-faced womenkind wearing the great picturesque sun-bonnets of the peasantry.' But they have much to offer. Tree-sheltered St Mary's Church in **North Stoke** is thirteenth- and fourteenth-century in origin, though on the site of an earlier church which was governed from Normandy by the Abbey of Bec. There are three sundials here: the most noticeable is the scratch dial incorporating the head and hands of a priest – the hours are simply scratched into the stonework round the gnomon or pin that casts the shadow. You will find this above the blocked south doorway. Could it be Saxon? Scratch dials of the seventh century have been found elsewhere.

The upper portion of the tower (which fell down in 1669) is partly brick, repaired in 1725. Inside, the thirteenth-century font has a Jacobean wooden cover; the carved pulpit is also Jacobean. There are fourteenth-century wall paintings in the

Above Shillingford Bridge – a tranquil setting for a riverside house

chancel of the martyrdom of St Thomas à Becket, the lives of St Catherine and St Stephen, and of kings. Rectory Farmhouse, nearby, is seventeenth- and eighteenth-century with an octagonal dovecot. North Stoke's most celebrated daughter was Dame Clara Butt (1873–1936), the contralto whose rendering of 'Abide with Me' and 'Land of Hope and Glory' so stirred our grandparents: she lived at Brook Lodge and died there in 1936.

We have to guess at what **South Stoke** looked like to the smocked peasantry of 1892, for much of it was destroyed by fire in the early 1900s. But some oldish houses round the church survive, and there is a pleasant flint-built pub, the Perch and Pike. St Andrew's Church, too, is thirteenth-century, remodelled in the fourteenth century and not much restored in later ages. Inside are a fourteenth-century octagonal font, a fragment of a seventeenth-century wall painting, various wall monuments (one to Griffith Higgs, 1659, described as 'Chaplain to the Queen of Bohemia'), and, in the south aisle, some thirteenth-century stained glass. Two houses nearby are worth a glance: Manor Farm, with its big square brick gabled dovecot, and Corner House, mainly Georgian but with a half-timbered section which might be Tudor.

STREATLEY (*Berkshire*)

Meaning 'grove or clearing by street'. On the A329 it is 9 miles northwest of Reading. The 'street' may be a branch of Icknield Way (pre-Roman) or the neighbouring Ridge Way, which joined it at a prehistoric ford here – it is wide but shallow. Two villages therefore developed here (the other one was Goring) each with its own priory. Walk down Streatley's main street to enjoy the Georgian houses: Streatley House itself is late-Georgian, large and square but with a graceful portico. St Mary's Church with its chunky Perpendicular tower, was

Wallingford Bridge acquired its balustrade in 1809 when it was widened; it originally dates from medieval times

substantially rebuilt in 1865 (Early English style). Between the street and the church is a range of malt-houses which in 1898 were converted into a village hall.

Should you wish to stretch your legs, you can – indeed I think you must – climb the hill behind Streatley for one of the most rewarding views the Thames Valley can offer: the climb, if you are reasonably fit, takes about ten minutes. From Streatley Hill you look upstream across the town to the silver thread of the river with the Gap looming all around. Two other beauty spots well worth walking to, Larden Chase and Lough Down, are owned by the National Trust. Both are on the left-hand side of the B4009 road as you enter Streatley from the Newbury direction. You may be forgiven if you spend most of your time at the Swan Hotel, and watching the life of the river go by from the hotel gardens. In the 1890s a contributor to *Punch*, signing himself, The Lazy Minstrel, sang: 'I'd rather much sit here and laze,/Than scale the hill at Streatley . . .' He went on to observe the new, athletic girls of the time, particularly one whose:

> . . . hands are brown, her eyes are grey,
> And trim her nautical array –
> Alas! she swiftly sculls away
> And leaves the Swan at Streatley.

SUTTON COURTENAY (*Oxfordshire*)

Meaning 'south village'. Situated $2\frac{1}{2}$ miles south of Abingdon on the B4016. It was granted to Reginald de Curtenai, ancestor of the Earls of Devon, by Henry II in 1161 and has much of the Middle Ages surviving in it. Part of it belonged to Abingdon Abbey, which had a retreat here. The grange (for visiting monks who came to collect rents), now known as the Abbey, is near All Saints Church which is mostly fourteenth-century, with an oak-roofed great hall. The Abbey is now a school and is not open to the general public.

The main street, with grass verges broadening into a village green by the church, is spacious and lovely, with houses of many periods. Near the church too is the Norman Hall (also known as the Court House), a stone-built twelfth-century house with narrow lancet windows and unrestored south door. Inside, it has an open timber roof with carving. Opposite the George Inn is Courtenay Manor House, built probably *circa* 1200, about the same time as the church. There have been later additions, but the round doorway survives: the gables appear to be Tudor. Inside is a lofty banqueting hall with a minstrels' gallery.

The church dates from the twelfth century, and mixes Norman and Early English styles. The Norman tower has a clock with only one hand. The brick porch, with its so-called parvis or living-room above, is sixteenth-century. Inside, the chancel is thirteenth-century and the nave about a century younger.

Sutton Courtenay, an attractive village of cottages and old timbered houses

There are a hexagonal Jacobean pulpit, box pews, and an elegant rood-screen. In the churchyard is buried Herbert Henry Asquith, 1st Earl of Oxford and Asquith, last Prime Minister of a Liberal Government (1908–16) who allowed Lloyd George to lay the foundations of the Welfare State. Asquith lived at The Wharf, down by the tree-canopied waters of Sutton Pool, which he regarded as 'the real essence of England'. Nearby are the graves of Eric Blair (George Orwell, 1903–50), author of *Animal Farm* and *1984*, and Martha Pye, who died in 1832 aged 117. There is also a yew tree believed to be 300 years old.

The name of Asquith's house reminds us that, before railways came, Sutton Courtenay was the river-port for the neighbouring villages which sent their farm-produce by water to London. When the toll-charging miller was bypassed by the new cut in 1809, the wharf area was left by nature to become the wonderland it is today. The mill, now no more, was by the Fish Inn. Beyond the village green, to the south, is another part with old cottages worth looking at; but don't go too far, for suddenly Didcot power station confronts you and the illusion of being in an old village in the nineteenth century is shattered.

WALLINGFORD (*Oxfordshire*)
Meaning 'ford of Wealh's people'. Situated midway between Oxford and Reading on the A329, it has gridded streets enclosed by ramparts – the town looks as if it has been planned. It could hardly have been done by the Saxons, who tended to use (or simply neglect) what was already existing, so it must have been the Romans. In this case it seems to have become a Saxon burgh or fortified town sometime during the ninth century. Certainly the ford, and the bridges that succeeded it, were strategically important to Aulus Plautius, William the Conqueror, and both sides in the Civil War. The Conqueror chose this point to cross the river before heading east around London. He appointed Robert d'Oyley as governor of the district, and d'Oyley in 1071 built a castle on a mound by the river. (There

are still traces of it in the gardens of Castle House, open to the public; and the ramparts can be seen in the open space known as Kine Croft.) Here Matilda was besieged by King Stephen – but in vain. By the Treaty of Wallingford Henry II secured the throne and in 1155 gave the town its first charter. The castle was defended by Colonel Blagge – the last Royalist stronghold to surrender – and in 1652 was destroyed by Commonwealth soldiers.

There may have been a bridge here as early as the seventh century, but the first known one was built in 1141. At one time it seems to have had a gatehouse at each end and a Mary Grace chapel in the middle, probably destroyed by Cromwell's artillery. In 1641 Colonel Blagge blew up four arches and replaced them with a drawbridge made of wood to improve the town's defences. The present seventeen-arch bridge dates from 1809, when it was built because of floods (that is why it is so long).

Tradition says that in the twelfth century Wallingford had ten – perhaps fourteen – churches. Now there are only three. The population decline after the Black Death in 1348 hit the town very badly. Today, St Leonard's Church is the oldest, with much Norman work, although the herring-bone decoration (you see it in the nave and the north door) may be older, possibly Saxon. St Mary-le-More, in the Market Place, much rebuilt, has a Perpendicular seventeenth-century tower which may have been repaired with material from the razed Castle. St Peter's (now disused), largely eighteenth-century, is a well-known river landmark, instantly recognizable by its open-work spire, like a hypodermic needle, designed by Sir Robert Taylor (1777). On the outer south wall is a monument to Sir William Blackstone (1723–80) whose *Commentaries* on the laws of England are still required reading for lawyers. He lived at Wallingford for some years and may have helped design St Peter's.

Walking about this busy market town (market day: Friday) is a great pleasure. Going up High Street from the bridge, you pass several well-cared-for houses of the sixteenth–eighteenth

The town hall in Wallingford was built in 1670. It houses a fine collection of paintings

centuries, among them Calleva House (early Georgian) and the gabled George Hotel. St Mary's Street leads up to Market Place, where the seventeenth-century town hall, open underneath because it is partly supported by Doric pillars, has a large Venetian window facing the square, and houses a collection of portraits (some by Gainsborough). Old and new harmoniously combine in the Lamb Arcade, a market for antiques and handcrafts, developed out of an old and long-neglected Georgian inn.

Wallingford's only author was Agatha Christie who lived for thirty-five years at Winterbrook, a Queen Anne house about 1 mile out of town with a view of the river across a meadow.

WHITCHURCH (*Oxfordshire*)

Meaning 'white or stone church'. This village is 6 miles west-northwest of Reading and is pleasing to see from the river, grouped round the church with its short shingled spire. The main street leads down to the river and the toll-bridge (built *circa* 1880) by which you cross to Pangbourne (*see* entry). It is easy to dismiss Whitchurch as 'Pangbourne's country cousin', but the lack of dramatic history should not deter the visitor. You can start by refreshing yourself at the Greyhound, and then stroll about.

St Mary's Church still has a Norman doorway and a fifteenth-century porch, but most of it was rebuilt in 1858. Never mind: there are bits of twelfth- and fifteenth-century sculpture over the doorway and porch, some good Victorian stained glass, and various monuments dating back to the fifteenth century. One (in the chancel) is to Richard Lybbe (d.1599) and his wife — the Lybbes were Lords of the Manor of Hardwick (*see* entry). Among the brasses is a fifteenth-century one to Thomas Walysch, 'trayer' (i.e. wine-taster to the Royal Family) and his wife.

Two Georgian houses worth a glance are the Rectory, with its classical porch, and the three-bayed Thames Bank, extended in the 1830s.

THE WITTENHAMS, Long and Little (*Oxfordshire*)

Derived from 'Witta's island and ham'. These villages are 4 miles east-southeast of Abingdon, off the A415. Owing to a U-bend in the river, the two villages are 1 mile apart by road but 3½ miles apart by water. Both villages are there because of the Sinodun Hills or Wittenham Clumps, whose history they share. Some of that history is conjectural. The ramparts on Castle Hill were an Iron Age fort: the hill was bound to be exploited militarily, and there are traces of the Romans too. Was this where the Atrebates made their last stand before yielding to them? Or was it simply a look-out beacon on the site of a temple? After Boadicea's revolt in AD 60 the British tribes were pacified until the invasions began, so there was less need for forts. Around Long Wittenham we find traces of Stone Age, Bronze Age and Iron Age; but the village we see today began

in Saxon times (a Saxon cemetery, possibly Christian, was excavated at nearby Freeacre). The Clumps can be climbed from Little Wittenham Lane by a footpath (about ½ mile) to the copse of birch trees on top; or from Day's Lock, by much the same route; or (slightly longer) from Long Wittenham. In each case the reward is the same: one of the great panoramic views of southern England, taking in the plains of the curling river, the Vale of the White Horse, Wallingford, Abingdon and the distant wooded hill of Nuneham Courtenay.

Little Wittenham was once Abbots Wittenham when the manor belonged to Abingdon Abbey. St Peter's Church near the river (you pass it on the footpath up to the Clumps) has a Decorated and Perpendicular tower, though most of the body was remodelled, in Early English style, in 1863. Inside are monuments to the Dunch family who flourished in the sixteenth and seventeenth centuries. There they are, in marble and alabaster, some lying down, others kneeling. One, Sir William, was married to Oliver Cromwell's aunt, Mary. Sir William's son, Edmund, was made (by Cromwell) Governor of Wallingford Castle and became Lord Burnel. A nice, cosy little church but rather dark. The village has a war memorial with only one name on it. Robert Gibbings, author of *Sweet Thames, Run Softly*, spent his last years at Footbridge Cottage in Little Wittenham and wrote the sequel, *Till I End my Song*, just before his death in 1958.

Long Wittenham is long all right — about ½ mile of it. If the village seems to straggle, this may be due to the fact that much of it was burned down in 1868. Long Wittenham Church, though its oldest parts (chancel, north window and other details) are Norman, has much of the thirteenth and fourteenth centuries and samples of many styles. The Norman lead font has a design in which bishops and nuns are featured, and in the south transept, also used as a vestry, is a sculptured piscina showing two angels guarding a knight (thirteenth-century). The heavily timbered porch is quaint and looks as if it is about

The village cross at Long Wittenham was once the market meeting-place

to collapse. (I have seen a photograph of it taken ninety years ago: it hasn't changed a bit.) Since 1322 the church has been cared for by Exeter College, Oxford, which was responsible for the carved woodwork inside, notably the Jacobean stalls, pulpit and screen.

Long Wittenham is a good place for studying cottages. Some of them are of cruck construction (which we saw in the Barley Mow, Clifton Hampden). One is even called Cruckfield Cottage – it may look bent but it is strong. Near the church is Church Farm, a timber-framed fifteenth-century house with an over-hanging first storey, and a thatched barn of the sixteenth century. The Plough Inn is the same period. The village cross was a meeting place where the market assembled centuries ago: it was traditionally known as a chipping or bargaining cross.

The Pendon Museum (open Saturday and Sunday afternoons), housed in a barn, is a companion to Didcot's Great Western Society Museum (*see* Didcot) – with scenes of transport and country life in the 1930s and an emphasis on railways dating back to the early 1800s, and many scale models.

CHAPTER FOUR

Middle Thames

Although the river does not properly touch Reading on the right bank, you are aware – and how! – of an industrial town and a railway centre, especially as you leave it going downstream. Yet well within 3 miles, the river has returned to the country, widening and curling amid islands that will soon be calling themselves eyots or aits, becoming grander and richer (in all senses of the word). Everything that goes to make the Thames will be there, only more so: bigger beechwoods on distant hills or coming steeply down to the water, even prettier lock-gardens, more boats, more people. (But also more room for more people, especially in explorable backwaters.)

About ½ mile above Sonning, on the right, the towpath is fringed with overhanging trees: this is Holme Park, now the Reading Bluecoat School, and the riverbank here is known as Thames Parade. Sonning Lock has a famous garden which, for thirteen years in succession (under the old Thames Conservancy), won the 'Best-kept lock and garden' competition cup. This was when Edward Light was keeper; his successor Mr Prince kept up the tradition too. Sonning Lock, in fact, has generally had out-of-the-ordinary keepers: one of them, appointed in 1845, was John James Sadler, described as 'parish clerk, beekeeper and poet'. Sonning Bridge, with eleven arches, dates mostly from the eighteenth century and is built of red brick. The river divides at this point where there used to be two bridges; the one you see today (starting on the Berkshire side), the other a quainter affair on wooden piles which was replaced about seventy years ago by a two-part iron bridge over backwater and mill-stream. On either side of the bridge is a famous hostelry, the French Horn (left) and the White Hart (right).

A luxuriance of trees, in which the white-boarded Mill can be seen, and we are in open country again. After 1 mile, a bridge on the right marks St Patrick's Stream, which leaves the river here and comes back to it lower down at Shiplake. This is a bit of Thames engineering: the river Loddon used to enter the river here, but now does so by Shiplake Lock. The land the stream encloses is known as Borough Marsh. Islands – or rather eyots – galore as we approach Shiplake: Buck, Hallsmead, the Lynch, Phillimore's. You can, it is said (but I have never done it), go down St Patrick's Stream for the whole of its length and thus rejoin the river, having bypassed Shiplake Lock. But old hands warn against doing this upstream because the current is strongly opposing you.

Shiplake – and Lower Shiplake – go on for 1½ miles, as we are prepared for the grandeur beyond Henley. Since Caversham the Thames has been flowing mainly north, though twisting so much that it is easy to lose your sense of direction. The river Loddon joins the Thames from the right, just below Shiplake Lock, near the railway bridge (not, unfortunately, one of Brunel's). You have to be a very fervent admirer of Alexander Pope to excuse his shortcomings as a nature poet when he wrote, 'The Loddon slow, with verdant alders crown'd.' Yes, there are alders, but slow? Just try rowing, or, worse still, swimming, against its current . . .

Towards Wargrave, the land flattens out again as the river begins to curve round Wargrave Marsh on the right. This is enclosed by Hennerton Backwater which leaves the Thames and returns 1 mile later just above Marsh Lock. Hennerton is beautiful as only the Thames can be, gracefully overhung by trees: it should be explored by punt or rowing boat, and you are warned that there is a very low bridge at the far end: duck for safety. On the mainstream way, more eyots – Hardbuck, Poplar, Ferry (but there is no ferry). The land on the right rises more steeply, the woods grow denser as the Twyford–Henley road comes to the riverbank. Marsh Lock, unusually, is situated bang in the middle of the river. It has an attractive lock-keeper's cottage, trees and a prize-winning garden, and is approached from the towpath by a long timber bridge over the weir. Bridge and weir are said to have been designed (at least partly) by the Reverend Humphrey Gainsborough, brother of the painter, who was minister of the local Congregational church. Parson Gainsborough, a friend of James Watt who invented the steam engine, was somewhat frustrated by the parsimony of the Thames Commissioners who used wood for their pound-locks: it could not withstand the wear and tear of barge traffic, and had to be rebuilt ten years later.

Below Marsh Lock, immediately on the right, is Park Place, a French Renaissance style house of the 1870s: you may not be able to see it because of the trees, but you know it is there by the golf-course into which its grounds have been converted. Its Victorian boathouse is on the riverbank. We are now within 1 mile of Henley, passing the Rod Eyot islets. It is a long time since we encountered a really well-proportioned stone bridge, but Henley Bridge, with the hospitable Angel Inn on the left, is exactly that. Five arches and a balustraded parapet, designed in 1786 by one William Hayward, are embellished with masks of Thames and Isis carved on each side of the middle arch by Mrs Damer: she was a cousin of Horace Walpole (he bequeathed Strawberry Hill to her) and the daughter of General Conway who owned Park Place. The Angel (sometimes called Angel-on-the-Bridge) recalls a tradition that a thirteenth-century bridge here had both an inn and a chapel on it.

Henley-on-Thames, if you do not know it, or have seen it only at Regatta time, should be explored. And if you feel like a stately home on dry land by way of a change, Greys Court, a National Trust property, is only 3 miles away.

From Henley, for the next 27 river miles or so (say, from Henley to Runnymede), if you are not navigating, you can play

Temple Island marks the starting point of the races at Henley Regatta

the old cruising game of Spotting the Celebrities. A large number of successful people, especially those in show business, acquire riverside retreats.

Henley Reach is dead straight for 2 miles, which is why it is such a good Regatta course. On the right, the Leander Club with Remenham Wood rising behind; on the left Phyllis Court, both looking so much less significant than they do in Regatta Week, when everything in Henley Reach is a landmark. Fawley Court, coming up on the left (if you can see it through the trees), is a white mansion attributed to Wren but altered by James Wyatt in 1771: having been for some time a theological college, it is now occupied by the Royal Navy. The county boundary comes down to the river a few yards before it, and the left bank is now in Buckinghamshire. In another $\frac{1}{2}$ mile we come to Temple Island, sometimes called Regatta Island because it is the starting point of the Henley rowing course. The temple on it – really more of a cottage – was built by James Wyatt (when he was remodelling Fawley Court) for the then owner, Mr Freeman. It is not just a folly: someone lives there.

Fawley Meadows were a sort of no-man's-land in the Civil War. As the river bends sharply to the right (and to the east), a house called Greenlands can be seen on the left. The original house (1604) was a Royalist stronghold (Henley was Roundhead), it was besieged for six months: cannon balls have been found in its gardens. Built in 1853, the present house was first owned by W. H. Smith M.P., founder of the book and stationery chain. It is now an administrative staff college.

Hambleden Lock and the great sweeping weir with Hambleden Mill on the left are something you don't forget. A public footpath goes across the weirs to the white weatherboarded mill, which was still working as recently as 1955. Now it spends most of its life being photographed, and is being converted into spacious flats with garages and a communal garden. The river here flows southeast for about $\frac{1}{4}$ mile, and turns almost due east opposite Culham Court, a square redbrick Georgian mansion,

built about 1770, whose terraced gardens, ornamented with topiary, come down to the river. Its first owner, the Honourable F. West, son of Lord de la Warr, had George III to stay and greatly impressed his royal guest by having hot rolls sent by relays of horses from his London baker. The present-day owner has a splendid view of Magpie Island downstream.

An S-bend in the river begins as we come to Medmenham Abbey on the left, beautiful, notorious, a little sinister and Gothick (in the bogus eighteenth-century sense). More islands and pretty backwaters; and by Frogmill on the right, attractive riverside houses. One of them was named Poison Ducks, derived from the Norman French. It may mean pike but it is more likely to refer to *poisson* ducts or fish weirs, especially eel traps (like basketwork sausages) which were still in use in the early 1920s.

On the Buckinghamshire side, there is a big slightly supercilious house on a hill called Danesfield, built of stone in Tudor style in about 1900 for Robert Hudson, who had just restored Medmenham. We now encounter two locks within $\frac{1}{2}$ mile. Just before Hurley Lock on the Berkshire side, is Ladye Place, a largely Edwardian mansion on the site of a much earlier house, the scene of a political plot in 1688. Much of Hurley is overrun by caravans in summer, but there is seclusion in the backwaters formed by several islands. Hurley Lock has a relic of the past – a timber weir-winch, once used to haul boats up the old flash weir that was here until 1773. Between Hurley and Temple Lock there is an impressive view, on the left, of eighteenth-century brick-built Harleyford Manor, in its wonderful wooded setting. It now acts as host or club house for the river folk who use Harleyford Marina.

Temple Lock, Temple village, Temple Mills – the Knights Templar were once powerful hereabouts, though there is no trace of them at the attractive lock – another sweeping curved weir, topiary in the lock-garden and an outsize chestnut tree.

If you can see its outline amid the trees, Bisham Abbey is the next landmark on the Berkshire side – a mainly Tudor building with a remoter past. Strange that it should now be the National Sports Centre. Beyond Bisham village are Park Wood and Quarry Wood, which we shall see again from the other side of Marlow. A little further on, to the right, is Bisham Church, to add to our collection of cosy riverside churches, so close to the water that it's almost in it, with its sturdy Norman tower and its tiled roof.

The first sight of Marlow has become a postcard cliché — one of those accidental groupings which no artist could improve on — the pinnacled church spire, Tierney Clark's 1836 suspension bridge and the lawn of the Compleat Angler Hotel. Beyond, the mesmerizing thrum of the weir (the water falls 7 feet 1 inch and the strong current below is known as Marlow Race). Spare some time for looking at Marlow (we had better call it Great Marlow) even if you only enjoy the view from the Angler.

Beyond the lock, Quarry Wood (*Toad* scholars think it may be the original of the Wild Wood) rises thickly on the right with Winter Hill beyond, and a group of islands ahead. Climb Winter Hill (225 feet) if you get the chance, for one of the great panoramas of the Thames Valley. The river runs straight northeast for 1½ miles, with a strange little prehistoric railway on the Buckinghamshire side — the branch line from Bourne End to Marlow, with Little Marlow in the distance. The boathouse of the Upper Thames Sailing Club and the profusion of sail (power and oar must give way to it) makes it clear that this is one of the best sailing centres on the river.

At Bourne End, the Thames turns violently south near the railway bridge, and in a mile Cookham Bridge is in sight. Cookham is dominated by Turk's Boat Yard (above and below the bridge) and in particular by Frederick John Turk, sixty-nine, ex-Merchant Navy and Keeper, since 1963, of the Swans. The entry to Cookham Lock, lined with woods (most magical in the gold of autumn), is probably the most beautiful on the river. Three forested estates, Hedsor, Dropmore and Cliveden, come

Turk's Boat Yard by Cookham Bridge. The proprietor, Mr John Turk, is at present Swan Keeper to Her Majesty the Queen

together near here. The river divides into several streams, two of which enclose Formosa, the river's largest island: the streams can all be explored except the one running through Hedsor which is private property.

Anyone trying to describe Cliveden Reach soon runs out of superlatives. The great Italianate house looks down upon the magnificent scene – and 'looks down' is the correct description, for I have always found it coldly supercilious. But the setting – the most dramatic we have seen since Goring Gap, with a forested riverbank 300 feet high in places – is breathtaking. Let scandal bring us down to earth. At the water's edge, near the site of the old *My Lady* ferry, is a gabled cottage which, in the early 1960s, was let by the late Lord Astor to an osteopath named Stephen Ward. Weekend goings-on involved a girl called Keeler, a Minister for War, the Russian Naval Attaché, and a landlord called Rachman.

Boulter's Lock has a fall of 7 feet 10 inches, the second deepest on the river (the deepest is Teddington), and is one of the few locks to have three pairs of gates to help the flow of craft in peak season. It is the busiest lock of all, and people come here for fun, not merely for the river: there's always the delightful possibility that someone may fall in. The lock-keeper, Bill Stacey, and his wife Jill reckon this happens at least once a week on average: they even keep a spare set of clothes for 'swimmers' as they call them.

Once through the lock, Maidenhead and Taplow soon begin. This reach is good for punting: the bottom is shingly so the pole doesn't stick in the mud. The river is divided again by long thin islands with a park-promenade on the right (Maidenhead) side and the riverside houses of Taplow on the left, preceded by the Taplow Court estate which has been following the river for ½ mile or so: the mansion itself, Victorian-Tudor with towers and gables, is sheltered by trees. Ahead is the balustraded Maidenhead Bridge, built by Sir Robert Taylor in the 1700s in stone with thirteen arches, to carry the all-important Bath Road, now the A4. Immediately to the left, above it, is Skindles Hotel, once the vortex of Maidenhead pleasure-seeking in the 1920s when Michael Arlen called it 'the hymen of London'. (Skindles is in Taplow.)

Maidenhead Railway Bridge. Built by Brunel in 1837–8 it has the longest brick-built span in the world

A few hundred yards further on is Brunel's famous railway bridge, handsome in red brick. In 1839 when it was built, heads were shaken: could any brick bridge of only two arches (the widest in the world at 128 feet) and a height of only 24 feet stand the strain of carrying the Great Western broad-gauge railway? It could. Turner painted it, and generations of cruisers have discovered that the arch on the Buckinghamshire side has an eerie echo. If you shout 'Ha!' it flings eldritch laughter back at you.

The river continues due south, past attractive houses with riverside gardens; opposite, on the Buckinghamshire side, is the Amerden estate. The Perpendicular tower of Bray Church appears among trees on the right. Just above Bray Lock, where Headpile Eyot begins, by the Waterside Hotel, the river makes a right-angle turn to the east. Bray village is a little more peaceful now that the M4 has syphoned off some of its through-traffic.

The lock has reason to be proud of its garden, another of those cupwinners. We meet the M4 below the lock, its roaring traffic carried across the river by a concrete bridge built in 1961.

We are now in Dorney Reach, and Dorney Church and sixteenth-century Dorney Court can be seen on the left. Monkey Island, long and narrow, does not encourage casual visitors: what was the 3rd Duke of Marlborough's fishing pavilion in the mid-eighteenth century is now a hotel. More islands, the largest being Queen's Eyot, and on the Berkshire bank two houses claim our attention. Down Place also has eighteenth-century associations; it is now a film studio specializing in horror films. Next to it is Oakley Court, a turreted Victorian castle whose grounds stretch along the river for nearly $\frac{3}{4}$ mile. The flattish riverbank opposite is Thames Field.

From now on, as the river wriggles this way and that, there are glimpses of Windsor Castle ahead. As the mainstream turns left (northeast), a mill-stream goes off to the right, thus forming the large island that contains Windsor Racecourse. Meanwhile, spare a glance for a rather sad little tree-fringed chapel, very old, with a weatherboarded belfry, on the left: this is St Mary Magdalene at Boveney. The lock, built in 1838 towards the end of the great canal-building era, can be avoided altogether if you're in a light craft that can be manhandled over the rollers. But it has trees and greenery and lilacs.

Elizabeth Bridge, just below the point where the mill-stream rejoins the river, carries the A355 link road between the M40, M30, M4 and north and south destinations. By now you will be seeing rowing-crews from Eton College, whose 'wet bobs' use this part of the river. On the left is Brocas Field, presented to the College by Lord Brocas, and the Eton boathouses; opposite, along the Windsor bank, Alexandra Gardens. (Both banks are now in Berkshire: the county boundary falls between Boveney and Eton Wick.)

Windsor Bridge (now closed to motor traffic) connects Eton with Windsor. Built in 1823, it has iron arches on granite piers.

From another island, Cutler's Eyot, we get that distant view, on the left, of Eton College that caused the poet Gray to think of its pupils as 'little victims'; which, when Keate was a flogging headmaster, they surely were. Yet Eton and the Thames love each other: 'The river throws its arm about Eton with an ample swing,' wrote Percy Lubbock more than fifty years ago. 'The Thames is a very lordly water, in these its middle reaches.' Here are the college's two bathing places, Athens and Cuckoo Weir; and the Masters' Boathouse. Romney Island and Romney Lock now appear: the backwater practically belongs to the College, and is the scene of water-spectacles on the Fourth of June. The lock, with its flights of granite steps, is an important stage in the annual Swan Upping: here the Dyers' and Vintners' swan men parade to receive the present senior swan-master, John Turk, and his men who, since they represent the Queen, have the privilege of entering the lock first. It was on Romney Island that Izaak Walton fished with Charles Cotton, poet and translator, John Donne, poet and Dean of St Paul's, and Sir Henry Wotton, Provost of Eton.

The river, which began to turn north at Windsor Bridge, completes one side of an inverted U at Black Potts railway bridge and turns south again, reaching Victoria Bridge; both this and the imminent Albert Bridge are believed to have been designed by the Prince Consort himself. Windsor Home Park now appears on the right and continues for a good $1\frac{1}{2}$ miles. The towpath is on this side but, for reasons of royal security, walkers should use the other side of the river, taking the B3021 through Datchet. If Victoria Bridge is associated with comedy (for it was here that Falstaff, in *The Merry Wives of Windsor*, was thrown into the Thames), so is the decorated stone Albert Bridge at the end of Home Park. In Queen Anne's reign a rickety timber bridge spanned the Thames at Datchet itself, then in Buckinghamshire. The bridge was always falling down. For many years Buckinghamshire and Berkshire wrangled about how to rebuild it. Finally a two-part bridge was built – half was made

of wood, and half of iron. It still fell down. In 1851 the Prince Consort solved the problem by recommending two bridges.

Beyond Datchet is the Queen Mother Reservoir, the largest in Britain with 8,300 million gallons, one of many reservoirs (they can be seen from an aircraft circling Heathrow) around Staines supplying the Thames Water area. Old Windsor Lock, with an island and a backwater, needs beautifying to bring it up to the standard set by Boveney, Cookham and others. It was the first to be repaired after World War II, and critics have accused it of a 'surfeit of concrete'. Beyond it, on the left, is Wraysbury, which has several reservoirs. The backwater leaves and rejoins the river (here called the New Cut) in a large U-bend of its own, enclosing Ham Fields. Just below its southern end is minute Friday Island.

After $\frac{3}{4}$ mile, a famous inn is seen among trees on the right, the Bells of Ouzeley. It dates only from the 1930s, but tradition has it that there was a hostelry here in the twelfth century. The name dates from the Dissolution of the Monasteries, when, it is said, the bells from Ouzeley Abbey were brought here in a barge and buried nearby. (No one has ever found them.) The county boundary falls just below the inn, and the right bank is now in Surrey. For the next $1\frac{1}{4}$ miles Runnymede dominates the scene on the right bank, with the Kennedy Memorial and Cooper's Hill in the distance. Magna Carta Island is on our left, and as we go through the shrine to democracy we may wonder a little whether the authors of *1066 And All That*, having read the wording of the great charter, were far wrong when they hinted that King John gave freedom and justice to all 'except the common people'. There are notices on Magna Carta Island, nevertheless, discouraging boating parties. Behind the island is Ankerwyke, an estate containing the ruins of a twelfth-century nunnery and a huge, very old (nearly 33 feet round) yew tree associated with King John.

At the annual Swan Upping between Sunbury and Pangbourne, a team of watermen mark cygnets that do not belong to the crown

Bell Weir Lock (there are rollers here too), built in 1817, is named after its first keeper, Charles Bell. The Runnymede Hotel was built in 1971 on the site of the old Anglers' Hotel. The weir here is recommended for fly-fishing. Ahead is Runnymede Bridge, and by now we are beginning to be aware of Staines as an industrial town, and a profusion of boatyards on the right for the next mile or so. Between Runnymede Bridge and Staines Bridge, just over $\frac{1}{2}$ mile, are two large islands, Holm Island and Church Island. Between them, on the left bank, runs Ashby Recreation Ground in which you may just be able to see the famous London Stone. You certainly won't be able to read the inscription on it which says, 'God preserve ye citty'. Did the name Staines come from the Stone? It has been there since 1285 and marked the old limit of the City of London's control over the river until 1857. Before 1857 there was a custom by which the Lord Mayor and Aldermen visited the Stone by barge, drank copious toasts and 'bumped' all Sheriffs and Aldermen who had not been made Freemen of the Waters. The stone also once marked the old boundary between Buckinghamshire and Middlesex. Now, confusingly, it marks the boundary between Berkshire and Surrey. Henceforth, downstream, both riverbanks are in Surrey for the time being. Above the stone, too, fishing is no longer free.

We have now arrived at Staines Bridge, a practical affair which does not quite qualify for the adjective handsome or noble but is not unpleasing to look at. It was built by John Rennie's son George and opened in 1832 by William IV. It seems that major Thames bridges usually have a pub at each end. In this case we have the choice of the Swan and the Bridge Hotel before continuing our downstream journey.

Reading to Staines - 39 river miles

BISHAM (*Berkshire*)

Probably meaning 'Byssel's ham'. Situated $1\frac{3}{4}$ miles south of Great Marlow on the A404. Not easy to approach from the river because of No Mooring notices. Church and abbey are associated historically. All Saints Church (late seventeenth-century tower) is mostly a restoration of 1849, but the chapel, containing monuments to the Hoby family, is almost wholly sixteenth-century. The Hobys, a family of diplomats, somehow survived the reigns of Henry VIII, Mary and Elizabeth I with honour and preferment. The monument to Lady Margaret Hoby (1605) is a work of art: sculpted swans decorate an alabaster plinth and obelisk. Her maiden name was Carey, and the swan is part of the Carey arms. Lady Elizabeth Hoby (her tomb, 1609,

Bisham Abbey was a religious house in Tudor times. Today it is a recreation centre

is here too) built tombs to her husband Sir Thomas (1566) and his half-brother Sir Philip (1588). She eventually married Lord John Russell, having prayed, 'Give me, O God, a husband like Thomas, or else restore me to my husband Thomas!'

Bisham Abbey, it is monotonous to report, was another victim of the Dissolution — in this case, a double dissolution. It began as 'preceptory' of the Knights Templar. In the fourteenth century, after the Templars were suppressed, William Montacute, Earl of Salisbury, who fought at Poitiers, built an Augustinian priory here (only fragments of the great hall, chapel, front door and porch remain). Here were buried four Earls of Salisbury and Richard Neville ('Warwick the Kingmaker') whose body was brought here after his defeat at Barnet in 1471. Henry VIII, with whose support the Priory had been established, seized it back after the Dissolution and gave it to Anne of Cleves (the 'Flanders mare' whose portrait had so flattered her) as a sort of consolation for divorcing her. Anne didn't care for it and gave it to Sir Philip Hoby, who built the largely Tudor house using materials from the old abbey. About this time a ghost appeared with a black face and white dress, like a photographic negative. It was of Lady Hoby who had punished her small son for blotting his copybook by shutting him up in a room with no window until he died. Her spirit floats about washing her hands like Lady Macbeth. Actual copybooks were found under the floorboards many years later.

The future Queen Elizabeth I was guarded here, for three years during her sister Mary's reign, by Sir Thomas Hoby.

BOULTER'S LOCK (*Berkshire*)

Situated $\frac{1}{2}$ mile north of Maidenhead. Boulter isn't anyone's name — it is simply an old word for 'miller'. Where there was a lock, there was often a mill, and Ray's Mill, on the island, is thus accounted for (it is now an hotel). Richard Ray, lock-keeper here for fifty years, retired in 1829, having also run the mill: he was one of the old breed of river-servants who are hard to find today. The lock was built in 1770 and was given a new mechanism in 1912. Plentifully wooded though the riverbank is, you could never call it secluded, especially with a busy road running parallel on the Berkshire side. People flock here all the year round, and the lock, for all its great size, can be choked with river-traffic at high seasons like Ascot Week. You cross a small bridge to get to the island, which has attractive gardens and a miniature golf-course.

Nearby are the offices of the District Navigation Inspector, whose team patrols 21 miles of the river, checking locks, water levels, boats and weirs. An obstruction (such as a derelict boat) in a weir can cause a water-level rise of nearly a foot in a few hours: there is an ever-present risk of flooding.

Boulter's Lock is really a complete village gathered round Boulter's Inn hotel and restaurant. It still has an air of Edwardian naughtiness, of punts and parasols, blazers and straw-boaters. One who loved it well was Fred S. Thacker, lifelong historian of the Thames to whose two great volumes, *The Thames Highway (1914–1920)*, all other Thames writers are indebted. Diligent researcher and charming stylist, he knew that the river was in danger of succumbing to the twentieth century, and envied the Boulter's lock-keeper with his own mill, from an age 'when England was wise to feed herself' and you could see 'Thames salmon leap below the weir'.

BOURNE END (*Buckinghamshire*)

From 'bourne' meaning stream. It is $1\frac{1}{4}$ miles upstream from Cookham on the A4094. The bourne is the river Wye or Wick which joins the Thames near the railway bridge, having given its name to High Wycombe on the way. The Upper Thames Sailing Club, the Bourne End Cruiser and Yacht Club and Bourne

Bray Church is surrounded by many old houses

111

End Marina conspire to fill the broad river with craft. Between here and Cookham, on the left bank, villas and gardens reinforce the impression of a 'commuter town', not that this is necessarily pejorative. Bourne End is described in a 1890s guidebook on the Thames as mainly open fields and looked like the National Trust's open space of Cocksmarsh on the opposite bank. So it is a community which has mostly sprung up since the end of the nineteenth century. It looks older than it is, for it is a model estate built as an experiment in the 1890s called Abbots Brook Estate, and is praised by architectural pundits as 'cosy make-believe' and 'a subtopian fairy world' – medium-sized half-timbered houses arranged along a trout stream! 'Picturesque' (Pevsner, not me) and somehow it works. Sir Reginald Blomfield designed the church built in 1889 in red brick, and left attractively bare inside. On the banks of the other (Wye) stream stands a handsome house of uncertain age, Mill House, surrounded by luxurious tree-filled gardens.

BOVENEY (*Buckinghamshire*)

Meaning 'place above the island'. It is 2 miles above Windsor. The island is presumably the large one accommodating the racecourse. The main interest of this hamlet is the odd little chapel of St Mary Magdalene standing alone on the riverbank. Built of rubble, begun in Norman times (early thirteenth-century) its nave and chancel are one. The weatherboarded belfry gives it a patched-up look; yet it wears its poverty with pride. Inside, there are sculptured pieces of figures from the life of Christ, perhaps from an old reredos. The chapel was once used by bargees in the days when there were wharves along the river. There is no electric light, only candles. If you find it locked, you can borrow a key from a house near the lock called The Old Place.

Boveney Court and Boveney Place are among several large timber-framed houses in the village, 'so heavily restored', says one authority, 'as to give doubts as to authenticity'.

BRAY (*Berkshire*)

Meaning 'brow of a hill'. Situated 1 mile south of Maidenhead. We'll talk about the Vicar in a moment. The village, despite busy roads and the nearby M4 traffic, still *looks* rural, with its crooked lanes and timbered and Georgian houses. The Hotel de Paris is no more, but the Hind's Head still flourishes. Chantry House, by the churchyard, is eighteenth-century. The Crown Inn's middle section is a timbered fourteenth-century hall. The Lych Gate, or Cottage, is an eighteenth-century mixture of timber, tiles and brick, with a gallery overlooking those who enter the churchyard. The Chantry Chapel of St Mary, also in the churchyard, is built of flint and was used as a school in the seventeenth century.

Bray's best-known resident (apart from the Vicar) was William Goddard, who died in 1609 but left a bequest to found Jesus Hospital in Holyport Road – you can see his statue in the gatehouse. Goddard, a prominent City merchant, provided for twenty-six poor people who must be over fifty years old; twenty of them must have lived in Bray for at least twenty years; the rest are freemen or women of the Fishmongers' Company which runs the charity. The seventeenth-century almshouses, gabled with tall chimneys, form a quadrangle. In order to build those chimneys, the founders were granted special exemption from Hearth Tax. Notice the splendid Parliament Clock in the porter's lodge. The almshouses were a favourite subject of the Victorian painter Fred Walker, A.R.A. (1840–75): his best-known picture of them is 'The Harbour of Refuge'. Walker (*see also* Cookham) fetched high prices at the turn of the twentieth century because he was thought to be the original of Little Billee in George Du Maurier's *Trilby*.

Ah, yes: the Vicar. The song, 'Whatsoever King shall reign, I'll be the Vicar of Bray,' gives the impression that he survived the reigns of Charles II, James II, William III, Anne and George I.

The Thames 'that runs so clear and green and weedy' – near Cookham Lock

Who was he, anyway? There were several slippery vicars — Simon Alwyn, Peter Pendleton, Francis Carswell — between Henry VIII and Elizabeth I. Simon Alwyn, Alleyn or Symonds is the one, according to Thomas Fuller's *Church History*. He turned coat as he did because he was so terrified by the sight of the heretics being burned at Windsor in Mary's reign. And, it was a rich living.

His big church, St Michael's, has a Perpendicular tower but the rest is mostly a restoration of 1859. There is a very early (1378) brass of Sir John de Foxley and his two wives, and a monument to William Goddard.

BURNHAM BEECHES (*Buckinghamshire*)
Situated 2½ miles northeast of Taplow. One of several excursions worth making while you're in the neighbourhood. Nearly 600 acres of wild (yet preserved) woodlands, part of the prehistoric forest that until the Middle Ages covered most of the Chilterns. It gives you some idea of how England appeared to the Romans. Burnham Beeches was acquired in 1880 for the pleasure of the City's people by the Corporation of London, which still adminsters them. You should see them in their autumn gold to enjoy them at their best. Dating trees is never easy, but some of the hollow pollard beeches may be as old as 800 years. Burnham Village has a flint church dating from the thirteenth century with interesting brasses and monuments; one of them to George Evelyn (d.1657), John's cousin. Quite a lot of Norman building survived the Dissolution at Burnham Abbey (founded 1266), and the village has many fifteenth- and sixteenth-century houses.

Dorneywood, southwest of Burnham Beeches, was built *circa* 1920 — a Tudor-style mansion with Georgian windows and (inside the porch) decorations by Rex Whistler. Unfortunately you cannot see over the house. But people visit it to see

Marlow — the river here was the haunt of writer, Izaak Walton, in the seventeenth century

its magnificent garden (National Trust, open Saturday afternoons in August and September by appointment). Dorneywood was presented to the nation with 200 acres in 1942 by Lord Courtauld-Thomson as a country retreat for a Secretary of State or Minister of the Crown (usually the Foreign Secretary).

Whether you like Gray's *Elegy* or not (and I hold it to be one of the great dead poems of our language) the churchyard at **Stoke Poges** (3 miles east of Burnham) is worth a visit. The poet's tomb, which he shares with his mother, is by the south wall of St Giles' Church, Norman but gabled. The Hastings Chapel was added about 1560. There is an odd window in one of the porches showing an angel riding — what? It can't be a bicycle: it must be a hobby-horse.

CLIVEDEN (*Buckinghamshire*)
Meaning 'valley among cliffs'. It is 2 miles north of Taplow off the B476. The first house was built here in 1666 for George Villiers, 2nd Duke of Buckingham, member of the Cabal and general libertine, Dryden's 'man so various . . . chymist, fiddler, statesman and buffoon'. Here he fought a duel with Lord Shrewsbury over Lady Shrewsbury, killing his man. The lady, disguised as a page-boy, watched with unseemly relish. There were additions to the house in the eighteenth century when, among several occupants, the Earl of Orkney (one of Marlborough's generals) and Frederick, Prince of Wales (George III's father) lived here. 'Rule Britannia', as part of James Thomson's masque *Alfred*, was first performed before him here. In 1795 the house was burned to a cinder; only the terrace escaped. Another house on the same site was also destroyed by fire in 1849.

The owner, the Duke of Sutherland, hired Sir Charles Barry, architect of the Houses of Parliament, to design a new house. The result is the nine-bayed and balustraded mansion we see, today, proud on its hill. Built in 1851, it was sold in 1870 to the Duke of Westminster, who in 1893 sold it to William Waldorf

Astor who became the 1st Viscount Astor. There was a period in which the Astor family owned both *The Times* and the *Observer*. Small wonder that Cliveden became the centre of political weekend parties. Whether Claud Cockburn's 1930s scandal sheet *The Week* was right in hinting that the 'Cliveden Set', led by Nancy Astor, the first woman M.P., was plotting to give Germany a free hand in Europe, we shall probably never know. The 2nd Viscount Astor, Nancy's husband, gave Cliveden to the National Trust in 1942. Today it is let to Stanford University of California, and only two rooms are open to the public (April to October, Saturday and Sunday afternoons).

The magnificent gardens, formal and otherwise, are open every day from March to December. Half-way down to the river is an Italian garden made into a cemetery for those who died at Cliveden when it was a military hospital during 1914–18. Queen Anne's Walk leads to the Blenheim Pavilion (by Leoni, *circa* 1735). The Long Garden has statues and topiary; there is also a water-garden and a rose-garden laid out in 1956.

Inside the house is a huge French Renaissance fireplace (genuine Francis I). This, and some Brussels tapestries depicting The Arts of War, are both in the Hall. The French panelling in the Dining Room came from the Château of Asnières near Paris, built in 1751 for the Marquis d'Argenson and occupied for some time by Madame de Pompadour.

For a glorious view of the Thames Valley, find Leoni's octagonal gazebo (1740). It was converted into a chapel by the 1st Viscount Astor, who is buried there.

COOKHAM (*Berkshire*)

Meaning 'hill at bend in river'. It is 3 miles north of Maidenhead. The High Street looks more like that of a town than a village, but many old houses have been quite skilfully turned into agreeable shop-fronts. There are too many visitors and cars, perhaps, in the summer; yet it is spacious, with much to look at. The big village green, named Cookham Moor, indicates what Cookham was like before most of its houses were built: there is a timber-framed cottage, Moor End, looking as if it might fall over at any minute, and Moor Cottage too; Malting and Forge House tell of trades no longer here. Churchgate House and Cottage, East Gate, Wistaria Cottage, Tarry Stone House – was ever such variety in one place? Most are seventeenth- and eighteenth-century. The last house is opposite the Tarry Stone, placed there in 1909, a big sarsen like a bit of Stonehenge: a notice tells you that 'sports were held' around it before 1507. Was it Druidical or a meteorite? Nobody seems to know.

In High Street are two world-famous inns, or rather hotels, named the Bel and Dragon and the King's Arms, and the house called Fernlea where Stanley Spencer the painter was born in 1891. Spencer, who died in 1959, expressed basic Christianity through the sights and ordinary people of Cookham. His 'Resurrection' (in the Tate Gallery in London) shows Jesus at the door of Cookham Church. Also in the Tate is his 'Swan Upping'. Famous too is his 'Christ Preaching at Cookham Regatta'. The villagers well remember the bony man with glasses and wild hair who pushed an old pram full of his painting materials and set up his easel anywhere with a notice that read, 'Mr Spencer would be grateful if visitors would kindly avoid distracting his attention from his work.'

You can see the pram (and buy a picture postcard of it) at the Stanley Spencer Gallery (open daily Easter to October, and weekends from November to Easter). The gallery is in King's Hall where Spencer as a boy went to Sunday school. The church he attended, Holy Trinity, beside the Thames, is built of flint and stone, with a sturdy tower (late Perpendicular), a Norman nave and a thirteenth-century north aisle and chapel. There may have been a church here in Saxon times, but the first mention of a church is in Domesday Book. The tower, unusually, has both a clock and a sundial.

The Bel and the Dragon Hotel at Cookham

Inside hangs Stanley Spencer's 'Last Supper'. Note the medieval tiles in the chancel. In the Lady Chapel are wood carvings from Oberammergau. There are many monuments of all ages, especially to the Babham family (dating from 1458 onwards), and some fifteenth- and sixteenth-century brasses in the chancel and north chapel. Flaxman's tablet to Sir Isaac Pocock (1810), who drowned in the river depicts his body in a boat cradled in his niece's arms, is touching. There is also a tablet to Fred Walker, A.R.A. (1840–75) (see Bray), illustrator, painter and wood engraver, whose drawings once appeared in the *Cornhill* and other magazines, and whose paintings of peasants in landscape often found inspiration on the banks of the River Thames.

DATCHET (*Buckinghamshire*)
It is 2 miles east of Windsor. Although my 1890s guidebook talks of 'suburban villas' here, Datchet is still a village with a green and a number of old houses. High Street, leading to the river, has a row of Georgian redbrick and several detached Early Victorian yellow-brick houses. Near the river are Datchet Lodge (to the right) and Old Bridge House (to the left), whose bow-front with iron verandah can be seen from the water. A small public garden comes down to the river where once there was a ferry and also a timber bridge.

The church of St Mary is Victorian (1860), although seventeenth-century tablets to the Wheeler family inside suggest an earlier building. The tower is octagonal and much-ornamented. There is some good Victorian stained glass.

Datchet was the home for some time of Sir William Herschel (1738–1822), who gave up his career as a musician to become private astronomer to George III. He and his sister Caroline often entertained members of the Royal Family. He discovered the planet Uranus. It is evident that Shakespeare knew Datchet and the whole district from *The Merry Wives of Windsor*. Near the end of Datchet Lane was 'the muddy ditch at Datchet Mead' where Falstaff was 'carried in a basket, like a barrow of butcher's offal, to be thrown in the Thames' and would have been drowned but that the shore was 'shelvy and shallow'. Which it still is.

DORNEY (*Buckinghamshire*)
Probably meaning 'isle of bees'. It is 3 miles northwest of Windsor on the B3026. To call Dorney 'a sleepy village' is a compliment. Its history is dominated by the Palmer Family, who lived at Dorney Court, a fine house with gables and tall chimneys dating from the late fifteenth century, though altered during the nineteenth and twentieth centuries. The Hall, with its handsome braced roof, is much the same as when it was built. Some of the fireplaces are original too. Charles II used to visit Barbara Villiers here, and in his honour the Dorney gardener, Charles Rose, grew the first English 'king-pine' (pineapple) from stock imported from the Barbados, and presented it to him in 1668. This is recorded in a painting by Hendrik Danckerts showing the 'Merry Monarch' looking extremely wary. There is a village pub called the Pineapple; and another called the Palmer Arms, an old coaching inn, which was once exclusively for employees of the Palmer estates.

The small stone and flint church of St James can be reached either down a lane alongside Dorney Court, or from the river near Queen's Eyot along a footpath, the Barge Path. Much remains of the original Norman building. The brick tower is Tudor, the font Norman, the pulpit seventeenth-century, the pews a little later. The musicians' gallery, all in oak, was built in 1634. Exceptionally pathetic is the alabaster monument to Sir William Garrard (d.1607), a Lord Mayor of London, and his wife and fifteen children (seven boys, eight girls) kneeling round him. Some of them hold skulls to show they died young.

DOWN PLACE (*Berkshire*)
This house is $\frac{3}{4}$ mile south of Bray village. Vampires, mutton pies and the House of Hanover come together here for it is now

a film studio, specializing in horror (Hammer Films were made here), and it was once the home of Jacob Tonson (1656–1736), publisher (shrewd fellow, he bought the copyright of *Paradise Lost*), and secretary of the Kit-Cat Club, presided over by the Earl of Dorset, to which the Whig wits of the time (Steele, Addison, Congreve, Vanbrugh and others) belonged. The Club took its name from Christopher (Kit) Cat, maker of mutton pies which were eaten by the clubmen. The Club's political objective was loyalty to the House of Hanover. At full strength it had thirty-nine members, all of whom were painted by Sir Godfrey Kneller: their portraits were presented to Jacob Tonson, and passed to his grandson who hung them in his house at Water Oakley nearby. They are now in the National Portrait Gallery in London. Tonson published many of his brother Kitcats – also Dryden, Rowe's edition of Shakespeare, and an edition of Beaumont and Fletcher.

ETON (*Buckinghamshire*)

Meaning '*tun* on the river'. It is $\frac{1}{2}$ mile north of Windsor. With your permission, we'll skip what the Duke of Wellington said about the playing fields. Eton is a town of about 3,500 people with a pleasant High Street full of old buildings such as the timber-framed Cockpit Café, where young Etonians are taken by visiting parents. The College, founded in 1440 by Henry VI when he was eighteen (he had been very impressed by William of Wykeham's school at Winchester), has several of its original buildings. The 'seventy indigent scholars' for whom the College was founded are now some 1,200, not so indigent, judging from the parental Rolls-Royces on the Fourth of June, Eton's speech day and river festival held on the nearest Saturday to that date. It commemorates the birthday of George III.

There is so much to see that I recommend the guided tour from the Tourist Office, Central Station, Windsor (afternoons, May to October). The Chapel is open 2–5 p.m., also in the mornings during school holidays; School Yard and Cloisters likewise.

Eton College, founded in 1440 by Henry VI, is famous as a rowing school and first took part in Henley Royal Regatta in 1861

College Chapel (Perpendicular, 1440–80) is similar to King's College Chapel, Cambridge, also founded by Henry VI. Its windows were shattered by a bomb in 1940 but it has eight new ones designed by John Piper. The same bomb damaged Upper School (built in 1690, attributed to Wren). Lower School, built in 1445, was the original classroom, and continued so for 200 years; the Long Chamber above is for the use of King's Scholars who live in College. Lupton's Tower, named after the Provost of Henry VIII's time, was built in 1520: its gateway leads to the Cloisters, part of which belong to the original building; the rest was added in the sixteenth and eighteenth centuries. Anyone who thinks of public schools as places of Latin and Greek should note that Eton had a Chemistry Laboratory as early as 1869 and Mathematical Schools in 1877.

FAWLEY COURT (*Buckinghamshire*)

Probably meaning 'grove with a clearing'. It is 1 mile downstream from Henley. The original house was built in 1684 for William Freeman (by Wren, some say), and remodelled in 'classical' style by James Wyatt in 1771 with an Ionic colonnade and gardens by Capability Brown. The gardens contain various eighteenth-century ornaments, and there is a flint-built dairy incorporating a genuine Norman doorway taken from a house in Henley. There seems to have been an earlier house here, owned by Sir Bulstrode Whitelock, in a no-man's-land between Cavaliers and Roundheads in the Civil War, and it suffered severe damage. Cannon balls have been found in the grounds. Inside are several eighteenth-century fireplaces, and the Saloon (says Pevsner) has 'the most splendid seventeenth-century plaster work in the county'. Fawley Court is now the Divine Mercy College.

Fawley village, which you can't see from the river, straggles along behind Henley Reach uphill to St Mary's Church. The church's tower is mainly thirteenth-century; the chancel was built in 1748 for the Freemans of Fawley Court, with furnishings taken from Canons, the Duke of Chandos's palace near Edgware; font, panelling, carved pulpit, pews and stalls are attributed to Grinling Gibbons. In the churchyard is the domed Freeman Mausoleum (1750).

HAMBLEDEN (*Buckinghamshire*)

Probably derived from 'Hamela's valley'. It is 1 mile north of Hambleden Mill. The part of the village you see from the lock and the mill is Mill End, on the A4155 Henley–Marlow road. Hambleden is the ideal unspoiled Chiltern village, in a valley full of beech trees, with a village green surrounded by old houses, and with a village pump. The gabled early seventeenth-century Manor House is the home of Viscount Hambleden.

The footbridge at Hambleden Lock crosses the weirs to Mill End and its famous mill

St Mary's Church embodies fragments of the original Norman church, whose central tower fell down in 1703. The existing flint and brick tower is dated 1721. In the north transept is a striking monument to Sir Cope d'Oyley (d.1633) in alabaster, carved by John Hargrave: the kneeling figures of Sir Cope and his lady are shown surrounded by their ten children. Lady d'Oyley was the sister of Francis Quarles, James I's Poet Laureate. There is a painting of the Virgin by Murillo, lent by Lord Hambleden. In the south transept is a recent altar made from carved oak said to have been taken from Cardinal Wolsey's bedstead. It bears his hat and arms.

In the churchyard is the Kendrick Mausoleum and monument. Dr Scawen Kendrick, rector here in 1724, built the large seven-bayed rectory (now known as Kendricks) northeast of the village.

At Mill End, by the river, are the mill, Mill House and Mill End Farm. Yewdon Manor, $\frac{1}{4}$ mile away, is mostly seventeenth-century with many gables. Near it, in 1911, a Roman-British villa was excavated: fourth-century coins, a mosaic floor and hypocaust fragments found here are now on exhibition in Aylesbury Museum. Hambleden Mill, probably sixteenth-century (although there is evidence of a mill here in 1338), was working until 1955, powered by a water-driven turbine.

HARLEYFORD MANOR (*Buckinghamshire*)

The manor is midway between Henley and Temple Locks, $1\frac{1}{2}$ miles southwest of Marlow. It is an extremely solid house built by Sir Robert Taylor for Sir William Clayton in 1755. There is a statue to Sir William in the grounds. The house is five bays square. Was there once a pillared portico? Sir Robert had a taste for the Palladian. The columns may have been removed and used round a circular building in the grounds known as the Temple of Vesta. Vesta was a Roman hearth goddess in whose temples an eternal fire was kept burning, tended by Vestal Virgins. Sir William Clayton seems to have been a man of taste:

it is not known who decorated the house inside, but in one room there are attractive plaster panels depicting sports and arts, and handsome chimney pieces in others. The gardens were laid out by Capability Brown.

Now an adjunct of Harleyford Marina, the manor plays host to innumerable river boats moored between the two locks; and a caravan park too.

HENLEY-ON-THAMES (*Oxfordshire*)

Meaning 'high grove'. Long before its Regatta (held annually) Henley was a fashionable and prosperous social centre, a riverside Cheltenham dating largely from about 1750 – hence all the Georgian buildings, some of which are sixteenth- and seventeenth-century behind eighteenth-century fronts. In medieval times Henley was an inland port, shipping timber, corn and malt to London. After 1700 it became a staging post for Oxford–London coaches. Now it has been labelled a commuter town, especially since the M4 motorway has been built. It is, however, still an entrancing place. It has over twenty pubs, many with bull and bear baiting yards. The oldest is probably the Bull in Bell Street (fifteenth-century). The Angel, a coaching inn by the bridge, has a stone and flint arch in the cellar which is believed to be part of an earlier bridge over the river before the present one built in 1786. The Bear is sixteenth–seventeenth-century, the Catherine Wheel is mostly Regency, the Old White Hart is fifteenth–sixteenth-century, the redbrick Red Lion, overlooking the river, was visited by Charles I in 1632 (his coat of arms was discovered over a chimney piece) and again during the Civil War. It was at the Red Lion that the poet Shenstone (1714–63) scratched this famous verse on a window:

> Whoe'er has travelled life's dull round
> Where'er his stages may have been,
> May sigh to think he still has found
> The warmest welcome at an inn.

St Mary's Church, big and spacious, has a tall sixteenth-century tower, thought to have been built by John Longland, who was born in Henley and became Bishop of Lincoln (1521–47). The fine chapel of St Leonard (fifteenth-century) has a battlemented parapet with gargoyles, and traceried stone windows. There are many monuments, some of them to rich benefactors of the town and church, such as William Hayward, who built the bridge. The finest monument is probably that to Lady Elizabeth Periam (d.1621), sister of the 1st Lord Bacon, in alabaster and black marble. Also buried here are General Dumouriez (1739–1823), the French commander who fled to England and advised the War Office on how to deal with Napoleon; and (in the churchyard) Richard Jennings, Wren's Master Builder of St Paul's Cathedral.

Despite a one-way traffic system, Henley can daunt a pedestrian; but to see its best features, concentrate on Market Place, Hart Street, New Street, and Friday Street. Bell Street is the main shopping centre. Near the church are some old almshouses, and Chantry House (built in 1420 as a school for poor boys, and now Church House). Notice, in Hart Street, two gabled Tudor houses: one of them belonged to William Lenthall, Speaker of the House of Commons during the Long Parliament. The Old Rope Walk is fifteenth-century.

Behind the Queen Anne style town hall (*circa* 1900) is a folly called Friar Park, built in 1896 by a rich solicitor, Sir Frank Crisp. In its Edwardian heyday it was full of French Flamboyant decoration, with figures of friars – you pressed a friar's nose to switch on the light. Was it all a huge expensive joke? Nobody seems certain.

The course for the Regatta begins at Temple Island and ends over a mile later at Poplar Point. Further on nearer the bridge is the Leander Club's boathouse. Opposite Poplar Point is the smart club, Phyllis Court.

The bridge at Henley-on-Thames, designed by Salopian William Hayward in 1786, has masks of Father Thames and the goddess Isis

HURLEY (*Berkshire*)

Meaning 'glade at a bend'. It is 5 miles east of Henley, on the A423. Turning a blind eye, if possible, to the holiday caravans that line the river here in summer, concentrate on the little green by the parish church of St Mary. This incorporates part of Hurley Priory, an eleventh-century Benedictine monastery built on the site of an Anglo-Saxon church. You can still see the refectory wall, now part of a private house, within a quadrangle known as Paradise. It is reputed that Edith, sister of Edward the Confessor, is buried here. The Priory was probably founded by Geoffrey de Mandeville soon after the Norman Conquest, and consecrated in 1086 by St Osmund, Bishop of Sarum.

The nave of the church, which is long and narrow with Norman windows and doors, is also part of the old Priory. The church (much restored in Victorian times) contains monuments to the Lovelace family of Ladye Place. Everything once revolved round the Priory: Ye Olde Bell, one of the oldest inns in the country, dates back to about 1135 when it was the Priory guesthouse. The cloisters were originally to the north of the present church; nearby is a round fourteenth-century dovecot and two tithe barns. In a crypt, covered by an inscribed stone, three skeletons wearing Benedictine habits were found. In the churchyard Dame Irene Vanbrugh, the actress, is buried.

It is said that there is a secret tunnel connecting the Old Bell to Ladye Place (named after the dedication of the Priory to Our Lady). After the Dissolution the Lovelace family moved in, and on the site of the Priory a fine Tudor house was built by John Lovelace (d.1558). His grandson Richard, 'a gentleman of mettle', distinguished himself in the Spanish wars and was eventually knighted in Ireland by the Earl of Essex – a proxy ennoblement which made Queen Elizabeth extremely angry. In 1627 he was created Baron Lovelace by Charles I.

In the vaults of Ladye Place (according to Lord Macaulay) the Lovelace family and other nobles met secretly in 1688 to plot the overthrow of James II, and his replacement by William

A secret passage is said to run from the Olde Bell, Hurley, to Ladye Place

of Orange. 'Beneath the stately saloon', Macaulay says, 'was a subterraneous vault, in which the bones of ancient monks had sometimes been found. In this stark chamber, some zealous and daring opponents of the government had held many midnight conferences during that anxious time when England was impatiently expecting the Protestant wind.'

The last Lord Lovelace married Byron's daughter in 1835. Two years later Ladye Place was demolished.

MAIDENHEAD (Berkshire)

Meaning 'maidens' hythe or landing place'. The place, like so many fordable points on the river, once had great strategic importance. It was here that the Saxon king Aella defeated the Roman Ambrosius Aurelianus. The Saxon grave, once thought to be Aella's, on Taplow Hill which was excavated in 1883, is now identified with a chieftain named Taeppa who possibly gave his name to Taplow. His jewelry, silver drinking horns, ceremonial deer's antlers and his huge iron sword are now in the British Museum in London. A thirteenth-century bridge further encouraged the town's growth. In the Civil War strategy came to the fore again; and in the eighteenth century Sir Robert Taylor's road bridge helped Maidenhead to become an important coach stop between London and Bath. Many travellers preferred to spend the night here so that they could cross Maidenhead Thicket, infested with highwaymen, in daylight. In the nineteenth century the Great Western Railway, and in the twentieth century the M4 motorway, influenced Maidenhead's role as a residential, commuter and industrial town. As in Reading, a good deal of town planning has been done. You don't come here to admire beauty, but there are attractions well worth landing for. The M4 makes London more accessible, but it also diverts traffic away from the town and it has been possible to create pedestrian and shopping precincts.

At Maidenhead Thicket (take the A423 from the town), instead of highwaymen, is the Courage Shire Horse Centre (open

Maidenhead looks across the river to Taplow

daily, except Mondays, during March to October, and also on Bank Holiday Mondays). This is a good place to take children: they can admire the splendid animals, visit Pets' Corner, and have rides in a brewer's dray. In riverside Guards Club Road is the Henry Reitlinger Bequest Museum (open Tuesdays and Thursdays, and the first Sunday in each month, April to September) – an exhibition of glassware, pottery, paintings and sculpture. It's free too.

In **Taplow**, on the Buckinghamshire bank. is Skindles Hotel, Taplow Court and St Nicholas Church. Taplow Court, a gabled Early Tudor style mansion, attributed to Sir Charles Barry, was built in 1855 for the Earl of Orkney, with a pompous square tower in the middle. The church, although mostly built in 1912, contains some interesting brasses from the fourteenth–sixteenth centuries, including one of about 1350 dedicated to Nichole de Aumberdene described as 'the earliest surviving brass of a civilian in England'.

MARLOW, Great and Little (*Buckinghamshire*)

Possibly meaning 'remains of lake'. It is 6 miles northwest of Maidenhead, on the A404 and A4155. Fifty years ago Great Marlow's population was about 2,000: now it must be more than 10,000. But before dismissing this very attractive town as a suburb of London, look at the care with which new buildings have been designed to harmonize with the old. Weir and lock are the famous beauty spot, and the modern development beyond has been built on the site of the old mill to resemble another white weatherboarded mill. Great Marlow looks a modern town, but there are plenty of Georgian houses, especially in High Street and West Street. A milestone dated 1822 in Market Place reminds us that Marlow was a staging post for travellers between London and Bath. The Cecil family of Hatfield, many of whom suffered from gout, had great faith in the waters there.

Albion House was where Shelley lived for some months in 1817–18 while writing 'The Revolt of Islam'. His second wife Mary Godwin wrote *Frankenstein* here, and Thomas Love Peacock wrote *Nightmare Abbey* at 47 West Street. Shelley often went rowing with them on the river, one of his favourite places being Bisham. The Grammar School, founded by Sir William Borlase in 1624, is a flint-and-brick building with modern extensions. Remnantz is a large early eighteenth-century house of brick; the Royal Military College was founded here in 1799 and moved to Sandhurst in 1811. The Old Parsonage in St Peter's Street, long and rambling with many gables, dates from the fourteenth century – probably the oldest house in the town. The Crown Hotel in Market Place, once the town hall, was built in 1807 by Samuel Wyatt.

There is much to see in Marlow: don't miss Marlow Place in Station Road, built about 1720 for John Wallop, Earl of Portsmouth, who made it available to the Prince of Wales; this may be the reason the capitals of some pilasters have a leek design on them. The George and Dragon (eighteenth-century), Ship

The suspension bridge beside the Compleat Angler at Marlow was designed by William Tierney Clark.

Inn (sixteenth-century, with original ship's timbers), Two Brewers, and the Compleat Angler (in memory of Izaak Walton who loved this part of the river) are all attractive hostelries.

All Saints Church, by the bridge, rebuilt 1832–5, with the steeple added in 1898, has a monument to Richard Davenport (d.1799) by Joseph Nollekens, and another to Sir Miles Hobart (d.1636), M.P. for the borough. The latter portrays his death in a coach accident in Holborn: Parliament voted the money for the monument because Hobart, a rebel against Charles I, had locked the door of the House against the king's messenger while a finance bill was being passed. For this he was imprisoned in the Tower. In the vestry is a picture of the famous 'spotted boy' (d.1811), a disfigured child from the West Indies who was exploited by a showman named William Richardson. They share a grave in the churchyard.

William Tierney Clark's suspension bridge (1831–6) is now the only extant example of his work: his Hammersmith Bridge was replaced, and the beautiful bridge at Budapest was destroyed in World War II.

Little Marlow, 2 miles along the road to Bourne End, is dominated by Thames Water's various works, but the coarse fishing is recommended here. The tiny village has an eighteenth-century Manor House, Spade Oak Farm (seventeenth-century) and the remains of a thirteenth-century tower. An ominous signpost says, 'No road beyond the cemetery'. Here, unexpectedly, is the grave of the prolific thriller writer Edgar Wallace.

MEDMENHAM (*Buckinghamshire*)

Meaning 'middle ham with island'. It is 4 miles west-southwest of Marlow, on the A4155. The Abbey claims our first attention. A Cistercian house was founded here in the early thirteenth century, but little of it remains. What you see today is partly late Elizabethan, partly eighteenth-century, with later additions. The Gothick 'artificial ruin' (very fashionable in those times) was added in the tenancy of Sir Francis Dashwood of West Wycombe, who leased the abbey from its owner Francis Duffield. Dashwood, born in 1708, came into his title and estates when he was sixteen and thenceforth dedicated his youth to vice and eventually to the Hellfire Club, which he founded in 1745: its motto was 'do what thou wilt'. Leasing the Abbey he made free with it: he filled a temple with phallic symbols and pornographic statues and paintings. The 'Knights of St Francis of Wycombe' obscenely mocked Roman Catholic rites, offered sacrifices to heathen gods, and gave the sacrament to an ape. They included, at various times, Cabinet Ministers, members of the House of Lords, a Governor of Bengal, a Regius Professor at Oxford, and the notorious John Wilkes, the only Lord Mayor of London released from the Tower to take up that civic honour. Members of the Club, on the way from London, stopped at Ladye Place at Hurley (*see* entry) to change into monks' habits before their 'nameless orgies'. Dashwood was also Chancellor of the Exchequer, the only one to admit he was drunk while making his Budget speech. The Abbey is used by the Royal Air Force.

Medmenham, nevertheless, is a pleasant village, well-wooded and sheltered by chalk hills. A road leads down to the river and almost enters the water where the ferry used to be. There are flint cottages of various ages and some fine Lombardy poplars. Lodge Farm (owned by the National Trust) is seventeenth-century, built of brick and flint and has gables. St Peter's Church, amid chestnut trees, has hints of a Norman foundation, and an eighteenth-century tower. Inside, there are one or two brasses of the same period. The village bears traces of conflict during the Civil War: the Thames Valley was mostly Royalist, and a Roundhead cannon ball was found in the wall of the village pub, the fourteenth-century Dog and Badger, when it was being restored. The mansion Danesfield is about 500 yards to the east.

MONKEY ISLAND (*Berkshire*)

The island is $\frac{1}{2}$ mile downstream from Bray Lock. The 3rd Duke of Marlborough built a pavilion or fishing lodge here in 1744, and as those anglers who have permits know, the fishing is good hereabouts. What is unexplained is why the duke, among his ducal eccentricities, chose to decorate the pavilion with paintings of monkeys – classic subjects such as the 'Triumph of Galatea', and rural sports which dukes pursue, such as hunting, shooting and fishing, albeit performed by monkeys. We know little of the 3rd Duke: was his view of *homo sapiens* so low? Did he anticipate Darwin? My guidebook of the 1890s accuses the then landlord of passing off these decorations as the work of Sir Joshua Reynolds. They are by a French painter named Clermont, of whom very little is known. The fishing lodge is now part of a hotel. To reach it by land, take the lane south from Bray over the M4 – remembering that the rest of the way belongs to the hotel. Is Monkey Island a place which is famous for being famous? Perhaps.

PARK PLACE (*Berkshire*)

It is $\frac{3}{4}$ mile southeast of Henley, on the A321. It was built by the Duke of Hamilton, and the original mansion (now demolished) was the occasional residence of members of the Royal Family (especially Frederick, Prince of Wales, who alternated between here and Cliveden). In 1752 it was bought, with 900 acres, by General Conway, Governor of Jersey, who engaged James 'Athenian' Stuart to lay out the park, incorporating an obelisk made from the original steeple of St Bride's Church, Fleet Street, London. The General's imagination ran riot; Gothick artificial ruins were added, and an underground passage leading to an artificial Roman amphitheatre, with the stones of a Druids' Temple (or was it a burial ground?) which he brought back from Jersey in 1785. From the river you catch a glimpse, in the rich ascending woodland, of Happy Valley which is embellished with 'Gainsborough's Arch', said to have been built of stones taken from Reading Abbey. The road between Wargrave and Henley passes bumpily over Conway's Bridge. Conway was the father of Mrs Damer who sculpted the decorations on Henley Bridge. The estate of Park Place was divided in the nineteenth century and a house called Templecombe was built in part of it. Today some of the General's Gothick and archeological interests can be seen around the golf-course at Park Place.

REMENHAM (*Berkshire*)

Meaning 'ham by the rim or bank'. It is $1\frac{1}{2}$ miles east of Henley off the A423. Visitors to Henley Regatta think of Remenham as a village – no more than a hamlet – which you don't have time to see because its lanes are part of the one-way traffic system. A church, a farm or two, a few cottages dotted about, yet it is a big parish taking in the river's Berkshire bank from Park Place in the south to Aston and Culham Court in the north (about 5 river miles round the U-bend). Much of it hangs on a hillside, giving lovely glimpses of the river. St Nicholas's Church, by the water, is largely Victorian, restored in flint in an attempt to recapture the style of the Norman original: thus it has a semi-circular apse at its east end. It fits well into its cosy setting, but critics have called it 'self-consciously quaint'. Inside is an attractive wrought-iron screen, thought to be Italian. The churchyard contains the grave of Caleb Gould, who died in 1836 aged ninety-two. He was lock-keeper at Hambleden from 1777 until his death, his longevity was attributed to eating 'onion-porridge' every evening for supper. He sold home-baked bread to the river folk of those days, never took to nineteenth-century fashions, and always wore an eighteenth-century long coat with silver buttons.

Aston (about $\frac{3}{4}$ miles east of Remenham) has a pub called the Flower Pot, and there is a pottery in the village.

ROTHERFIELD GREYS (*Oxfordshire*)

Meaning 'field or open grazing land'. It is 3 miles west of Henley, on the Peppard road. A small village with a great house, Greys Court, which belonged to the de Grey family from the Conquest until the end of the fifteenth century. A fortified manor house, it was built in 1347 by Sir John de Grey, one of the original Knights of the Garter, who fought at Crécy. The Grey family died out and the manor reverted to the Crown. In 1516 Henry VIII gave it to Robert Knollys (whose son Francis became Lord Treasurer of the Household to Elizabeth I). His grandson (some scholars think he was the model for Shakespeare's Malvolio) succeeded in 1596.

In 1708 the house passed (by marriage) to the Stapleton family. In 1935 it was bought by Sir Felix Brunner and presented to the National Trust. The house is open to the public Monday, Wednesday and Friday (not Good Friday), April–September; gardens daily (except Sunday) in the afternoon. Amid the remains of the fourteenth-century walls and a crenellated tower is a mainly Jacobean manor house (built by the

The Magna Carta Memorial at Runnymede is situated at the foot of Cooper's Hill

Knollyses) including the seventeenth-century stables. Beside the tower is the Bachelors' Hall, so-called because a Latin inscription over the door says, 'Nothing is better than the celibate life'. The early Tudor well-house has a donkey-wheel which provided the Court's only water-supply until 1914.

In the stables was housed the Carlisle Collection of miniature rooms which the National Trust has now moved to North Yorkshire. A pity: it was an additional attraction for children on wet days. Instead, we have a touch of crime, for it was here that Robert Carr, Earl of Somerset (favourite of James I), and his wife Frances Howard were confined when they were awaiting trial for murder; they poisoned Sir Thomas Overbury, the poet, who died in the Tower in 1613. They were guilty of conspiracy all right, but only their accomplices were hanged.

The church contains a splendid brass to Robert de Grey (1387) and richly carved monuments to the Knollys family.

RUNNYMEDE (Surrey)

Meaning 'council island meadow'. It is 2 miles west of Staines on the A308. So did modern democracy begin here on 15 June 1215 when Bad King John sealed what would now be called a draft of a Great Charter? Lawyers who drafted the Bill of Rights and the United Nations Charter certainly thought so. 'Given by our hand in the meadow that is called Runnymede', the document says, 'between Windsor and Staines, on the 15th day of June in the 17th year of our reign.' It is assumed that the King and his entourage came from Windsor and the Barons from Staines. Did the two parties occupy opposite banks of the river and then meet on Magna Carta Island in the middle? Or was the King's camp on Ankerwyke? It is not certain. On Magna Carta Island is a Gothic cottage built in 1834: in it is a flat stone on which John is supposed to have rested the document while sealing it. The little Magna Carta Museum (visit by appointment, apply to the warden) at the Windsor end of the meadows contains a photocopy of the Charter.

Runnymede was not always such a treasured heritage. From the late eighteenth century to the 1880s it was a racecourse, and in 1921 the Commissioners of Woods and Forests tried to sell it. It was eventually presented to the National Trust by Lady Fairhaven in 1931 in memory of her father-in-law. The area and lodges at either end were laid out by Lutyens. There are three memorials. The tower superbly situated on Cooper's Hill, with views over the Thames Valley, was designed by Sir Edward Maufe and built in 1953. It marks the Commonwealth Air Forces 1939–45 memorial which contains 'the names of 20,456 airmen who have no known grave'. Maufe also designed the Magna Carta Memorial, a small temple presented by the American Bar Association in 1957 as a tribute to 'freedom under law'. A short distance away is the Kennedy Memorial which stands on 1 acre of land which the Queen gave to the American people in 1965 'in memory of John F. Kennedy, born 19 May 1917, President of the United States, 1961–63, died by an assassin's hand 24 November 1963.'

Cooper's Hill should certainly be climbed for the view. Pope, as if foreseeing the memorials, wrote that 'eternal wreaths shall grow'. A better poem about it was written by Sir John Denham (1615–69), gambler, Royalist, High Sheriff of Surrey and sometime Governor of Farnham Castle. When his rival, poet George Wither, a Roundhead, was captured, he persuaded Charles I to spare him, on the grounds that while Wither lived 'I shall not be the worst poet in England'.

SHIPLAKE (Oxfordshire)

Meaning 'stream where sheep are washed'. It is 3 miles south of Henley on the A4155. It is a long village, spread out for about 1½ miles on the Oxfordshire bank of the river. Lower Shiplake, more modern, may be mainly 'landscaped gardens and cabin cruisers', but that is what the residential river is for. Old Ship-

Sonning Lock – lock-keepers on the Thames usually work from 9 a.m. to dusk

lake is gathered round the church of St Peter and St Paul, re-built by G. E. Street in 1869. It stands above the river on a knoll. There are still traces of fifteenth-century carving, thir-teenth-century lancet windows, a fourteenth-century tower, and some seventeenth-century monuments. But the glory of this church is the fifteenth-century stained glass, brought here from the abbey of St Bertin, St Omer (France), where it had been buried since the French Revolution. It was rescued by the Reverend J. P. Boteler in 1828–30. It shows lives of various saints, Peter of Luxembourg's Vision of the Crucifixion, the Coronation of the Virgin, and many Angels and Seraphim.

One who knew the church before its restoration was Alfred Lord Tennyson who was married here in 1850. His engage-ment to Emily Sellwood had been temporarily broken off be-cause of her family's doubts about his religious orthodoxy, but the vicar, Mr Rawnsley, favoured the match and married them. Before the wedding Emily stayed at Holmwood, a Georgian house 1 mile northwest. Holmwood was the home of Swin-burne's parents during 1865–79, and Swinburne came here frequently to sober up, helped by his friend and keeper Theodore Watts-Dunton. Another very different author, George Orwell (Eric Blair) as a boy lived at a house called Roselawn, situated in Station Road.

Shiplake Court, near the church, built in the early years of the twentieth century, has been described as English Renais-sance in style: it is now a college and its stables have been con-verted into classrooms. Also by the river is Shiplake House, Regency-Victorian with a wrought-iron veranda.

SONNING (Berkshire)

Meaning 'Sunna's people'. Situated 4 miles from Reading, off the A4. The Thames village that has everything – old humped bridge, several famous inns, a beautiful setting in a river hollow,

a warren of narrow streets full of thatched and timber-framed cottages, a mill, and its history going back to the Saxons. Just one problem – try to avoid the high tourist season if you want room to move.

In Saxon times the Bishop of Salisbury had a palace here: it survived into the reign of Elizabeth I, and you can still see a fragment of its high brick wall on one side of the churchyard. Excavations in 1916 revealed the foundations of a fifteenth-century hall, gateway, and one wing of an older manor house. It was probably here that Isabella of France, child wife of Richard II, was protected after her husband lost his throne in 1399 before being returned to her father Charles VI. Still earlier, Sonning was part of the diocese of Ramsbury, Wiltshire.

St Andrew's Church, although almost completely remodelled in the nineteenth century, has traces of a Saxon building, a Norman aisle and an arch with fifteenth-century carving, and some Tudor brasses; an oak screen and a curious Saxon coffin lid built into a buttress of the north aisle. Among several hostel-ries are the French Horn, in the part of the village called Sonning Eye; the 500-year-old White Hart; the black-and-white timbered Bull; and, on the main road, the Shoulder of Mutton and the Flowing Spring.

In order to enjoy Sonning, you should concentrate on Thames Street, Pearson Street and High Street. Among several Georgian brick houses is the Dower House (probably a little earlier) in Pearson Street. In Thames Street is The Deanery, designed by Lutyens 1899–1901 with gardens by Gertrude Jekyll. In the days of the Bishop's Palace there was a Deanery here. The first owner of the Lutyens house (which has characteristically 'noble' chimneys) was Edward Hudson, founder of Country Life. The house recently changed hands for £650,000. The Robert Palmer almshouses dating from 1850 are in Tudor style. Among trees on the Sonning Eye side is the restored mill, which has recently been converted experimentally into an out-of-town theatre.

Windsor, the site of the largest inhabited castle in the world originally built nine hundred years ago

STAINES (*Surrey*)

Probably derived from 'stone' – perhaps a milestone. It is 6 miles east of Windsor on the A30. You wouldn't go to Staines for a holiday, but it is an important residential and industrial town, and if you happen to find yourself there it is as well to have a few facts about it. The first documentary mention of Staines is in AD 969 and it is also mentioned in Domesday Book. But there is evidence of a Roman village here, on the main road from London to the West, and of one of the earliest bridges across the river, possibly a ford reinforced with logs. This bridge is mentioned in an *Itinerary* of Antoninus.

The only old part of Staines, which now has a population of over 56,000, is round the parish church which gives you an idea of how the town looked a century ago when some 5,500 people lived here. St Mary's Church, set apart in a quiet quarter near the park containing the London Stone, has a tower whose lower half dates from the early seventeenth century and the top section, part of a general rebuilding, is of 1828. St Peter's, in Laleham Road (you see it from the river), designed by Fellowes Prynne, is a good, self-confident late Victorian church of the 1890s, all of a piece, with stained glass and a very large tracery screen filling the chancel arch.

High Street has one or two old buildings dating back to about 1700, including the Blue Anchor Inn. The Italianate town hall is from the 1870s. Clarence Street, between High Street and the bridge, has some late Georgian houses. Staines is a place to replenish stores, being an excellent shopping centre (market days Wednesday and Saturday).

STONOR PARK (*Oxfordshire*)

Meaning 'stony ridge'. It is 3 miles north of Henley on the B480. A colourful house, parts of which date back to the twelfth century, set on a Chiltern hillside covered with beech woods. Much altered and added to over the centuries, it all somehow blends into a memorable picture. It has strong Roman Catholic associations. The Stonor family have had a private chapel here since the thirteenth century. The Chapel of the Holy Trinity as it appears today is a remodelling (in 1960) of what it looked like in 1800 after eighteenth-century 'Gothick' alterations.

The main house (open to the public from Easter to September) was first built some years before 1300 by Sir Richard Stonor, who added the chapel soon after. This was enlarged by his son Sir John, who also added a house for six priests. Further enlargements by Sir Walter in the sixteenth century gave the house a rambling appearance which Sir Francis tried to smooth out with a new façade and gables . . . so it went on. The Stonors intermarried with other Catholic families such as the Blounts of Mapledurham and in the mid-sixteenth century gave shelter to St Edmund Campion (1540–81), the Jesuit who preached privately, and was tortured and executed in the Tower. At Stonor he had a printing press in a secret room called Mount Pleasant. Interesting as the house is, the grounds are worth visiting for themselves.

WARGRAVE (*Berkshire*)

Meaning 'grove by weirs'. Situated 4 miles southeast of Henley on the A321. Much of it hangs on a hillside above the Hennerton Backwater, along a narrow road that can cause traffic problems in the summer season. A pity, because it is an attractive place with a waterside pub and some Georgian houses – such as Wargrave House, on the corner of High Street, and the Bull Hotel. A few timber-framed houses, two seventeenth-century pubs and a Queen Anne vicarage. Of the original church, which was Norman on a Saxon foundation, very little remains, and for once we cannot blame villainous Victorian restorers: the church was burned down in 1914, allegedly by suffragettes. What was left intact was the 1635 creeper-covered brick tower.

The churchyard contains the grave of a forgotten author, Thomas Day (1748–89), who died after being thrown by an unbroken horse while trying to demonstrate that animals can only be tamed by kindness. His best-known work, *Sandford and Merton*, humourless and didactic, set out to show that virtue is a good thing, and enjoyed a vogue in its day. There used to be a tablet to him in the church, with an inscription by his friend Richard Edgeworth, Maria's father, but it perished in the fire. Also buried here is Madame Marie Tussaud (1760–1850), founder of the famous waxworks exhibition in London whose Chamber of Horrors has given more pleasure than poor Day's virtue.

WINDSOR (*Berkshire*)

The name possibly means 'landing place with windlass' or perhaps 'winding shore'. Everyone comes to see the Castle; but Windsor is a fascinating town in its own right. If your time is limited, you can join a guided walking-tour from the Information Centre at the Central Station (the guides speak several languages). This includes the old Guildhall area, the Castle, the State Apartments and (optionally) St George's Chapel, the finest of all Windsor's attractions. There is also a 10-mile bus tour, taking in Eton and its College, Datchet, the Long Walk and the Home Park.

The pillared *Guildhall*, begun in 1686 and completed by Wren, is in High Street. It contains a splendid exhibition of royal portraits and a display of Windsor's silver plate (open daily, afternoons only, Easter to September). There is a story that the town, fearing the Council Chamber above would sag, insisted on more pillars; Wren supplied them, but deliberately left a gap between them and the ceiling to prove they were not needed; you can see it today. Beside Guildhall is Market Cross House (seventeenth-century).

Still in High Street, the parish church (1872) contains Grinling Gibbons carvings and a painting, 'The Last Supper', by Franz de Cleyn. Nearby, in St Albans Street, is the *Royal Mews Exhibition* of the Queen's horses and carriages. Here,

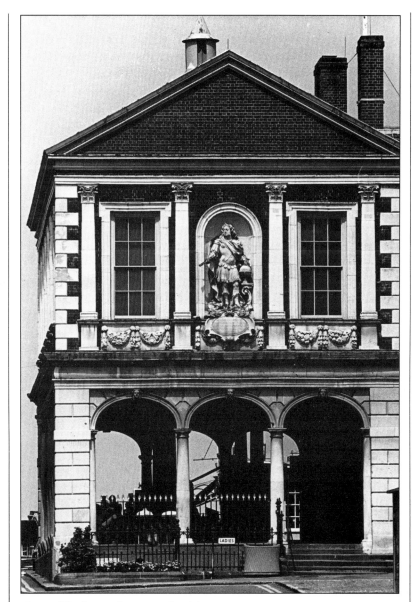

The Guildhall, Windsor, completed by Wren

among others, is the Scottish State Coach used at the Royal Wedding in July 1981. There is also a display of gifts received by the Queen for her Silver Jubilee in 1977. At Combermere Barracks, St Leonard's Road, is the *Household Cavalry Museum* (open daily except Saturdays, and on Sunday too during the summer). Among exhibits covering the history of this famous regiment from Charles II to the present day is an outstanding collection of uniforms and swords.

Madame Tussaud's *Royalty and Railways Exhibition* at Windsor and Eton Central Railway station is a remarkable display of Queen Victoria's Diamond Jubilee and the arrival of her guests at Windsor. Exhibits include the railway station, the Royal Train and the Royal Waiting Room.

The *Castle*, all 13 acres of it, the largest inhabited castle in the world, was founded more than 900 years ago by William the Conqueror – as one of a ring of fortresses around London to consolidate his conquest (but he never lived in it, preferring, it is said, his own palace at Old Windsor). Henry II added the Round Tower, Edward III extended the residential parts and began a long tradition of chivalry by founding the Order of Knights of the Garter. Subsequent monarchs nearly all added something. The general appearance or profile we know today is mostly the work of Sir Jeffry Wyatville, instructed by George IV, who spent a million pounds on the apartments alone.

The main entrance to the Castle is by Henry VII's Gateway on Castle Hill. There is a private entrance at the bottom of Thames Street by way of the Hundred Steps (there are actually 133). The *State Apartments* are open only when the Queen is not in residence. She spends Christmas, Easter and Ascot Week at Windsor, and also entertains guests on State Visits. You are advised to check whether the Apartments are open by telephoning the Information Centre (Windsor 52010). They contain wonderful collections of porcelain, furniture, armour and pictures: Rubens, Rembrandt and Van Dyck are among painters represented. *Queen Mary's Doll House*, designed by Sir Edwin Lutyens and presented to Queen Mary in 1923, is in a room nearby. A never-failing attraction for children, it is more than 8 feet long and 5 feet wide, contains miniature books and paintings by contemporary artists, and the plumbing and electric lighting really work. Next door to it is the *Exhibition of Drawings* from the Queen's priceless collection. The display, which is changed from time to time, usually includes work by Holbein and Leonardo da Vinci.

The Castle Precincts are open daily from 10 a.m. until sunset. St George's Chapel (*see* below) is open all the year round from 10.45 a.m. until either 3.45 or 4 p.m. except during January when it is cleaned.

St George's Chapel, in Perpendicular style, was begun by Edward IV and completed by Henry VIII. It took fifty-one years to build, and has been very little altered since Henry VIII finished the heraldic badges in the roof in 1528. The richness of decoration, with the fan-vaulting in the Choir, is breathtaking. Ten kings and queens are buried here: Edward VII and Queen Alexandra, Henry VIII, Charles I, George V and Queen Mary, and others beneath the Albert Memorial Chapel. (Queen Victoria and her Prince Consort are buried in the Royal Mausoleum in Home Park nearby.) Each stall in St George's Choir bears the arms and banners of the twenty-six Knights of the Garter who sat (or sit) there. Here, too, is the huge two-handed sword, nearly 7 feet long, of Edward III.

Windsor Great Park, 4,800 acres of what was once a royal hunting forest, has the famous *Long Walk*, a 3-mile avenue created by Charles II and extended by Queen Anne, who took it as far as Ascot. Along this way the Royal Family ride to the races during Ascot Week, beginning in cars and changing to open horse-drawn carriages at Duke's Lane, just past the Copper Horse. This equestrian statue of George III, riding in a Roman toga without stirrups, is the place where Elizabeth II lit the first of a chain of bonfires throughout the country to celebrate her Silver Jubilee in 1977.

CHAPTER FIVE

Approaching London

If the last memory we have of Staines is a large gasholder, I must remind you of our agreement at the start that gasworks can be beautiful. People need gas. On the same principle, we must not be dismayed, as we approach London, by the increasing incidence of bungalows and of waterworks and reservoirs (people need water and 75 per cent of London's water is supplied by the Thames). Even the tolerant Sir Alan Herbert, writing about this part of the river, used words like commuters, suburbia, 'summer holiday dwellings on stilts', and 'well-kept prettiness rather than beauty'. We must be serendipitous.

After $1\frac{1}{2}$ miles, with a 90-degree turn to the east, we are at Penton Hook Lock and (off to the right) the marina. Here too the so-called Abbey River leaves the mainstream and rejoins at Chertsey Lock. The Hook is a channel of the river which makes a U-bend that has been bypassed. Today it is pleasant to cross the weirs, but this place was once sinister; it was a burial ground during the Great Plague of 1665. The lock cottage (1814) is most attractive: there is one almost exactly like it at Sunbury Lock. On the left bank is Laleham (and beyond it the huge Queen Mary Reservoir) – a village much more attractive than the view from the river suggests: all you see, said William Morris a century ago, is 'enormous willows and queer suggestions of old houses'. Thus you cannot see Laleham House (or Abbey) amid its wooded grounds, though you can see the site of Chertsey Abbey on the opposite bank. A nice Georgian ferry-man's cottage shows where Laleham Ferry used to be.

Above Chertsey Lock the M3 motorway crosses the river, followed by old Chertsey Bridge which has seven arches, built in 1780–5 by one James Paine. Most of Chertsey is a mile to the south, so the river here can afford to be rural. An S-bend of about $1\frac{1}{2}$ miles, followed by another bend to the east as we pass round Chertsey Meads, and Pharaoh's Island (also known as Dog's Ait), lies ahead. So, almost immediately, does Shepperton Lock. Below it, on the left, the river Wey joins the Thames by Thames Lock. Wey Navigation, now owned as far as Godalming by the National Trust, was 'canalized' as early as the seventeenth century, that is, it was dug out as far as Guildford, and extended to Godalming in 1764. Then, in the great canal boom towards 1800, a new canal linked it to Basingstoke, and another to the Sussex Arun. Thus it was once possible to travel by boat or barge all the way from Weybridge to the English Channel. Today the Wey is a popular boating river (where you generally have to work the locks yourself) and it is navigable by canoe for some 35 miles upstream as far as Farnham.

D'Oyly Carte Island, just below Shepperton Lock, once belonged to the Savoy-Gilbert and Sullivan family. Now a strange thing happens. The mainstream ahead is not the natural course of the river, which, left to itself, does a violent M-shaped wriggle to the left towards Shepperton village. The straight channel, bypassing the village altogether, is the Desborough Cut, dug as recently as 1935 and named after Lord Desborough, philanthropist, athlete and longest-serving chairman (1904–37) of the old Thames Conservancy during its most constructive period. No doubt his Cut has saved many people a lot of time, and left Shepperton more peaceful than it might otherwise have been; but Shepperton is worth visiting, and fortunately the M-wriggle is navigable, so let us take it and enjoy the village grouped about the church, and the luxuriant lawns of Shepperton Manor coming down to the water's edge. (One slope is known as Mrs Lindsay's Lawn.) There is a lot of water around Shepperton, where the river can look like a flood (it sometimes is) or a lake dotted with islands. This is one of the many places on the Thames where Izaak Walton fished.

And talking of Walton, we come, within ¼ mile of the end of Desborough Cut, to Walton Bridge, or rather bridges: the long, many-arched bridge is nineteenth-century but was repaired when its brick central arch collapsed in 1859. This was found to be too weak to bear the weight of modern traffic, so it was reinforced with an ugly parallel structure of steel. Just above it, where the river bends, is a place known as Cowey Stakes (is 'Cowey' a corruption of 'causeway'?). It is thought that a ford existed here in Roman times – a curved one whose outline was marked by a row of stakes. Was it here that Caesar crossed the river to pursue Cassivellaunus? Or did Cassivellaunus put the stakes there to deter the Romans? Archeologists excavating the river bank here in 1879 found many Ancient British weapons; and Caesar's own account of 54 BC lends support to the story. The stakes were removed about 1800 because they were a danger to navigation.

In Walton Reach, below the bridge, we have Shepperton Marina on the left, and two notable riverside pubs, the Angler's Inn and the Swan, on the right. (I have lost count of the number of Swan Inns we have encountered since the Source.) We pass a little chain of islands, starting with Wheatley's Eyot, as we approach Sunbury Lock, with the Weir Hotel on the right bank. Sunbury has two locks side by side; the first pound-lock was built of timber in 1811 (and the original lock-house is still there); the present lock was built in 1925. Sunbury – now more town than village – looks inviting from the river, with its odd but dominating church tower and cupola, and the narrow Thames street which contains most of old Sunbury. It is well supplied with pubs, and you will find the Flower Pot, the Magpie and the Phoenix close to the water.

The Phoenix shares its name with Phoenix Island, now coming up on the left, followed by Sunbury Court Island and Sunbury Eyot: you can't see Sunbury Court itself from the river

Desborough Cut, built in 1935, bypasses the village of Shepperton

because of new houses built in between. Over to the right (you can't see much of them – well, do you want to?) are some large reservoirs with grand names – Knight, Bessborough, Elizabeth II – stretching away towards East Molesey. Tiny Purvis Eyot marks the boundary between Surrey and Greater London, at least for the left (north) bank of the river: the south bank continues to be in Surrey for the next 3¾ river miles. The larger island, Platt's Eyot, with West Molesey Wharf opposite, prepares us for the view of the square pinnacled tower of Hampton Church and so-called Garrick's Temple, an octagonal little pavilion with an Ionic portico on its lawn at a bend where the river begins to turn south. On the opposite bank, not so long ago, stood the obtrusive grandstand of Hurst Park Racecourse. Today it is a housing estate.

The last island before we reach Molesey Lock is Tagg's, which is joined to what we must no longer call the 'Middlesex' bank by a bridge. All hereabouts seems to be boatyards, and what on earth a genuine all-timber Swiss chalet is doing here, you may well wonder; yet it pleases the eye. (It has been here since 1900.)

Ash Island, by Molesey Weir, is attractive, but cannot be explored because it is private. But the very long, tree-lined lock is among the prettiest on the river, with gardens and a swimming pool nearby.

Ahead is Hampton Court Bridge, a brick-and-stone structure by Lutyens (1930) which I think we may call noble, except when you are driving a car over it at rush-hour times. This replaced a serviceable but plain iron bridge, which in turn replaced a weird structure of 1753, described vaguely as 'rococo'; a seven-arch affair each span of which rose like a hump, embellished with turrets like Chinese pagodas. Just before you pass under Lutyens' bridge, notice the 300-year-old Mitre Hotel covered in creeper on your left.

As the name Molesey suggests, the river Mole is ready to enter the Thames, with its tributary the Ember Brook, and it does so just below the Jolly Boatman Inn on the right. Between the Mole and Hampton Court Bridge is a triangular public garden known (I cannot tell you why) as Cigarette Island. The Mole, whose source is near Turner's Hill in Sussex, can be navigated by canoe for over 30 miles — as far, it is said, as Horley. It had a mysterious reputation among sixteenth- and seventeenth-century poets, who seem never to have explored it. There was a legend that it disappeared into a tunnel by Box Hill: 'Sullen Mole', wrote Pope, 'that hides his diving flood.'

And now, on the left, we have, for 2 miles or more, the park of Hampton Court, as the river turns southeast past Thames Ditton Island, bending suddenly again, northeast and then north, past Ravens Eyot towards Kingston. Here you get views of the great palace (on the left bank). Of Thames Ditton itself you see little but the spiky spire of the parish church, a house or two, and many bungalows. Ditton Reach, where the river is wide and fairly straight, is good for sailing. It is not easy to see where Thames Ditton ends and Surbiton begins; but on the right, soon after the river bends to the north, Thames Ditton Marina roughly marks the spot and just below it is the boundary between Surrey and Greater London. From now onwards, until further notice, we have Greater London on both sides of us. This is also the southernmost point the Thames ever reaches.

By Ravens Eyot, still on the right, begins Queen's Promenade, announcing that Surbiton is turning into Kingston upon Thames. On the opposite bank, Hampton Court has become Hampton Wick. Kingston, not seen to advantage from the river, is the biggest townscape we have faced since Staines. A fine place for shopping, and plenty of history to see, but explore it on foot — the one-way traffic-system is confusing if you don't know it, and the traffic itself spoils the view of anything interesting.

Did you ever hear of the river Hogsmill? This stream enters the Thames amid the boathouses on the right, a few yards above Kingston Bridge. It rises somewhere among the mental hospitals between Ewell and Epsom, and its humble course takes in New Malden and the A3 (Kingston bypass). Kingston Bridge, with five stone arches, could be called elegant. It was opened in 1828, and is almost the twin of Richmond Bridge (which, however, is more than fifty years older). It was widened in 1914. There was a bridge here in the thirteenth century, and there may have been one before that. It was built of timber, and until the eighteenth century was the second up-river bridge from the sea, the first being London Bridge. A wooden bridge was still here in 1710; on it, we are told, two seats were provided so that pedestrians could 'avoid carts and enjoy the delightful prospect'.

The road bridge is followed quickly by a railway bridge. Kingston is a great rowing centre, and its rowing club enters for events everywhere, including the town's own regatta. Its boathouse is just beyond Steven's Eyot which we come to after

Canbury Gardens on the right. On the left bank is Teddington, and as we pass long, thin Trowlock Island we begin to hear the rumble of Teddington Weir ½ mile ahead. This weir and its locks are of critical importance to the whole river and to London. Daily 1,535 million gallons of water pour over Teddington Weir. From now on, the Thames is a tidal river, which is the reason Teddington has the biggest lock system of all. There are three locks: the Barge Lock, 650 feet long (which can be shortened by an extra pair of gates in the middle), the Old or Launch Lock (first built of timber in 1811), 178 feet long; and the tiny Skiff or Coffin Lock, built in 1858 and less than 50 feet long. About 400 yards below the locks, on the right, you will notice, among the trees, an obelisk inside iron railings. This is the boundary stone between the Thames Water Authority's jurisdiction (which has been looking after us since Cricklade, 132 river miles back) and that of the Port of London Authority which now takes over until we are deep into the Estuary.

This could well be the point at which we consider whether we are going further downstream, and if so, how. I suggest we go ashore, crossing to the north bank by the little suspension bridge, and think it over in one of Teddington's riverside pubs, the Anglers or the Tide End Cottage. I had better confess that I have only done this part of the journey by river steamer. The nearer to the Estuary you get, the more professional your seamanship needs to be, and the stouter your craft. I am no more than a 'put-put' motor-launch driver, one of the boys, not the men. Sir Alan Herbert, Thamesman supreme, used to beat his breast about this sort of thing. Below Teddington the Tideway, he pointed out, merges into London River, from which, in summer, people sail up the Medway, down to East Coast river mouths, calling at yacht clubs at Greenwich, Erith, Gravesend, even Southend, and dropping names like Hole Haven, and Canvey Island.

Barges at Teddington Lock. Beyond this point, towards London, the Thames becomes a tidal river

But not yet. The river, sinuous as ever, having veered north-west by Trowlock Island, now goes due north for nearly 1 mile, and past Strawberry Hill (on the left) is Horace Walpole's and Pope's Twickenham (which they fashionably called Twitnam and Rugby football fans call Twickers). Then a sharp bend to the northeast as we pass Ham Fields on the right and get a sight of the Duke of Lauderdale's Ham House and its seventeenth-century garden. In summer one of the river's last surviving ferries, a private-enterprise one, operates between Ham and Twickenham.

The river widens to receive Eel Pie Island, long, fat, and joined to the north bank by a concrete footbridge. This Edwardian picnic place is now rather over-developed. It takes its name, a Victorian guidebook tells us, from 'the popular refreshment provided there'. No more, alas. Round the island's northern tip appears Twickenham's semi-Palladian church, followed by Orleans House and York House, the birthplace of Queen Anne, and both associated, during the nineteenth century, with the exiled Royal Family of France. Hammerton's boatyard ushers in Marble Hill, a Palladian house built early in the eighteenth century by George II for his mistress, the Countess of Suffolk: it was later a temporary home for George IV's Mrs Fitzherbert. Its park continues along the river, while on the opposite bank Petersham Meadows make a rural effect before the towpath becomes a kind of promenade leading up to Richmond ½ mile away, and as the Thames bends northwest again we have a splendid view of Richmond Hill. (Even more splendid is to stand on Richmond Hill and look down at where we are now.)

Richmond Bridge, with five arches, reminds one of Kingston Bridge (and why not, for the same James Paine had a hand in its design?), but is more handsome still. It was widened and very slightly flattened in 1937. The tiny Corporation Island is on the left below the bridge, with the Castle Hotel on the right. It seems that we have still not completely left Twickenham behind, for

The London Apprentice, a popular riverside pub at Isleworth

the next road bridge (preceded by a railway bridge), an austere affair in concrete (1933) rather like Waterloo Bridge, is called Twickenham Bridge. It is immediately followed by Richmond Lock, the last lock on the downstream journey, with a foot-bridge to the left bank. The river, flowing northwesterly for a short distance, bends north again round the Old Deer Park on the right, with Isleworth Eyot on the left. Behind the north tip of the eyot is the only old and 'villagey' part of Isleworth, gathered round the parish church with a famous eighteenth-century inn, the London Apprentice, almost next door — tra-ditionally a haunt of smugglers in the days when Isleworth was an inland port. A landmark on the right, in the middle of the Old Deer Park, is Kew Observatory.

Since the next bit of river is Syon Reach, we anticipate with some eagerness the appearance, on the left, of Isleworth's proudest possession, Syon House, in its magnificent grounds.

On the opposite bank, the Old Deer Park has now become the Royal Botanic Gardens at Kew with their pagoda and great palm house; and we also see Kew Palace (1631), originally known as the Dutch House, one of several Royal residences here. On the opposite bank, the river Brent, which links up with — indeed, becomes — the Grand Union Canal, joins the Thames at the site of Brentford Dock. (You could turn left and go to Birmingham if you wanted to.) Brentford, distinguishable from far away by an outsize gasholder, is not a place you would go to for a holiday, but it is not without interest: in particular, it has a wonderful stately home within 1½ miles of the river, Osterley Park. Beyond the dock are three small islands the last of which is Brentford Eyot.

At Kew Bridge we know we are in London, with tall office blocks and a traffic jam at one or both ends. And yet, no sooner have we shot the bridge than a bit of the eighteenth century suddenly appears on the left, the waterside village of Strand-on-the-Green. Purists say 'the' should be omitted from the name, but they can give me no sound linguistic reason for so doing. A pity about the railway, which crosses the river here on its way to Richmond; you must just mentally blot it out. Just before it is a tiny island called Oliver's Eyot.

On the right bank the towpath looks a little more 'country-fied' again as we approach Chiswick Bridge. You will not need to be reminded that this is the finishing point of the Oxford and Cambridge Boat Race. The exact point is marked by the University Stone. We follow the race's course of 4 miles and 374 yards in reverse until we reach Putney Bridge, wondering perhaps at the capriciousness of cross-winds and currents, and trying to guess why the two crews toss for the chosen side of the river. Now that this is all part of London, the next gener-ation away will never know that we used to talk about the Surrey side and the Middlesex side.

What can one say about Mortlake, whose High Street and church join us along the right bank? The best known landmark, a favourite with Boat Race commentators, is the brewery and, adjoining it, the Ship Inn, which was the old winning post of the race. Opposite is the curve of Duke's Meadows, full of sports grounds, as the river bends northeast again. Barnes Bridge carries a railway from Waterloo to points west. Barnes itself, on the right, has become a fashionable place to live, not only along Riverside which soon becomes Lonsdale Road and Barnes Terrace but farther inland towards the Common.

The best of Chiswick is yet to come. Meanwhile, we have an electricity station on the left, a small reservoir on the right – and suddenly, by Chiswick Eyot, there it is: Chiswick Mall. It then becomes Upper and Lower Mall, Hammersmith, and contains terraces of fine, mainly eighteenth-century houses with cosy little gardens at the water's edge and the occasional risk of flooding – the late Stephen Potter, who lived here in the 1920s and early 1930s, told me he sat in his basement room watching water squirting through the keyhole during the great floods of 1929.

More reservoirs on the Barnes side, but some of them are now disused, and instead there are the new buildings of St Paul's School which left its redbrick Victorian home in Hammersmith Road in 1968 for the damper but ultra-modern place it now occupies.

Just before Hammersmith Bridge, let us give a bow, a wave, or any other gesture of loyalty, to No. 12 Hammersmith Terrace, where A.P. Herbert lived and died. It is in a row of eighteenth-century houses built (the tale goes – but it is such a usual tale along the Thames) originally for royal mistresses. As for Bazalgette's suspension bridge (1887), which replaced another (prettier) one by Tierney Clark, it is a glorious anachronism and a traffic bottleneck, and its critics have abused its flamboyance in phrases such as 'ornate in brown, cream and gilt, like some vast coffee-cake decoration'. But just you sign a petition for its abolition and see where you get. You will be annihilated by loyal Hammersmithians, Thamesmen, and Boat

Race watchers everywhere. Mind your head – there's only 14 feet 3 inches at high water.

The river bends south again – more reservoirs on the right, with many kinds of waterfowl, and they quickly give way to Barn Elms Park and playing fields. At the end of Barn Elms, a streamlet called Beverley Brook joins the Thames, having risen near Motspur Park and travelled through Richmond Park. Here was another Boat Race landmark: a great castle of brick, Harrods Depository but now closed. On the left bank, how different: Fulham Football Ground is unmistakable, followed by Bishops Park, once the private grounds of the Bishop of London when he lived at his official residence, Fulham Palace.

Boathouses, boats and crews, and sailing dinghies, throng this bit of river above Putney Bridge, which ends this stage of our river journey. The Star and Garter, near the water, is well-known to rowing men and women. Putney Bridge is unique for it has a *church* at each end rather than a pub.

The Harrods Depository, now to become a block of flats

Staines to Putney - 27 river miles

BARNES (*London S.W.13*)

Probably meaning 'the barns'. On the south bank of the Thames, between Putney and Kew, it was once part of the manor of Mortlake, held by the Dean of St Paul's, who still has rights over Barnes Common. Barn Elms, the manor house, was the home of Sir Francis Walsingham in Elizabeth I's time, and of the poet Abraham Cowley in the seventeenth century. From 1884 to 1939 it housed the famous Ranelagh Club. In a cottage nearby (now gone) the Kit-Cat Club used to meet (*see also* Down Place). The promenade in Barn Elms Park was a fashionable place for duels in the seventeenth and eighteenth centuries. William Cobbett lived on the estate for a couple of years in the 1820s and wrote a book, *Advice to Young Men*.

Today Barnes is very much a village (largely, residents say, because there is no Underground Tube station). Many actors live here. Barnes Terrace, facing the river (but the ground-floor view is obscured by a flood barrier) contains some fine eighteenth- and nineteenth-century houses with wrought-iron balconies and bow windows. The composer Gustav Holst lived at No. 10. All Saints Church, Lower Common South, has some fine windows by Burne-Jones. Barnes is particularly well off for pubs, some of the best by the river. The pretty little High Street leads from the river straight to the village green (which has an appropriate pond).

BRENTFORD (*Greater London*)

Meaning 'ford over river'. There is no county hall here, but Brentford was once the county town of Middlesex. It was an important centre of government in Saxon times, and was granted a market and toll-bridge by Edward I. It was a popular resort for Londoners in the sixteenth and seventeenth centuries.

The market tradition survived the centuries, and the old street market, once held at Kew Bridge, was moved further into Brentford in the 1890s.

Boston Manor, Syon House and Osterley Park (*see* entries) are all within easy reach of Brentford. Boston Manor (which, like Osterley, has an Underground station named after it) is a big square house with a Jacobean porch dating from about 1623. It is now a public park. About 1 mile to the northeast is Gunnersbury Park, where there once stood a house said to have been designed by a pupil of Inigo Jones. On the site, a country mansion was built and acquired by George II's daughter, Princess Amelia, who sold it to a Rothschild. It was then inherited by Lionel Rothschild, head of the family bank. He gave it beautiful landscaped gardens including a Japanese garden of which his guest the Japanese ambassador said, 'We have nothing like it in Japan.' A museum of local history and transport (coaches belonging to the Rothschilds) is open in the afternoon.

The only 'villagey' part of Brentford today is round The Butts, the other side of the High Street from the dock area, where there are a few eighteenth-century houses. The parish church of St Lawrence is mostly eighteenth-century with a fifteenth-century tower and Victorian refurbishment within. Relics of a much earlier church include a 1528 brass to one H. Redman who, an expert says, 'may have originally designed Hampton Court'.

Finally, Brentford offers two of the most original exhibitions in the country, both near Kew Bridge. The Kew Bridge Engines Museum revives the Age of Steam for young and old (open weekends; tea room), and the British Piano Museum (housed in a converted church which used to be known as St George by the Gasholder) has pianolas and player pianos (one belonged to Queen Victoria's daughter Princess Beatrice), a violin which plays itself and accompanies itself on the piano, barrel-organs, mighty cinema organs, very old gramophones and nickelodeons. It is open during weekend afternoons.

CHERTSEY (*Surrey*)

From 'Ceorot's Island'. Situated 4 miles south of Staines on the A320. The best of Chertsey is along the river, but there are attractive features in the town if you look for them amid the traffic. There was once a great Benedictine abbey here (only traces remain but you can see the ground plan and where the fishponds were). It was founded by Erkenwald in 666, ruined by the Danes, refounded by King Edgar and given a new building by Hugh of Winchester in 1110 with extensions in the thirteenth century. It stood on Chertsey Mead, near the confluence of Abbey River and the Thames. After the Dissolution some of its materials were used to build Hampton Court. Of the town's three main streets, named London, Guildford and Windsor, the third is probably the most interesting: it contains Curfew House (1725), built in a style which has been called 'Vanbrughish', architect unknown, originally a school. The 'curfew' refers to a bell in St Peter's Church which commemorates Blanche Heriot who, during the Wars of the Roses, saved her lover from execution at curfew time by hanging on to the clapper (like the Hunchback of Notre Dame) as the bell tolled. It is still rung in her memory from Michaelmas to Lady Day, and an American poet, Rose Hartwick Thorpe, wrote a song about it, 'The curfew must not ring tonight.'

Charles James Fox had an estate at St Ann's Hill (near where the M3 and M25 cross) – the hill is worth climbing on a clear day when you can see the City. The poet Cowley lived in a house in Guildford Street, and Thomas Love Peacock in his youth lived at Gogmoor Hall.

Shakespeare, in *Richard III*, tells us that Henry VI's body rested at Chertsey Abbey on its way for burial at Windsor. It came from Blackfriars by water – 'not taken from St Paul's' by road, as Shakespeare implies.

CHISWICK (*London W.4*)

Meaning 'cheese farm'. Another riverside village despite the noisy concrete flyover behind, where the A4 becomes the M4 motorway. Its glories date from the seventeenth and eighteenth centuries, many of them along the river front. A notice on Chiswick Eyot reads Danger – River; another, Trespassers Will Be Drowned. Chiswick Mall has a wonderful, long, varied façade of desirable houses such as Strawberry House and Walpole House. The latter was once the Preparatory School for Young Gentlemen, attended by Thackeray, who used it in *Vanity Fair* as Miss Pinkerton's Seminary for Young Ladies where Becky Sharp and Amelia Sedley were 'finished'.

Chiswick House, originally built by Lord Burlington, was badly damaged in World War II but has been beautifully restored

At the Mall's western end is St Nicholas Church, full of monuments and tombs, among them William Hogarth's (d.1764) with an urn on top. Near him are two men he did not get on with in his youth, Lord Burlington, patron of architects and decorators, and William Kent, one of his protégés. James McNeill Whistler was also buried here in 1903. Hogarth's own house (open daily, except Tuesdays and Sunday afternoons October–March) is rather too close to the Great West Road for comfort: the artist spent fifteen summers here. It contains his possessions and many of his engravings.

Farther west is Chiswick House and its park (1729), which David Piper calls 'the most elegantly sophisticated public amenity of London' (open daily in summer, Wednesday to Sunday in winter). It is a miniature Palladian villa with a rotunda, designed by Lord Burlington, and decoration and garden layout by Kent. (Hogarth had no patience with these foreign fashions.) You can see the stages by which the house grew in the drawings kept in Burlington's library. In the gardens is a gateway by Inigo Jones (brought from Chelsea). There are statues by Rysbrack, and portraits inside: one, by Kent, is of Alexander Pope, who lived in Chiswick before moving to Twickenham. The house was built, not as a home, but as a meeting place for artists, writers and statesmen.

Chiswick House was badly bomb-damaged in World War II and there was a risk of demolition. It was saved by the Department of the Environment with no expense spared.

FULHAM (London S.W.6)

Meaning 'fuller's ham' or possibly 'place of fowls'. Place of fruit and vegetables would be more appropriate, since Fulham was one of the riverside villages whose market gardens supplied the metropolis. Fulham Road, linking Chelsea, Walham Green and Parson's Green, is very long, and the streets off it have 'come up', as Chelsea, culturally, has gone down. At the extreme western end, just before Putney Bridge, is Fulham Palace, once the Bishop of London's residence; its gardens and elegant plane trees became a public park in 1921. We are pursued, in this book, by gasworks, and it is my duty to tell you that Fulham, in 1829, had the first gasworks in Britain, on the site of Sandford House, where Charles II used to visit Nell Gwyn.

In recent years Fulham has become trendy yet mature. It has some good pubs, notably the Queen's Elm in Fulham Road, where many artists and writers gather. It takes its name from a tree which used to be there, under which Elizabeth I sheltered from a thunderstorm (foolish virgin!). Fulham has a famous football club; also the Hurlingham Club, which used to have two polo grounds until one of them was turned into a park, and Queens Club (tennis). Two authors frequented Fulham: Samuel Richardson, who in 1739 wrote *Pamela, or Virtue Rewarded* in a summer-house at 40, North End Crescent; and Rudyard Kipling, who spent his school holidays with his aunt, Lady Burne-Jones, at The Grange, North End Road. Both houses have gone, and blocks of flats have risen in their place.

HAM HOUSE (Surrey)

From *hamm* meaning 'flat meadow or enclosure'. Situated 2 miles south of Richmond, off the A307 by Ham village. Owned by the National Trust and administered by the Victoria and Albert Museum, Ham House is one of the largest Stuart houses in the country. Severe, built of warm brick, it has been found 'sinister' by critics who may have been influenced by the ruthless reputation of the Duke of Lauderdale whose lavish rather than elegant taste it reflects. Built originally in 1610 for Sir Thomas Vavasour, with additions by the Earls of Dysart, it was acquired in the 1670s by Lauderdale, a favourite of Charles II and a member of the Cabal, the King's inner circle of advisers many of whose meetings are believed to have been held here. The Duke and Duchess redecorated the whole place in the

Ham Village is clustered around its common, with several fine houses

fashion of the day, and much of their splendid collection of furniture is still in its original rooms. The gardens (free) have been restored and planted to their original plan, including an intricately designed knot garden. The house (which is a 'must') is open daily (except Mondays) and on most Bank Holiday Mondays, 2–6 p.m. April–September, and 12–4 p.m. October–March. If it's fine, you can have tea in the rose garden.

The house contains some magnificent family portraits: Sir Peter Lely's study of the fleshy Lauderdale flatters him not at all. There are paintings by Van Dyck and Kneller in the Great Hall, and others by Italian, Flemish and Dutch artists. In a room over the chapel is a collection of period costumes and weaving, including a French trousseau of the eighteenth century; and a collection of miniatures (one by Nicholas Hilliard). In other rooms are French, Dutch, Italian and English tapestries, and some seventeenth-century Flemish tapestries on classical themes after the style of Poussin. Tapestries by Bradshaw (eighteenth-century) hang in the Queen's bedroom, originally decorated in 1675 for Charles II's Queen Catherine of Braganza.

Lauderdale, living in the age of Newton and the Royal Society, with all his faults, was a learned man. So he was well advanced in the contemporary fashion for having a library, which he placed at the disposal of his friends. Next to it is a library closet with paintings of chemists in their laboratories.

Many rooms have plaster ceilings by Joseph Kinsman, a seventeenth-century craftsman much influenced by Inigo Jones. The imposing wooden staircase (*circa* 1637) is richly decorated with carved fruit baskets. In the Queen's closet is a *scagliola* (stucco like marble) fireplace. The paintings in the White Closet are thought to be by Verrio . . . one could go on.

While you are in the district, **Ham Village**, gathered about Ham Common, is worth a stroll. By Ham Common is Beverley Nichols' cottage with its beautiful garden. Sudbrook Lodge (seventeenth-century) and Ormeley Lodge (eighteenth-century with elegant Corinthian doorway) are worth noting.

HAMMERSMITH (*London W.6*)

Meaning 'the hammer smithy'. It is difficult to say where Chiswick ends and Hammersmith begins: Lower Mall, Upper Mall and Chiswick Mall link up together along the waterfront. Certainly Chiswick has more beauty, but Hammersmith, despite the fearsome traffic of the Broadway and the flyover, has plenty to offer. The best of Hammersmith is by the relatively quiet river. There are two good pubs, both associated with Sir Alan Herbert who lived nearby: the Dove, whose terrace overlooks the water, which claims a vaguely literary clientèle, and the Black Lion, of whose skittle club he used to be president. In the shadow of Sir Joseph Bazalgette's suspension bridge (odd to think that the designer who supervised most of the building of the Thames Embankment in London in the nineteenth century was also responsible for much of London's drainage system) Herbert learned to sail and navigate, naming his favourite cruiser *Water Gipsy* after the title of his best-selling novel about river and canal people.

At 26 Upper Mall is Kelmscott House, an eighteenth-century building once lived in by Sir Francis Ronalds, inventor of the electric telegraph. It was known as The Retreat when George MacDonald, the Scottish poet and novelist, lived there in the 1860s. He is forgotten today, but he was a friend of Tennyson, Browning, Carlyle and William Morris, to whom he sold the house in 1878. Morris renamed it Kelmscott after his Oxfordshire country house (*see* Kelmscot). Here he spent the last years of his life (1890–6) with his printing press and carrying out experiments in book design and typography, all influenced by medieval design, with ornate capitals and borders. His famous Kelmscott *Chaucer* took two years to print. In his London coach house he wove 'Hammersmith carpets'. The house is owned by a Trust and the William Morris Society wishes to turn it into a Morris Centre.

Hampton Court Palace has fine gardens with flower borders beautifully kept, many with seventeenth-century features

Two more of Hammersmith's authors are Rider Haggard, who wrote *King Solomon's Mines* (1885) at 69 Gunterstone Road, and Ouida (Marie Louise de la Ramée) who lived at 11 Ravenscourt Square.

HAMPTON (*Greater London*)

Probably meaning 'meadow homestead'. Situated $1\frac{1}{4}$ miles west-northwest of Hampton Court. A place people drive through on their way to and from London Airport with barely time to notice how many houses and streets are named after seventeenth- and eighteenth-century personalities such as Garrick, Wren, and Johnson — some of whom lived, and others visited, here. From the river it looks like a village, the group held together by the (mainly 1831) church. Garrick Villa, which the actor bought in 1754, was decorated and remodelled by the Adam brothers in 1774. The villa is connected to the lawn of Garrick's Temple (at the water's edge) by a tunnel under the road: it is believed that this was Dr Johnson's idea. The temple, in its garden, was designed by Capability Brown. It was built (a pardonable vanity on Garrick's part) to house Roubiliac's statue of Shakespeare for which he himself was the model. The statue is now in the British Museum in London.

Horace Walpole has described the gaiety of the Garrick household, the fêtes and illuminated garden parties they gave at night, attended by the grand acquaintances which Garrick's unique position in the theatre had won him. Garrick died in 1779 leaving a fortune of £100,000. His widow, Eva Maria, a Viennese dancer, survived him by forty-three years, dying in 1822. Sadly, she failed to keep many of his possessions. Dr Johnson, with whom in his youth Garrick had walked all the way from Lichfield in Staffordshire, to London, loved Hampton. 'Ah, David,' he said, 'it is the leaving of such places that makes a death bed terrible.'

The Great Palm House at the Royal Botanic Gardens, Kew, keeps tropical plants in temperatures of 20° Centigrade

HAMPTON COURT PALACE (*Greater London*)

On the A308 2 miles west of Kingston. Cardinal Wolsey in 1514 began to build what was to become the largest palace in England at his newly acquired manor of Hampton. He surrounded it with a moat and installed an ingenious water-supply and sewage disposal system. The latter lasted until 1871. The former conveyed water from Coombe Hill springs, $3\frac{1}{2}$ miles away on the other side of the river, by conduits under the Thames near Kingston, to the Palace. Wolsey, hoping to stave off his fall from power, prudently offered the Palace to Henry VIII who, having objected to its grandeur, made it grander still. The ghosts of two of his wives are said to roam here — Jane Seymour, who died giving birth to the future Edward VI, and Catherine Howard. Charles I was kept a prisoner here for some time. William III and Mary, helped by Wren, added the south and east façades, Fountain Court, gardens and probably the Maze. The Hanoverians seldom came here (George II was the last monarch to live here) and Queen Victoria, in 1839, opened the palace to the public.

Today the gardens are open daily (free); State Rooms, Great Hall, Lower Orangery and Great Vine are also open daily (May–September, Sundays 11–6 p.m.; similar, but slightly shorter hours for the rest of the year, Sunday afternoons only). The Real Tennis Court, Banqueting House, Kitchen and Upper Orangery are open April–September only. The Palace is closed Maundy Thursday, Good Friday, Christmas and New Year's Day. The mellow redbrick buildings, which contain about 1,000 rooms, are good to look upon. They provide many 'grace and favour' houses for servants of the Crown.

How to begin to summarize the wonders of the place? An astronomical clock (1540) by Nicholas Oursian, over Anne Boleyn's Gateway in Clock Court. The vast Tudor kitchen. The Great Hall, with its hammer-beam roof, built by Henry VIII, has magnificent tapestries, ten of them, illustrating the life of Abraham. In the Tilt Yard, where Henry jousted when he wasn't playing Real Tennis, you can obtain light refreshments. The Great Vine, planted in 1769, produces black grapes.

And the pictures: there seems always to have been a priceless collection here. Not only royal pictures, but masterpieces acquired by Charles I from Italy – Titian's 'Lucretia', Giorgione's 'Shepherd with a Pipe', Tintoretto's 'Nine Muses'. When we come to Charles II's reign, as you would expect, the walls fill up with girls – 'Windsor Beauties', women of his court painted with suitable abandon by Lely, and the rather more lady-like creatures whose looks suited the taste of William and Mary. Holbein, Veronese, Correggio and Andrea del Sarto are also represented.

In the Orangery are Mantegna's cartoons for the 'Triumph of Julius Caesar', recently restored. Some of the State Apartments have painted decorations by Laguerre, Thornhill and Verrio, who also decorated the walls and ceiling of the Banqueting House with classical subjects. There is much sculpture everywhere, including pieces by John Nost and Grinling Gibbons, and also ornamental ironwork, especially that of Jean Tijou, who came over with William III and made that screen for the Fountain Garden.

You could spend all day in the gardens alone. Long Water ($\frac{3}{4}$ mile) made for Charles II lies in an avenue and stretches towards the Thames with a feeling of infinity similar to Versailles. Home Park (625 acres) is almost surrounded by the river, and Bushy Park (on the other side of the road), 1,100 acres and full of deer, has a wonderful avenue pointing, in the same infinite way, towards Teddington, with the Diana Fountain (*circa* 1640) in the middle.

KEW (*Surrey*)

Meaning 'place on a promontory'. Kew has a village as well as the Gardens and it clusters round Kew Green, near the southern end of Kew Bridge. Here are a few Georgian houses, and St Anne's Church (1714), with its unusual octagonal cupola at the east end. In 1851 a mausoleum for the Duke and Duchess of Cambridge was added. The entrance to the Royal Botanic Gardens (there are others) is just off the green.

It is extraordinary that a place can combine science and beauty so marvellously. The Gardens are part of the Ministry of Agriculture. Their 280 acres are open daily until dusk. Kew Palace is also open daily, 11–5.30 p.m. Monday–Saturday, 2–6.00 p.m. Sunday, from April to mid-October (closed Maundy Thursday and Good Friday).

The Gardens began as a royal riverside playground in the eighteenth century. Queen Caroline, wife of George II, built follies such as a Hermitage and a Merlin's Cave filled with wax figures. The then Prince of Wales and his wife Augusta came to live in the White House, and after his death she landscaped the grounds and built more follies, including the conspicuous multi-storey Chinese Pagoda, 163 feet high, designed by Sir William Chambers (inside it, nothing but stairs!). George III, not yet mad, inherited Kew from his mother, and had some more landscaping done by Capability Brown. He influenced the development of pure science by appointing Sir Joseph Banks, just back from his global voyage with Captain Cook, as horticultural adviser. In the nineteenth century Joseph Paxton and others came into the service of Kew – yet it was Decimus Burton, architect of the Athenaeum Club and Hyde Park Corner, not Paxton, who designed the Palm House (1844–8) which anticipated the Crystal Palace. By now the Gardens belonged to the public, having been rescued in 1841 from the neglect into which they had fallen under George IV. Soon all the main elements were there – Palm House, Temperate House, herbarium, library, and museum.

Kew Palace is the general name for the Dutch House, built in 1631 with Dutch gables and brickwork. The Royal Family lived here for about a century until 1818. Simply furnished, it is

Kew Palace, built in 1631, was the home of the Royal Family during the eighteenth century

much as George III knew it. A seventeenth-century garden has been created behind it. The Orangery, built in 1761 for Princess Augusta, is one of several Classical pavilions Chambers designed for the estate – his Pagoda, inspired by his Oriental travels, was out of character. The rustic Queen Charlotte's Cottage (1772) was used by the Royal Family as a summer house. Among many odd small buildings dotted about the Gardens are the Temples of Arethusa, Bellona and Aeolus (places to sit when out walking). King William's Temple (built for William IV) used to contain busts of the Royal Family, but the walls inside are now covered with tablets commemorating battles fought by the British Army from 1760 to 1815.

There are two Museums of Economic Botany. One contains exhibits of plants useful to mankind. The Wood Museum (in Cambridge Cottage) has a display of timber. On Victory Hill is a flagstaff 225 feet high made from a Douglas fir nearly 400 years old which was presented by British Columbia in 1959.

KINGSTON UPON THAMES (*Greater London*)

Meaning 'royal manor'. Does the name mean simply an estate owned by a king? Tradition says that seven Saxon kings were crowned here, on the Coronation Stone on its lawn next to the Guildhall. There were some minor kings (whose names we don't know) in the seventh century or earlier, and certainly two West Saxon kings, Athelstan (925) and Edward the Martyr (975) were crowned here; and the place was important enough for Egbert to call a council here in 838. Kingston received its first charter from King John in about 1200. The town was fought over in the Wars of the Roses and the Civil War. It has a lively market which has been held since the seventeenth century; and if you come here for no other purpose, there is Bentall's huge department store.

Market Place has some bits of old Kingston. Market House (1840), formerly the town hall, is vaguely Italianate with an unexpected statue of Queen Anne (1706). Perhaps the oldest surviving structure in the town is the twelfth-century Clattern Bridge over the river Hogsmill. All Saints Church (flint and stone), just behind Market Place, was once Norman but now looks Victorian, although the brick top of the big square tower is early eighteenth-century. There are brasses dating back to 1437, and effigies by Flaxman and Chantrey. The west window has some good Victorian stained glass depicting God the Father with angels and prophets. In London Road the Lovekyn Chapel (of St Mary Magdalene), founded in 1309, is now part of Kingston Grammar School.

To the northeast, Kingston Hill and Coombe Hill show traces of Cardinal Wolsey's Conduit (*see* Hampton Court). One Conduit House is in the grounds of Coombe Springs, Coombe Hill. This district was developed in Victorian times with large houses, many of which have disappeared (except for their gatehouses). The pioneer developer seems to have been John Galsworthy's father; so it was natural that Soames Forsyte should build near here (there is a modern house in Coombe Hill Road called Robin Hill after one of Soames' houses). Kingston Hospital is in Galsworthy Road. The author of *The Forsyte Saga* was born in 1867 at Parkfield, Kingston Hill, while his parents were waiting for their new house to be finished (it stood in 24 acres). Much of Galsworthy's youth was spent at Coombe Leigh – now a school, Coombe Ridge, in George Road.

LALEHAM (*Surrey*)

Probably meaning 'willow ham'. It is 2 miles south of Staines on the B376. The village has been accused of not making the best of its river front; well, the willows (and some bungalows) are there, and it is an agreeable enough place if you don't make demands on it. Matthew Arnold was born here in 1822, at a house in Ashford Road (now gone). His father, Thomas, tutored here (1819–28) before becoming headmaster of Rugby, where he reformed the public-school system. Matthew, poet and civil servant, is buried (1888) in the churchyard of All Saints Church, where there is a brass tablet in his memory. He lies there with three of his sons.

The church looks Victorian, but has an eighteenth-century very solid ivy-covered tower, all in brick, with a parapet. The north chancel (Lucan Chapel) is also of brick, early sixteenth-century. There are bits and pieces of an original Norman building, including the arcades, and a modern (1926) stained-glass window showing St Christopher carrying the infant Jesus. A wall painting of about 1810 (not very clear) shows Jesus with Peter on the Sea of Galilee.

Plenty of old houses, especially on or near the green and Ferry Lane (no ferry, of course). Muncaster House and The Coverts are early eighteenth-century, and Thatched Cottage, with its pretty veranda, in Regency style. Near the church, Church Farm is late seventeenth-century, and Dial House dates itself 1730 by its sundial. The biggest house is Laleham Abbey in a splendid park with many trees. Built in 1803–6 for the 2nd Earl of Lucan, it is plain but dignified with a large Doric portico. For many years the home of the Lucans, including the general who commanded the cavalry at Balaclava (but not the missing 7th Earl), it is now a religious community.

MARBLE HILL PARK, Twickenham (*Greater London*)

Marble Hill House (open daily except Friday) is a small Palladian villa whose lawns run down to the river in 66 acres of park. It was built during 1723–9 for Henrietta Howard, mistress of George II (Pope called her 'Chloe'). Dean Swift said, 'Mr Pope was the contriver of the gardens, Lord Herbert the architect, and the Dean of St Patrick's [Swift himself] chief butler and keeper of the ice house.' They may have contributed ideas, but the real architect was Roger Morris and the gardens were laid out by Charles Bridgeman. Here Mrs Howard received the world of fashion and the arts. They included Horace Walpole, who enjoyed her titbits of Court gossip. The house, which has big Ionic pilasters on its north side, has

Marble Hill House, a Palladian villa at Twickenham

a very large room, two storeys high, containing a pillared fireplace decorated with cherubs; otherwise the house is intimate rather than grand. Threatened with demolition by a speculative builder, who wanted to build a housing estate over the whole park, it was saved by local government bodies, and the Greater London Council has restored and decorated it beautifully. The view over the river towards Richmond Park is superb.

Orleans House, a near neighbour, is not the original house built for James Johnstone, Queen Anne's Secretary of State for Scotland. That house was demolished in 1927 except for odd bits such as the Octagon (by James Gibbs, 1720), an impressive room which gives some idea of the original style which Defoe thought 'much the brightest figure' in Twickenham. Louis-Philippe had two periods of exile here, 1800–14 and 1815–17, and his brothers the Duc de Montpensier and the Comte de Beaujolais spent much time here. Afterwards Don Carlos, claimant to the Spanish throne, made the house his residence.

Another neighbour, *York House*, handsome and unfussy (*circa* 1700) is now used as council offices, nicely set in flower gardens. Once owned by the Earl of Clarendon, it was presented to the Duke of York, who had secretly married his daughter, Anne. Other notable tenants were Count Starhemberg, the Austrian ambassador, Anne Damer the sculptress (*see* Henley), the Comte de Paris of the French Royal family, and more recently Sir Ratan Tata, an Indian industrialist, who owned the house in 1906–18 and embellished the gardens with sculpture best described as curious.

MORTLAKE (*London S.W.14*)

Probably derived from 'Morta's water meadow'. Situated on the river between Chiswick and Barnes it is still a riverside village if you concentrate on the old parts. The church of St Mary was originally founded in 1543 but was also rebuilt in 1885 and 1905. Nevertheless a good Perpendicular tower remains, 'built', we are told, 'by order of Henry VIII' (why?), and an octagonal font of about the same age. Adjoining is an attractive seventeenth-century vestry. In the church is a sample of the famous seventeenth-century Mortlake tapestry — a local craft founded in 1619 and carried on until the Civil War. Several good monuments include an allegorical relief to Viscountess Sidmouth (d.1811). Her husband, better known as Henry Addington, was Prime Minister 1801–4. He is remembered now by a contemporary rhyme, 'Pitt is to Addington as London is to Paddington.' He is buried in the churchyard.

Along the river towards Chiswick Bridge are a few Georgian houses, and High Street has some more: No. 123 is the finest and was also painted twice by Turner. It has a Tuscan portico. In St Mary Magdalene Roman Catholic cemetery, south of the parish church, is an extraordinary monument to Sir Richard Burton, traveller and translator of the *Arabian Nights*, in stone

Osterley House displays its Tudor origins in its red brick and towers but the pillared portico was designed by Robert Adam

covered with crescents and stars, set up by his widow in 1890. The only other local celebrity appears to be Dr Dee, the astrologer also lived here and was consulted by Elizabeth I. There is a monument to him in St Mary's.

OSTERLEY PARK (*Greater London*)

Probably meaning 'glade on a hillock'. Situated $1\frac{3}{4}$ miles north-northwest of Isleworth, off the A30. Robert Adam achieved the almost impossible here: he transformed an Elizabethan house with turrets at the corners into something 'classical' — in such a way as to improve it. Originally built about 1577 for Sir Thomas Gresham, founder of the Royal Exchange in the City, it was afterwards owned by Coke, the Lord Chief Justice and Sir William Waller, the Roundhead general. Eventually it was acquired by the Child banking family, two of whom, Francis and Robert, commissioned Chambers in 1756 to redesign it. Adam took over in 1762 and worked on the house until 1780. Robert Child's daughter, Sophia, inherited the house and married the Earl of Jersey, whose descendant the 9th Earl gave it to the National Trust in 1949. It is open daily (except Monday), April to end of September, 12–4 p.m. October–March. Park open all year 10–8 p.m. or sunset.

Adam gave the house, which stands in 140 acres of parkland, a high flight of steps leading up to a grand Ionic portico. This followed the Italian Neo-classical vogue for making the first floor (*piano nobile*) the principal part of the house. Adam's exquisite (some would say effeminate) taste in furniture and decoration, and his delicate feeling for colour, are supreme here, as at Syon House (*see* entry). The only oddity is perhaps the Etruscan Room, whose design was influenced by Greek vases found at Pompeii in the mid-eighteenth century. Almost everything is as Adam left it. There are Beauvais tapestries (1786) in the 130-foot gallery, and a special room for Gobelins tapestries (1775) showing the loves of the gods, designed by Boucher; a State Bedroom with a huge cupola over the bed;

and in the library panels painted by Zucchi. Many carpets were designed by Adam himself.

The park has conservatories, one of them semi-circular, and a chain of lakes dating from 1596, with many fine cedar trees and an eighteenth-century Doric temple. Only the M4 motorway spoils the view. Strange to think that in the summer of 1940 the whole place was handed over to Sir Edward Hulton, publisher of *Picture Post*, as a Home Guard training centre specializing in the lessons of guerrilla fighting learned in the Spanish Civil War.

PETERSHAM (*Surrey*)

Meaning 'Peohtre's ham'. It is 1 mile southeast of Richmond. Not many villages can claim to be almost wholly sixteenth- and seventeenth-century, but this one can (very nearly). You can walk to St Peter's Church across meadows from the right-bank towpath. This church is tiny and full of interest. The earliest parts are thirteenth-century, nave and tower (brick) seventeenth-century, and the interior furnishings largely eighteenth-century. The cheerful (1624) monument, with lively effigies, to George Cole, his wife and grandson, is how most of us would like to be commemorated. In the churchyard is buried Captain George Vancouver (d.1798), the explorer, who gave his name to the capital of British Columbia.

Vancouver lived in a seventeenth-century house between two early eighteenth-century houses, Manor House and Petersham Lodge, both in River Lane. The Manor has a fine doorway with Ionic columns. The Lodge, with rococo decoration and a rotunda in the garden, was built by the Duchess of Queensberry and later decorated by Sir John Soane. John Gay, author of *The Beggar's Opera* and a frequent guest of the Queensberrys, did much of his writing in the rotunda. Dickens also knew Petersham well, stayed at Elm Lodge in Petersham Road, and swam to Richmond Bridge. On special occasions, such as the publication of a new novel, he celebrated at the old Star and Garter Hotel. Much of *Nicholas Nickleby* was written at an eighteenth-century house, 230 Petersham Road.

Near the church, Petersham House, late seventeenth-century, has a fine domed Regency porch. Montrose House, early eighteenth-century, of yellow and red brick, has a Doric porch and good iron gates. Rutland Lodge (River Lane), built in 1666 for the Lord Mayor of London, was gutted by fire in 1967, but the exterior survives and you can see what a beautifully proportioned house it was. Gort House (early eighteenth-century) and Douglas House (1700), on the way to Ham, are among several other good period houses that are worth looking out for during a visit to the village.

PUTNEY (*London S.W.6, S.W.15*)

Meaning 'Putta's landing place'. Always a great rowing centre, Putney has a river full of boats in the spring and summer. A

Boathouses of famous rowing clubs line the riverbank at Putney. Here there are good views of the start of the University Boat Race

century or more ago, before rowing became standardized, you could see all manner of craft – wherries, skiffs, scullers, shallops, gigs, cutters and funnies. Boathouses line the riverbanks. Putney Bridge (by Bazalgette, 1884) replaced a timber bridge which, we are told, was 'executed in 1729 by the King's Carpenter'. At its southern end is St Mary's Church, rebuilt in the eighteenth century on a medieval foundation – the three-stage tower is of this period. The chantry chapel of Bishop West of Ely (who was born in Putney) is early sixteenth-century. The church, though not vandalized in the Civil War, was the scene of a Council of War in 1647 when four Roundhead commanders, Fairfax, Ireton, Rich and Fleetwood, we are told, 'sat round the communion table with their hats on'. Another church, All Saints, Lower Common, designed by Street (1874), has pre-Raphaelite windows.

It has been said that Putney's Golden Age was in the nineteenth century, when colourful Italianate villas were built on Putney Hill. At the foot of the hill is No. 2 The Pines (now No. 11) where the poet Swinburne was taken by his friend Watts-Dunton to deal with his health problem. Swinburne's health improved, but his poetry didn't. Edward Gibbon, of the *Decline and Fall*, was born in Putney in 1737.

RICHMOND (*Surrey*)

'Richmond Green', Pevsner says, 'is one of the most beautiful urban greens surviving anywhere in England.' It also contains most of Richmond's early history, so let us begin there. It was always a favourite resort of royalty. Only fragments remain of the Old Palace (such as the Gateway and Old Palace Yard) which stood on the southwest side of the Green, the jousting place. Edward III died here, Henry V and VII rebuilt it. One of Henry VII's titles was Duke of Richmond in Yorkshire, thus he named the palace – its old name was Shene (Sheen). Elizabeth I died here, we are told, 'on a great pile of cushions'. To the south of the Green is Trumpeter's House (*circa* 1700), so called

because statues of trumpeters used to stand each side of its Tuscan portico. The Wardrobe (early eighteenth-century), a terrace, was built with some of the Tudor brickwork and so gives some idea of the Tudor palace. Nearby is Maids of Honour Row, built in 1724 for the maids of honour of the then Princess of Wales, who lived at Richmond Lodge. On the southeast side are large eighteenth-century houses, and to the north some nineteenth-century villas. The only jarring note in the old world harmony is Richmond Theatre with its turrets and cupolas (1899). The Old Palace fell into disuse and was eventually demolished in the eighteenth century. The Old Deer Park, to the north, was its garden and park. Bordering the river, it contains Sir William Chambers' Observatory, 'completed at the time of the transit of Venus in 1769'.

A town of many churches, Richmond has two of outstanding interest, one for its associations, the other for its grand design. St Mary Magdalene, in George Street, was founded in Henry VII's time – the tower arch is about 1500 – but most of the church is eighteenth-century with later additions, such as the flint and stone chancel (1904). There are monuments to Edmund Kean the actor (1839) who lived on the Green, and poet James Thomson, author of 'The Seasons', who died in 1748. St Matthias (1858), in Friars Stile Road on a hill, is the work of Sir George Gilbert Scott the Elder. Tall in every way, especially its spire, it is Victorian architecture at its best.

The famous view from Richmond Hill, best seen in Terrace Gardens, is everything it is cracked up to be. Many painters have painted it, notably Turner and (in one of his rare landscapes) Reynolds. You see the Thames leading towards Ham, the park of Marble Hill and other Twickenham houses, with wooded Glover's Island in the foreground, and in the far distance Windsor Castle. Such an abundance of riverside trees upset a visiting American from the Far West in the mid-1850s. 'That valley', he said 'wants clearing.' On the way up to the Hill are many interesting houses: we have space to note only two, The

Wick and Wick House, next to each other. The Wick (by Robert Mylne, 1775) has an oval drawing-room whose window looks out on to the Thames. Wick House, less attractive from the outside, was built in 1772 by Sir William Chambers for Sir Joshua Reynolds. Not far off is a Richmond landmark, the Star and Garter Home for invalid ex-servicemen (Neo-Georgian, 1924).

Richmond Park, 4 square miles with eleven entrances, the largest public space in Greater London, was first enclosed by Charles I in 1637 as a royal hunting ground, which it remained until the eighteenth century. It still has herds of red and fallow deer. The royal connection is preserved in some of the private houses within the Park: White Lodge, built 1727–9 by the Earl of Pembroke as a hunting lodge for George II, is one. Queen Victoria, Edward VII, and George V and Queen Mary when Prince and Princess of Wales, spent much time here, and it was the birthplace of the late Duke of Windsor. It is now part of the Royal Ballet School (some rooms are open to the public during August). Thatched House Lodge was built circa 1727 for Sir Robert Walpole, with one wing added in 1872. The thatched house is a summer-house in the garden, with two rooms painted circa 1780 and attributed to Angelica Kauffmann. The lodge is now the home of Princess Alexandra and her husband, the Hon. Angus Ogilvy.

SHEPPERTON (Surrey)

Meaning 'abode of shepherds'. It is 2¼ miles east of Chertsey on the B375. The true village is the old square by the river, with church, rectory, three pubs and some old houses. St Nicholas Church was rebuilt in 1614 after a ruinous flood, its oblong tower was added in 1710. This has two outside staircases, one leading to a public gallery, the other to a private gallery called the Manor House Pew. The rector during 1504–13 was William Grocyn, a great Greek scholar and friend of Colet, More and

Richmond Bridge was built by James Paine in 1774–7 and was widened in 1937

Erasmus. Erasmus visited Grocyn here, but why should his ghost haunt the rectory, as tradition says? In Victorian times a frequent visitor to the rectory was J.M. Neale, credited with speaking twenty-four languages and author of 136 hymns (including 'Jerusalem the golden' and 'Good King Wenceslas').

The Rectory, very handsome, has an early eighteenth-century front (seven bays of brick) concealing a large timber-framed hall which may be as old as 1485. Its lawns are 200 years old. The Manor House, seen only from the river, is circa 1830, stuccoed, and has a veranda. Its lawns reach down to the water. The village square has a row of eighteenth-century houses, among them Warren Lodge and the King's Head Hotel (the king was Charles II, and some local opinion likes to think that he stayed here with Nell Gwyn. If so, it must be over 300 years old). Other old houses, among them the sixteenth-century Ivy Cottages, are in Church Road.

The so-called Shepperton Film Studios are in neighbouring **Littleton**, on the brink of Queen Mary Reservoir. **Lower Halliford**, on the northwest, has literary associations: Thomas Love Peacock bought a riverside house in Walton Lane (1823) for his mother. He then bought the house next door and knocked them into one, now called Elmbank, and eventually retired there himself. His daughter married novelist and poet George Meredith. She died in 1861 and is buried in the churchyard.

Part of the riverbank is called War Close. So was there a battle between Romans and Britons after the Romans crossed the Thames at Cowey Stakes? Certainly both Roman and ancient British relics have been found in the district.

STRAND-ON-THE-GREEN (London W.4)

Meaning 'shore'. It is immediately below Kew Bridge. A true urban village, ½ mile long on the north riverbank. Many of the houses, ranging from the seventeenth to the eighteenth century, were once fishermen's cottages. In spring they are covered in clematis and wistaria. Purists may think the whole place has been 'tarted up', but the effect is seductive. No through traffic, lots of moored boats, and a low stepped wall as a safeguard against flooding. One or two houses have Dutch gables. Notice Springfield House and Zoffany House. In the latter lived John Zoffany R.A., from 1780 to 1810, he of the 'conversation pieces'. For his 'Last Supper', he is believed to have used local fishermen as models for the Apostles. Zoffany is buried at Kew Green. There are modern houses too, designed to harmonize with the old ones: one of them is named Number Nought. Three good pubs: the Bull, the Bell and Crown, and the City Barge. The last refers to the Lord Mayor of London's barge the *Maria Wood* which was often moored here (the City Corporation used to levy tolls on barge traffic). Lord Mayors of the past seem to have had a high old time patrolling the river and calling at waterside pubs on the pretext of inspecting everything.

SUNBURY (*Surrey*)

Meaning 'Sunna's stronghold'. Situated 5 miles west of Kingston, on the A308 and B375. Once again, you can see the original village which is now part of the town. The village (the old part) is fortunately by the river, and much of it is in Thames Street. The parish church of St Mary the Virgin stands on the site of a prehistoric settlement. It was built in 1782: only the tower and nave remain, for it was altered in 1856 to what has been called a 'quasi-Byzantine' style. Pevsner finds this 'peculiarly revolting'; others are content to say 'quaint'. In the churchyard is an old yew, said to be the one described in Dickens' *Oliver Twist* where Bill Sikes and Oliver Twist heard the clock strike seven on the way to the Shepperton robbery.

The Flower Pot Inn, Victorian with a Doric porch, is associated with the church through its sign, which shows the Virgin, and a lily in a flower pot. Along the waterfront are several eighteenth-century houses, among them Wilmary, Orchard House and Darby House. Hawke House (1703) was the home of Admiral Hawke, the victor of Quiberon Bay in 1759. The

Syon House has fine interiors designed by Adam and its rose gardens cover several acres

Three Fishes Inn in Green Street is seventeenth-century. The only big mansion is Sunbury Court, $\frac{1}{4}$ mile downstream (but not completely visible from the river). Dating from about 1770, it has a central redbrick pediment with Ionic pilasters. In its Saloon are Arcadian paintings by the Swedish artist Elias Martin who lived in England 1768–80. Sunbury Court is now a Salvation Army Youth Centre.

SYON HOUSE (*Greater London*)

It is $\frac{3}{4}$ mile north of Isleworth off the A315 London Road. 'The most splendid house in Middlesex'. Only of course it isn't in Middlesex any more. Another transformation by Robert Adam – especially of the interior decoration. Syon's history began more than 500 years ago, when Henry V, trying to expiate his father's sins, especially his part in the murder of Richard II, founded a Brigittine monastery near Twickenham (named Syon). It afterwards moved to its present site between Isleworth and Brentford, on the opposite side of the river to Kew Gardens. With the Dissolution, Henry VIII seized Syon, and Catherine Howard was imprisoned here before her execution. As if to reward him for his greed, the ugly story goes, Henry VIII's coffin rested here on its way to Windsor, mysteriously burst open and his body was partly eaten by the famished dogs of the household.

In 1547 both abbey and park were given to the Duke of Somerset, Lord Protector of the Realm, and in particular of the boy king Edward VI. Somerset, having built himself a house, was accused of treason by John Dudley, father-in-law of Lady Jane Grey, and executed. Dudley, in the ruthless manner of Tudor society, acquired Syon for himself and was created Earl of Northumberland. He too was executed. So far Syon had brought nobody much luck. In 1750 it was acquired by Sir Hugh Smithson and his wife, daughter of the 7th Duke of Somerset who petitioned the King to recreate the Earldom of Northumberland then extinct. So it was that Sir Hugh assumed the name Percy and became the 1st Duke of Northumberland. He commissioned Robert Adam to 'improve' the building, inside and out, giving him almost *carte blanche*. Adam worked on it for ten years (1762–72) while Capability Brown laid out the gardens.

The Percy Lion, brought from Northumberland House in the Strand, stands proudly over the entrance. Each room was planned as a whole, furniture, colours (the use of white has a subtle effect on all surrounding hues), even people and their clothes. The Great Hall, in black and white marble, full of statues like a Roman atrium, was designed to have footmen in blue and gold livery flitting about. The Long Gallery (136 feet long) was designed with special features to amuse the ladies after dinner while the men drank, 'finished in a style to afford variety and amusement'. The Dining Room had to be splendid, Adam said, because the English spent so much time there. The Red Drawing Room has a ceiling painted in the fashionable 'Pompeiian' style (Pompeii had recently been excavated) by Cipriani.

Syon has always had a tradition of gardening. Lord Protector Somerset, advised by his physician William Turner (1515–68), the 'Father of English Botany', planted trees; his mulberry trees still bear fruit. Capability Brown's gardens have been well maintained in the twentieth century. Rare trees were planted in the park by the 3rd Duke of Northumberland, who also built the Great Conservatory in the 1830s. Odd that this should face Kew across the river! In 1965, 55 acres of the park around a lake were set aside to form a garden centre, presided over by the present Duke. It is both a national horticultural exhibition and a business, selling plants and gardening equipment. There is a particularly beautiful rose garden. The gardens also contain an aviary, butterfly house and aquarium, and the British Leyland Heritage Museum is situated in Syon Park.

TEDDINGTON (*Greater London*)

Meaning 'place of Tudda's people'. It is $1\frac{1}{4}$ miles northwest of Kingston. The old derivation 'tide end town' is now frowned on by scholars, but the idea is preserved in a riverside pub, Tide End Cottage. It was a village when Master Noël Coward was born (at a house in Waldegrave Road) on 16 December 1899, but grew into a well-to-do suburb between World Wars I and II. Today, Teddington and Twickenham, linked by Strawberry Hill, are almost indistinguishable except for what remains of their 'villages'. The Coward family were the mainstay of the choir and life of St Alban's parish church, rebuilt in 1889–96; it is very tall and cold with a green copper roof. It is also the most prominent building in Teddington except for the Thames Television Studios in Broom Road. It is nearly all nave: the rest was never finished. Next (or opposite) to it, in Ferry Road, is the old, much smaller parish church, St Mary's, containing some Tudor brickwork, much eighteenth-century restoration and a nineteenth-century chancel. The church was remodelled in 1753 and seems to follow John James's ideas at Twickenham parish church. There is a tablet to 'Margaret Woffington, spinster': this is Peg Woffington, star of the eighteenth-century stage, who specialized in impersonating foppish males such as Sir Harry Wildair in Farquhar's *The Constant Couple*; and played Polly Peachum in *The Beggar's Opera*. Her cottage is now a restaurant. Peg died in 1760 aged thirty-nine. A vicar of this church (for some fifty years) was Stephen Hales, who was also a scientist and a Fellow of the Royal Society. There is a monument to Sir Orlando Bridgeman, Lord Keeper to Charles I, to whom Thomas Traherne, rector of St Mary's (1672–4) was chaplain. Traherne, whose metaphysical poems were not recognized as his until 1903, is buried in the church. Also buried here is John Walter, 'founder' of *The Times*.

R. D. Blackmore, author of *Lorna Doone*, built himself a house with a large orchard in Teddington (Gomer House, now gone, in what is now Doone Close). Here he ran a market garden for some years. Shortly before his death in 1900, he was invited to be godfather to Master Noël Coward. This he refused, because he had already been godfather to Noël's older brother Russell, who had died at the age of six – Blackmore felt he had brought bad luck to the family.

Other Teddington celebrities were William Penn, Quaker and founder of Pennsylvania; William T. Brooke, who in 1896 found Traherne's manuscripts at a secondhand bookstall; and Richard Bentley (1662–1742), scholar and critic, who helped Horace Walpole to design Strawberry Hill at Twickenham (*see* entry).

THAMES DITTON (*Surrey*)

Meaning 'turn by a dyke or ditch'. Situated 1 mile southeast of Hampton Court, off the A309. A village for fishermen before World War I, where the river (I am told) can still be fished despite so many boats and the area being very built up. It has

Twickenham Village boasts several handsome Georgian houses especially in Sion Road

regattas in the summer. Yet, around St Nicholas Church, the nucleus of a village can still be seen. The church, of flint and stone, with thirteenth-century weatherboarded tower and spikey spire, has a crudely carved Norman font showing scenes such as the Lamb and the Cross and an ibex falling on its horns. It also has an unusual Easter Sepulchre, brasses and sixteenth-century monuments, one with a bust to Sidney Godolphin (1645–1712), statesman and adviser to James II, William III and Queen Anne.

The big house opposite the church is a Georgian building given a new façade in the twentieth century. Once known as Boyle Farm, it is now a children's home. High Street leads down to the river, and at its north end is the sixteenth-century Swan Inn, and, nearby, a little suspension bridge (1914) over to the island. At Giggs Hill (to the southeast) is the headquarters (Neo-Georgian) of the Milk Marketing Board.

TWICKENHAM (*Greater London*)

Probably meaning 'Twicca's enclosure'. Situated $2\frac{1}{4}$ miles northwest of Kingston. 'Twit'nam' was the great place, in the sixteenth and seventeenth centuries, for building villas beside the Thames and no expense was spared. Pope, Kneller, Hudson (Reynolds' teacher), above all Horace Walpole all built houses here. Thus the original village is to be found mostly between St Mary's parish church and Lebanon Park, with many Georgian houses (for example, in Sion Road). The church has a fifteenth-century tower of Kentish ragstone, but the rest was rebuilt (1714–15) by John James, architect of St George's, Hanover Square, London. The Tuscan façade, with its pilasters, is seen from the river. Inside are monuments dating back to 1642, and tombs sculpted by Scheemakers, Rysbrack and others. There are two monuments to Alexander Pope, and one to his parents; and another, outside, to his nurse, Mary Beach.

Pope's Villa, in Cross Deep, is not the house on which the poet spent so much loving care from 1719 onwards: all that remains of that house is a tunnel under the road (The Grotto, open on Saturdays) connecting his two gardens. It is embellished with shells and rock crystal and mirrors to illuminate them by reflected light. Here Pope wrote the 'Essay on Man' and 'The Dunciad'. The Neo-Tudor house on the villa's site is now a convent school.

Horace Walpole's 'little plaything house', Strawberry Hill, has fortunately been well preserved. It is now a teachers' training college (St Mary's, open by appointment Wednesday and Saturday afternoons). Walpole acquired it in 1747 when he was thirty, and went on altering and extending it until 1776, using at least four architects. The result is not only Gothic but also *Sharawaggi*, the 'Chinese want of symmetry' which turned a cottage into a castle without ceasing to be a home. The Long Gallery, the Holbein Chamber and Little Cloister, the Tribune (chapel), the Great Bed Chamber, the Round Tower, the Beauchamp Turret are all choice bits taken from other buildings — it is eighteenth-century amateurism run riot!

We have only sampled one part of Twickenham. There is so much else. Sandycombe Lodge, in Sandycombe Road, was built by Turner the painter and completed in 1813. Henry Fielding lived for a few years in what is now Holly Road and wrote part of *Tom Jones* there. His cousin Lady Mary Wortley Montagu (Pope's friend until they quarrelled) lived in Heath Road. For other riverside houses, *see* Marble Hill Park.

WALTON ON THAMES (*Surrey*)

Probably meaning 'place by a stream or well'. It is $2\frac{1}{2}$ miles west-southwest of Hampton Court, on the A244. A town to live in, perhaps, more than to visit; its village qualities mostly disappeared in the late 1960s as a new shopping area (with multistorey car park) and blocks of offices and flats invaded. Yet there are rewarding things if you seek them out. The Old Manor House (*circa* 1500), timber-framed, has a hall complete with gallery and screen. This was once the home of John Bradshaw (1602–59), president of the court that condemned Charles I to death. At 47 High Street lived another Parliamentarian leader, Henry Ireton. Prince Louis of Battenberg, father of the late Earl Mountbatten, had a house here and so did Sir Arthur Sullivan.

The chief repository of Walton's history is St Mary's Church, built of flint and stone with a brick parapet. The north arcade is Norman (late) – circular piers with scalloped capitals. Much of the rest is fourteenth-century. The north aisle and roof of the nave are about 1630. The church has some fine monuments. The finest is Roubiliac's large statue to Richard Boyle, Viscount Shannon (d.1740), commissioned by his daughter in 1755, she being, we are told, 'justly sensible of the inexpressible loss of her respectable parents'. She is shown grieving over an urn, while he looks remarkably cheerful as he leans against a gun with a tent in the background (he was a field marshal). This sculpture has been pronounced, in Baedeker's phrase, 'worth a special journey'. There are other monuments by Chantrey and Elias Ashmole; the latter's is to William Lilly, the astrologer (1602–81) and publisher of almanacs of prophecy, who lived in Walton. A brass to John Selwyn (d.1587) shows him riding a stag, which he did to impress Queen Elizabeth I, steering it towards her and killing it at her feet. A 'scold's bridle' of iron is kept at the west end: it is only a model – the original, presented to the parish in 1633, was stolen in 1964.

WEYBRIDGE (*Surrey*)

It is 2 miles southeast of Chertsey. A large suburb, in parts luxurious and very expensive (St George's Hill, for example, favoured by pop stars); in other parts, dominated by industrial estates such as the one near the old Brooklands motor-racing circuit (now an airfield, mainly for helicopters). British Aircraft Corporation has a factory here.

Oatlands Park, near the river, was the site of a palace built (or rather rebuilt on a medieval core) in 1538 for Henry VIII. Here he married Catherine Howard. Elizabeth I, James I and Charles I often used the palace, and Cromwell demolished it. Nothing remains but part of a Tudor wall in Thames Street and an arch. The present house in the park was built on the site of a hunting lodge for the Duke of York in 1794 by Henry Holland, and converted into a hotel in 1856 (mid-Victorian Italianate).

Weybridge still has a village green (Monument Green) with the seventeenth-century Ship Hotel and a tall Doric column in memory of Frederica, Duchess of York (d.1820) who lived at Oatlands. The column originally stood at Seven Dials in London. There is also a Chantrey monument to her in St James's Church, with a typical kneeling figure. The church (at the west end of High Street towards the confluence of Wey and Thames) was built in 1848 by John Pearson. The outside is rather forbidding except for the thin broach spire which is its recognizable feature. Inside, twenty different kinds of marble decorate the chancel.

Surviving from an earlier church are some good brasses (mostly under the tower) – one to John Woulde (d.1598) and his two wives and children; another to Thomas Inwood (d.1586) and his three wives; another (?fifteenth-century) full of crudely represented skeletons.

Other churches are all dated to the second half of the nineteenth century, the first great expansion time for Weybridge as a residential suburb, helped by the new railways. The church of St Charles Borromeo (Roman Catholic) has attached to it the domed Mausoleum of King Louis-Philippe, who died in exile at Claremont, near Esher, in 1850. In Church Street the library and museum have exhibits of the history, archeology, costumes and handicrafts of northwest Surrey.

The Thames with swollen riverbanks viewed from Richmond Hill. Above Teddington Lock the river is tidal

CHAPTER SIX

To the Sea

Leaving Putney Bridge, we are immediately confronted with another more workaday bridge (carrying the District Line of London's Underground in the direction of Wimbledon). On the left, the desirable residences of Hurlingham Court and Rivermead Court, followed by the grounds of the Hurlingham Club with its mid-eighteenth-century house — a sort of country club in London. Trees and green lawn on the opposite bank — in Wandsworth Park, ¼ mile of it. Wandsworth takes its name from the river Wandle. A few hundred yards further down, on the right, what looks like a thin canal joins the river, hard by the inevitable gasworks. Who could imagine that the Wandle flows through pleasant small South London parks and has its beginning way beyond Croydon? Or that Izaak Walton recommended it as being full of leaping trout? Take heart: there are plans to reclaim it. You must by now have smelled beer. Beside the Wandle is Young's Brewery, where unchanging Real Ale is made; and the most reassuring sight in Wandsworth is Young's old-fashioned dray drawn by stately shire horses.

Wandsworth Bridge ushers in more industry, with Fulham power station on the left. On the right bank, as the river bends north, Battersea comes into view, and the railway bridge that meets us ¼ mile later carries a line that is fated like others in the neighbourhood, to disappear into the general 'spaghetti' of Clapham Junction. And over to the right are the tall blocks of flats that have replaced streets of hovels. The next power station on the left takes its name from Lots Road, its bare smokestacks at one time a byword for the ugliness of industry. They stand beside Chelsea Creek, once a stream called Gunter's Creek that enjoyed a short career as a canal in the nineteenth century. I

don't recommend trying to go up it — it leads to a real humdinger of a gasworks. Better to turn your eyes right across the river to the heliport and a little further on to admire the proud way Battersea parish church, St Mary's (mostly 1776), looks out upon the scene. Beyond is a new development of houses and flats called Morgan's Walk and offices over the bridge.

Lots Road, having been joined by Cremorne Road, reminding us that there were once pleasure gardens here (where Whistler watched the fireworks), suddenly becomes Cheyne Walk, whose elegance increases beyond Battersea Bridge. Just before the bridge, there is a friendly jumble of houseboats: here a variety of people live rate-free (except for water and electricity), some of them not unconnected with the theatre. It's a thing to do when you are young and romantic . . . Battersea Bridge (1890) replaced the rickety wooden affair of 1771 that Turner and Whistler loved to paint. Turner ended his days at the scruffy end of Cheyne Walk (No. 118), where he lived under the name of Puggy Booth. Cheyne Walk — the tall, posh part — recedes from our view as we see it from the river, separated from the water by the gardens, the result of the great Embankment of 1872. Beyond it is Chelsea (see entry).

If you love suspension bridges, the Albert Bridge, also joining Battersea to Chelsea, will delight you. Designed by Rowland Ordish in 1873, it puts maximum strain on the 'chains', so that there is a notice requiring soldiers to 'break step' when crossing it. You can feel it bouncing — but it is perfectly safe. At rush-hours, however, one-way traffic is insisted upon. The bridge looks glorious at night. Beside it is Cadogan Pier, finishing point of Doggett's Coat and Badge Race (see page 18).

About 700 yards downstream, it should be possible to catch a glimpse, still on your left, of Charles II's — some say Nell

The riverside walk at Strand-on-the-Green, one of the best-preserved villages on the tidal Thames

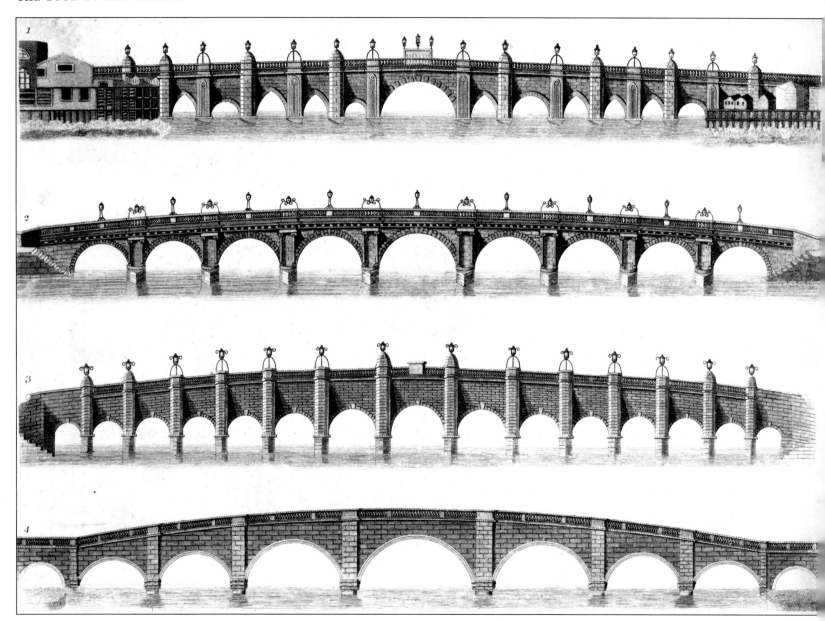

Gwyn's — noble Royal Hospital, designed by Christopher Wren and home of the Chelsea Pensioners, followed by a narrow bit of greenery which is Ranelagh Gardens.

On the right (south) bank, for the last $\frac{1}{2}$ mile, we have been passing Battersea Park and what remains of it in its 1951 guise of the Festival Pleasure Gardens, created when a benign Government tried to cheer up the rationed, bomb-damaged masses with a fun-fair, an Emett railway, a music hall and tree walks. Today it is nearly all gone, and we must improve our minds by looking at the out-of-doors Henry Moore sculptures which, unfortunately, you can't see from the river and also enjoying the gardens particularly during rhododendron time.

Strange to encounter, so soon, another suspension bridge and one built as recently as 1937. Chelsea Bridge is not so filigree-pretty as the Albert Bridge, but it doesn't rock when heavy vehicles cross it, being designed on a different engineering principle. Nobody needs to break step. It is followed immediately by a functional, rumbling railway bridge, called Grosvenor Bridge, carrying the Brighton and the other Southern Region lines into Victoria Station.

For some time we have been approaching Battersea Power Station: we first saw it as we passed under the Albert Bridge. Then it was misty in the distance. Now suddenly it rises starkly (on the right). Designing a power station burning solid fuel that needs smoke stacks is always difficult, and this design of Sir Giles Gilbert Scott all in pink brick, is as near to beauty as you are likely to get. It is no longer operational, and although completed in 1935 is scheduled for preservation. The fourth chimney was unnecessary — the architect simply put it there for the symmetry of the building.

Pimlico is the district on our left. Its name is said to mean a drink, a sort of eighteenth-century cocktail whose recipe has been lost. Its squares and avenues and pillared porticos were

Some of London's bridges across the Thames: London Bridge, Blackfriars Bridge, Westminster Bridge and Kew Bridge

designed in the 1850s by Thomas Cubitt, who also built Belgravia. But you don't see much of his work from the river. You do see modern blocks of flats, beginning with Dolphin Square (1937), the largest in Europe if not in the world, 1,200 flats housing about 4,000 well-to-do people in luxury; and then Churchill Gardens Estate, built by Westminster City Council after World War II, designed to use the waste heat from Battersea Power Station on the opposite bank.

The new Covent Garden fruit and vegetable market appears on the right, appropriately, for this is Nine Elms which, before the railways were built, was all market garden. The market came here in 1974 from its old site (between the Strand and Long Acre). We are now entering an area, on the South Bank, of planning controversy. During the next decade the riverside skyline will be altered, if certain planners have their ways, so as to turn dereliction into monstrosity. One such area is Vauxhall Cross, coming up on our right. The notorious 'Green Giant' plan for a huge tower block (500 feet) was rejected but replaced by another plan involving a tower. The debate continues. We shall see other such areas along the South Bank. Meanwhile, here is Vauxhall Bridge (1906) with sculptures, similar to those on the Albert Memorial, of Agriculture, Architecture, Engineering and other skills. No more Vauxhall Gardens, alas, where Pepys went by boat for pleasure.

On the left is Millbank (yes, there were once real windmills here, blown by stiff breezes as the Thames turns northward). Instead, the Tate Gallery, built on the site of a huge prison in 1897, cowers in the shadow of the Vickers Building (real name: Millbank House). The Tate houses our national collection of modern art and of British painting before 1900 (including Thamesmen like Turner and Whistler), modern foreign painting and modern sculpture. Every so often it attracts wide publicity by experimental works such as one arrangement of bricks on the floor. The restaurant was decorated by Rex Whistler. The Vickers Building which is next door has its stern critics, but the use of glass, and the angle at which it is set, somehow please me.

On the right, the Albert Embankment has mostly offices to offer us – the National Dock Labour Board, Decca, and the Headquarters of the London Fire Brigade (very important for riverside blazes). By now we should be getting glimpses of St Paul's Cathedral, once the peak of the City, now belittled by skyscrapers. Even the torpedo-like tower of Westminster Cathedral, over on the left, no longer stands alone. Lambeth Bridge (1932) replaced a nineteenth-century suspension bridge, which in turn replaced an ancient horse-ferry (hence Horse-ferry Road, which approaches the bridge from the Victoria direction). Below the bridge we get our first proper sight of the Houses of Parliament, sparing a glance for two big office blocks (pride of the 1930s) on the Millbank side, both belonging to ICI. Lambeth Palace, curiously self-effacing in its 700-year-old castellated way, is the Archbishop of Canterbury's London residence. St Mary's Church nestles beside it: five archbishops (and Bligh of the *Bounty*) are buried there.

The Palace of Westminster (not much left of the original) begins with Victoria Tower Gardens, which contain a statue of Mrs Pankhurst the suffragette; the tower itself (believed to be the biggest square tower in the world, 336 feet high) contains Parliament's archives, two million documents including every Act of Parliament since 1497. Lords and Commons are guarded by the Clock Tower (Big Ben, named after Sir Benjamin Hall, first Commissioner of Works in 1859 when it was cast, is the deep, cracked bell that strikes the hours). Opposite is St Thomas's Hospital, one of the great teaching hospitals, founded in the thirteenth century and with its Victorian buildings now modernized.

Westminster Bridge is not the one Wordsworth stood on in 1803 to compose his sonnet 'Earth has not anything to show more fair'. It was built in 1862 by Thomas Page to replace a structure erected in 1750 designed by a Swiss engineer, Charles Labelye: in 1750 it was London's only river bridge other than London Bridge. From Westminster Pier, pleasure steamers ply up and down the river, to Greenwich and Hampton Court. Now, on the right, we have County Hall, the pillared palatial headquarters of the Greater London Council; on the left, Norman Shaw's 1888 redbrick 'old' New Scotland Yard, no longer full of detectives (they now live in Victoria Street), the white-stone Air Ministry, and pinnacled Whitehall Court. This is the Victoria Embankment, facing (on the South Bank) Riverside Walk. Once we have passed under Hungerford Bridge, with its parallel footway, which takes part of the Southern Region railway into Charing Cross Station, the walk leads on to the Royal Festival Hall, the Queen Elizabeth Hall, and the National Film Theatre.

On the north bank (and it really is north, now that the river begins a stiff bend to the east just above Waterloo Bridge) are Shell-Mex House (nicknamed 'Big Benzine'), Cleopatra's Needle (nothing to do with Cleopatra – just a granite obelisk of *circa* 1500 BC brought from Heliopolis and presented to Britain in 1819 in gratitude for Nelson's victory at the battle of the Nile in 1798), and the Savoy Hotel (1889). All these look across the river at the colossal Shell Centre, abused by aesthetes (but the view from the 25th floor is breath-taking). I once stood on Waterloo Bridge with the late Sir Francis Meynell, who was composing a sonnet on Shell Centre. It began: 'Earth has not anything to show more square'.

Waterloo Bridge, three graceful concrete arches by Sir Giles Scott, completed (despite bombs) in 1945, replaced John Rennie's beautiful stone bridge of 1817. The view from the bridge, upstream and downstream, is magnificent, but hold on to your hat – there is a perpetual westerly wind which has twice blown my umbrella inside out.

Below the bridge, on the left, is London's only floating police station: you will already have noticed the black-and-cream

The *Cutty Sark* at Greenwich

patrol launches of the Thames River Police chugging about, and this Pier is where they forgather – later we shall see their headquarters at Wapping. High above Waterloo Pier is Somerset House, originally built in 1547 for the Duke of Somerset, Protector of the boy-king Edward VI; but what you see now is mostly the work of Sir William Chambers in the 1770s and 1780s, designed as Government departments: at present it houses the Principal Probate Registry (people's wills dating back to 1382). Elizabeth I and various other queens lived here as princesses; or to put it more pithily, 'Queen Elizabeth slept here: Civil Servants sleep here now.'

On the right is Sir Denys Lasdun's National Theatre, admired by purists, but to me, who cannot understand a windowless building, it is like a French Foreign Legion fortress. We are on the brink of another contentious south bank area known as 'Coin Street'. Opponents think it will ruin the Thames frontage if more towers like London Weekend Television's are built; proponents say it will revivify the whole area and make living in the City worthwhile. Or will it all end up as office blocks which will become 'listed buildings' in AD 2083?

On the north bank we have just passed into the City with a capital C – that square mile of commerce and tradition which earns so much in 'invisible exports'. The transition happened at Temple Steps, marked by the City's griffins, decorative dolphins on lamp-posts and policemen wearing 'Roman' helmets. Above and behind, is the Temple – Inner and Middle – a sort of barristers' university. Below, in front, three moored ships claim our attention. *Wellington*, the 'only floating Livery Hall' of the Honourable Company of Master Mariners; and *Chrysanthemum* and *President*, respectively a training ship and the headquarters of the Royal Naval Volunteer Reserve. Captain Scott's *Discovery*, in which he sailed to the Antarctic during 1901–4 has been moved to St Katharine's Docks where it is hoped she will stay indefinitely on view to the public together with other historic ships and barges.

Which brings us to Blackfriars Bridge, first of the four bridges whose 'sustentation' (lovely medieval word) is the responsibility of the Corporation of London through an ancient Trust Fund. (The other three are Southwark, London and Tower Bridge.) Joseph Cubitt built Blackfriars Bridge in 1865–9; its predecessor, which lasted a century, was called Pitt Bridge after the Elder Pitt. The parallel railway bridge brings trains from southeast England into Blackfriars Station.

Redevelopment areas, now, to both the left and right. Left, the Mermaid Theatre with an 'Elizabethan' stage, opened on 28 May 1959 to the bells of St Paul's – a lease of Puddle Dock having been granted by the City Corporation to 'Bernard Miles and other poor players of London'. About 500 yards further down, you can just see the small square of Queenhithe Dock, very important in the Middle Ages until ships became too big to get through the narrow arches of Old London Bridge. On the right (we are now in Southwark) is Bankside, in Shakespeare's day a 'liberty' full of brothels and beer-gardens, amenities not permitted in the City itself; and above all, his own Globe Theatre. Bankside Power Station (only one smoke-stack) sits in the middle: designed by Sir Giles Gilbert Scott (1935), it is now disused and will probably be 'listed' like its sister at Battersea. At Cardinal's Wharf, almost opposite Queenhithe, is the little house with a red front door where Sir Christopher Wren lived while St Paul's Cathedral, across the water, was a-building.

Southwark Bridge (built by John Rennie 1813–19 but rebuilt in 1913–21) is followed quickly by the railway bridge into Cannon Street Station. On the Southwark Bank we now have the decayed St Mary Overy or Clink Street area (Clink Street once led to Clink Prison) which developers of office blocks have their eyes on: they will never dare to touch the seventeenth-century Anchor Inn, close by the brewery once owned by the husband of Dr Johnson's friend Mrs Thrale. As we approach

Warehouses in the Pool of London. Many are now disused and there are schemes to find new uses for these buildings

London Bridge, Southwark Cathedral, founded 1106 as St Mary Overy, now almost swamped by commerce and a railway, holds its tower as high as it can.

The Fishmongers' Hall (1834), on the left above London Bridge marks the starting point of Doggett's Race. Just beyond it is the Monument, with its head of gold, Wren's reminder of the Great Fire (1666): 311 steps to the top, but worth it for the view. London Bridge (1973), very functional in concrete, isn't a patch on its predecessor, Rennie's 1831 bridge of stone, which was bought by the McCulloch Oil Corporation, transported bit by bit to America and re-erected at Lake Havasu City, Arizona. Did McCullochs expect to get the Tower Bridge instead? The Corporation of London vehemently denies it. As for our own London Bridge, if you are a Freeman of the City you are entitled to drive your sheep across it.

We now enter the Pool of London: sea-going vessels cannot go further upstream. On the left, the fine steeple of Wren's St Magnus the Martyr, followed by old Billingsgate Fish Market (the market has now been removed to the Isle of Dogs). As I mentioned earlier there is a scheme by *avant-garde* architects Richard Seifert and Partners to build a new Old London Bridge here, enormously wide and clad in mirror glass, containing offices, flats, shops, pubs, restaurants and – a skating rink. To the right is HMS *Belfast* (1938), veteran of World War II, the Royal Navy's largest cruiser. Opposite her, as we approach the Tower Bridge, is Tower Pier and Stairs, where Sir Winston Churchill's coffin was placed aboard a launch for its penultimate journey to Waterloo Pier. The Tower, for me, is the most sinister thing on the Thames: did anything good ever happen there? But Tower Bridge, already out-of-date for traffic when it first opened in 1894, is a delightful Gothick folly. Its bascules, now electrified, do not rise as often as they used to before the Port of London moved towards the Estuary. In 1951 they rose while a bus was still crossing the bridge. The driver accelerated smartly, jumped the gap and saved both his bus and his passengers.

St Katharine's Docks, on the left after Tower Bridge, have been successfully redeveloped from Telford's warehouses of 1828 into a yacht marina, with veteran vessels like the *Nore* lightship and HMS *Discovery*, a World Trade Centre and the vast new Tower Hotel. Next to it are the London Docks, closed in 1969 and awaiting future plans. On the right bank is St Saviour's Dock, Bermondsey, featured in Dickens' *Oliver Twist*. Both here and at Execution Dock in Wapping, opposite (look for a warehouse with a big letter E on it), pirates were hanged – including Captain Kidd in 1701. On the right bank, just below St Saviour's, is Cherry Garden Pier, where tall upstream vessels are supposed to hoot for Tower Bridge to lift its bascules.

We are now (on the right bank) in Rotherhithe. Alongside the river, Rotherhithe Street contains two well-known pubs, the Angel (which hangs over the water just like the Prospect of Whitby on the Wapping side) and, further downstream, the Mayflower, near the southern end of the Rotherhithe Tunnel (1908) under the Thames. If you look carefully at a row of neglected houses, you may be able to see one called The Little Midshipman, once the studio of Tony Armstrong-Jones before he became Lord Snowdon. On the Wapping side, notice the Thames Police Headquarters – the police patrol 54 miles of river between Staines Bridge and Dartford Creek.

A northeast bend into Limehouse Reach before the river turns due south gives us Shadwell on the left, with Regent's Canal Dock leading, via London Zoo, to the Grand Union Canal and so to Birmingham and the Midlands. St Anne's Church, Limehouse, was a welcome sight to returning clipper ships a century ago. On the right, the seemingly endless 400 acres of the Surrey Commercial Docks, closed in 1970, used to specialize in timber. Towards the end of them is Greenland Dock (1696),

OPPOSITE Battersea Power Station, a dominant but evocative landmark on the London river
OVERLEAF The bird's-eye view of London's great river and its city from the National Westminster Tower

once the base of the English whaling fleet. 'Once' – it's nearly all 'once' in dying Dockland. Yet the air vibrates with schemes to reclaim it – an airport, a new light railway, an 'enterprise zone', even a river-bus service, and all the ingenuity of the London Docklands Development Corporation. The actress, Joan Littlewood even planned a Palace of Fun on the Isle of Dogs . . .

Rotherhithe, on the right, has now become Deptford, with the redbrick remains of the Royal Navy Victualling Yards, once the Royal Docks where many of the ships that defeated the Spanish Armada were built, and where Elizabeth I knighted Drake aboard the *Golden Hind*. On the left we have almost rounded the Isle of Dogs, more politely known as Poplar, containing West and East India and Millwall Docks. (Why dogs? Because, in the days of Greenwich Palace, the noisy royal hounds were kept there.)

Now, as the river's U-bend flattens out before Greenwich Pier, prepare for one of the grandest sights of the river: the Royal Naval College (designed by Wren, of course), the *Cutty Sark*, Sir Francis Chichester's *Gipsy Moth IV*, the Trafalgar Tavern – the whole place is full of national and heroic achievement. It was entirely appropriate that Sir Ranulph Fiennes's Transglobe Expedition should have begun and ended here, on the prime meridian. (For the best view of Greenwich, take the pedestrian tunnel under the Thames and look at it from the Isle of Dogs.)

Blackwall Tunnel, on the other side of the Isle, also runs under the river from East Greenwich to Poplar (two one-way tunnels). In Blackwall Reach, the writhing river crosses the meridian three times. Another U-bend, another turn east, and we can see that new engineering wonder, the Thames Barrier, £435 million of flood prevention between Woolwich (south bank) and Silvertown (north). Then Woolwich Free Ferry, looking rather like a pleasure steamer, carrying cars and people between North and South Woolwich and the Royal Albert Docks. A huge new river bridge is planned hereabouts, between Beckton (Essex) and Thamesmead (Kent), the 'new town' built on Erith Marshes, 3 miles east of Woolwich. Marshes and creeks on both sides now, as the river broadens, past the Ford Works at Dagenham, and past Erith (where two small Kentish rivers, Darent and Cray, join the Thames).

By Purfleet, on the Essex side, Long Reach begins – 3 miles dead straight, over the Dartford Road Tunnel, to Greenhithe, looking rather pretty with chalk cliffs behind. Now there is less to look at, more atmosphere to absorb as we begin to smell the sea. 'The earth,' says one Thamesman used to navigating here, 'seems to be suspended from the sky.' Down St Clements Reach; Northfleet Hope ('hope', that ancient mariner's word for a 'marshy inlet'); past Swanscombe Marshes, where they found a skull that changed our ideas about the age of *homo sapiens sapiens*; and at last to Gravesend (with Tilbury opposite). Gravesend, where the river is 1,000 yards wide, and if you take a mouthful of water it is half-salt, half-fresh; Gravesend, so much less gloomy than its name, the gateway to the open sea, the true gateway to London's river; where Customs men control incoming ships, and up-river ships take on river pilots. It is a town full of what Alan Herbert called 'the beauty peculiar to business on the water', giving us our first sight of really big vessels. See you in the Elephant's Head.

OPPOSITE The Estuary – the Thames meets the sea near Southend at the end of its long journey from Thames Head
PREVIOUS PAGE Woolwich – the Thames here is still a working river with the Port of London downstream at Tilbury

Putney to Gravesend – 40 river miles

BANKSIDE (*London S.E.1*)

Situated on the south bank, between Blackfriars and Southwark Bridges. Street names alone preserve the history of this warehouse wilderness – Bear Gardens, Rose Alley, Barge House Street, Thrale Street, Paris Garden, and a few you won't find on the map, Maid Lane, Foul Lane, Love Lane and Melancholy Walk. Never mind the power station, which has been compared to a crematorium; Bankside is worth visiting for two things – the Bear Gardens Museum and the superb views across the water of St Paul's Cathedral, especially at sunset, from the Anchor Inn (seventeenth-century, and claiming Dr Johnson among its clientèle). The Museum (open Saturdays and Sundays, April–September, at other times by appointment: ring 01-928 6342) offers a permanent exhibition of the theatre in Shakespeare's time and also performs plays. Under the bottling plant of Courage, Barclay and Simonds' brewery is the site of Shakespeare's Globe Theatre (1599, burned down in 1613, rebuilt and then pulled down in 1644). Warehouses now, but whorehouses then: one was called the Cardinal's Hat. Cardinal's Wharf, by Wren's little house, is still there in outline.

To Bankside came Elizabeth I and James I to entertain their foreign ambassadors with bear-baiting; also Samuel Pepys to see a bullfight and the tossing of a dog ('very good sport' – then a twinge of conscience – 'a rude and nasty pleasure'). The Hope Theatre (which was also a bear garden) was opened in 1613 by Philip Henslowe: it saw the first production of Ben Jonson's *Bartholomew Fayre*. Rose Alley commemorates Henslowe's Rose Theatre (1592–1603), which employed most dramatists and actors of the day including Shakespeare.

There are not many barges and lighters left on the Thames, but they produced one local character who is remembered on Bankside. Harry Harris (1880–1962), whose family had been licensed watermen for six generations, became dock lighterage manager here. His grandfather claimed to remember Old London Bridge with houses on it. But it was on Southwark Bridge that Harry distinguished himself: he celebrated Mafeking Night (1900) by walking end to end along the parapet.

BATTERSEA (*London S.W.11*)

Meaning 'Beaduric's island'. It is on the south bank between Wandsworth and Chelsea Bridges. Battersea, like Clapham, has 'come up' in the past twenty years, and may almost be thought of as South Chelsea. The one thing every true Briton knows about the place is the Dog's Home at 4 Battersea Park Road. Old Battersea (not much remains) can be seen from the river. York Road, parallel to the river between Wandsworth Bridge and the railway bridge, is named after a palace for the archbishops of York that was here from Edward IV's reign to Mary I's. In the seventeenth and eighteenth centuries 'Battersea enamelled ware' was famous (it is still valued today), and the district was noted for market gardens specializing in celery.

The parish church of St Mary (rebuilt 1776), in Church Road, contains older monuments such as Roubiliac's to Lord Bolingbroke (1678–1751) who was born in the Manor House (now gone). He is remembered by Bolingbroke Grove which runs alongside Wandsworth Common. In St Mary's, Blake was married, and from the vestry window Turner painted Thames sunsets. Near the church, in Vicarage Crescent, is Old Battersea House, with William de Morgan's collection of paintings and pottery. Battersea Park nearby offers a lake, boating, fishing,

St Mary's Church, Battersea. Turner painted many Thames sunsets from the church

a subtropical garden, tennis, an athletic track, flower gardens, sculpture, a picnic area, an Easter Parade and a tiny zoo. It was laid out in the 1850s, using spoil from the Royal Victoria Dock, Blackwall, to reinforce marshland where once, in 1829, the Duke of Wellington (aged sixty), then Prime Minister, fought a bloodless duel with the Earl of Winchelsea. Over a woman? Lord, no – just Catholic emancipation.

CHELSEA (London S.W.3)

Meaning 'landing place for chalk or lime'. On the north bank between Battersea and Chelsea Bridges. Bounded on the north by Fulham Road and on the south by the river, Chelsea stretches roughly the length of King's Road, from smart Sloane Square to the greyer World's End with its antique shops. All the world knows the Chelsea Flower Show, held in May in marquees at the Royal Hospital, approached from the north by Royal Avenue (originally designed to stretch all the way to Kensington Palace). In 1960 half of one side of the Avenue was knocked down to build a supermarket, which began the decline of Bohemian Chelsea.

Chelsea's Royal Hospital (designed by Wren) in its dignified setting of grass and trees can be visited (weekdays 10–12 p.m. and 2 p.m.–dusk; Sundays 2 p.m.–dusk; tips expected). Next door is the National Army Museum (weekdays 10–5.30 p.m., Sundays 2–5.30 p.m.) which moved here from Sandhurst in 1971. The museum tells the history of the British Army from Henry VII's time to 1914 – the two World Wars are dealt with at the Imperial War Museum. It also has an art gallery including works by Reynolds, Romney, Wootton and others. The old soldiers, who wear dark-blue uniforms in winter, parade in their summer scarlet on Oak Apple Day (29 May) in honour of Charles II, their founder. In the Centre Court there is a bronze statue of him wearing a kilt, by Grinling Gibbons. It is wreathed with oak on Oak Apple Day. King's Road was once the Merry Monarch's private coach-road to the West.

Chelsea Embankment, surmounted for about 1 mile by Cheyne Walk and its great houses, has Chelsea Old Church (All Saints), which was badly damaged in the Blitz in World War II. The south chantry chapel was built by Sir Thomas More for his first wife in 1532. There are other monuments: to Lord Dacre and his wife (1595), a Pietro Bernini design for Charles Cheyne, Viscount Newhaven, erected in memory of his wife (1669); tablets to William Frend de Morgan and Henry James; and, in the churchyard, a tribute to Sir Hans Sloane (d.1753 aged ninety-two), a physician and botanist, who gave his Physic Garden (along the Embankment) to the Apothecaries' Company.

Crosby Hall, on the corner of Cheyne Walk and Danvers Street, was partly transferred from Bishopsgate where it was founded in 1466 by a City wool merchant, Sir John Crosby. It belonged at one time to the Duke of Gloucester, afterwards Richard III, at another to William Roper, More's son-in-law. Now it belongs to the British Federation of University Women. Inside, it has a hammer-beam roof, a medieval fireplace, Jacobean furniture and a copy of Holbein's painting of the More family. Many literary and artistic figures have lived in Chelsea. Strange that one of the least-read writers today attracts many visitors to his house, 24 Cheyne Row (National Trust), open weekdays (except Tuesday) and Sunday afternoon – Thomas Carlyle, the Sage of Chelsea.

CITY, The (London E.C.2)

The square mile of concentrated business activity extends roughly from the Barbican to the river, and from Temple Bar (and Steps) to the Tower. Most of it is contained in the line of Londinium's second-century Roman wall, bits of which can still be seen. Here the dome of St Paul's Cathedral is surrounded by the towers of commerce such as National Westminster, Kleinwort Benson, the Stock Exchange, the Bank of England, Lloyds (the only insurance market of its kind in the world), and the Metal Exchange. The City enjoys the panoply of the Lord

Mayor and his Procession, the gorgeous halls of City Livery Companies, the 'funny' clothes worn by officials with titles like Common Cryer and Serjeant-at-arms; Guildhall, where the Common Council meets to rule the City; and the new, madly expensive Barbican development with its lofty blocks of flats and its ambitious cultural complex.

All this and twenty Wren churches built after the Great Fire of 1666 (some of them have lunchtime concerts and lectures). Much City business is conducted informally by businessmen who know each other, meet casually on the pavement, or chat on the telephone or in a wine-bar; observing the Stock Exchange motto, 'My word is my bond'.

DEPTFORD (*London S.E.8*)

Meaning 'deep ford'. Situated on the south bank, $1\frac{1}{2}$ miles west of Greenwich. The ford was over the little river Ravensbourne, which enters the Thames at Deptford Creek, the old boundary between Surrey and Kent near the dominating power station. Samuel Pepys came here to discuss, with John Evelyn of Sayes Court, the foundation of the Royal Society. Of Sayes Court (demolished 1729) nothing remains but part of the gardens, now a park. The estate never recovered from being lent to Russia's Peter the Great, who came in 1698 to study shipbuilding. Among other rough pleasures, he loved to be pushed in a wheelbarrow through Evelyn's trim hedges. Peter's favourite tipple in local taverns was hot brandy and pepper. On the site of the old Royal Navy Victualling Yard is the Pepys housing estate (locals pronounce the name 'Pepsi'). Some eighteenth-century buildings remain: a colonnaded terrace and, on the riverfront, two fine rum warehouses, now the Pepys Library and the Deptford Sailing Centre. There are more such houses in Albury Street.

The old parish church, St Nicholas (tower *circa* 1500, the rest mainly 1697), was badly bomb-damaged in World War II. It contains the graves of famous seamen, including Captain George Shelvocke (d.1742), Alexander Selkirk's rival to being the original of Robinson Crusoe. In the churchyard is buried playwright and poet Christopher Marlowe, killed in a Deptford tavern by one Ingram Frizer. Why? Was it just a quarrel over the bill? Or was Marlowe a government agent, and his death a political murder?

DOCKLAND (*London E.* and *S.E.*)

Situated on both banks, from Tower Bridge to Tilbury. The London Dockland Development Corporation, in competition with other development areas of Britain, advertises aggressively to industry: 'Why move to the middle of nowhere when you can move to the middle of London?' The whole business has been bedevilled for years by disagreement between developers and local government. Should the docks somehow be revived, now that containerization has made new ships so much larger that it is much easier to dock at Tilbury, 25 miles downstream? Or can new ideas supply both employment and housing, and also creative excitement? Something of the kind has already happened at St Katharine-by-the-Tower, which has become a tourist playground. Telford's docks were built in 1825–8 and his warehouses (which once stored wines, tea, coffee, tobacco, sugar, spices, rubber and wool) have become flats and offices; crumbling, rat-infested buildings have been restored; new shops, restaurants and a Dickensian pub have arrived, with a giant hotel and a World Trade Centre which opened in 1972. Three basins have been converted to form a marina for large yachts, there are rare Thames sailing barges, and an historic ship museum.

There is a £150-million scheme for Surrey Docks . . . But there are small schemes too — such as for market gardens and nature conservancy. Dr Goode, a Greater London Council ecologist, has attracted the rare black redstart to 2 acres near Tower Bridge; and Hilary Peters started a dairy farm on wasteland near Greenland Dock.

GRAVESEND (*Kent*)

Meaning 'end of the grove'. Situated 26 miles from London on the A226. It has both a riverside and a seaside smell, with perhaps Kentish mudflats predominating. Frobisher and Cabot set sail from here. In Victorian times it became a resort: the Pier Hotel, Clarendon Hotel (with garden), the Three Daws inn, the 1818 brick Customs House (not the modern one with the aerials and radar) give some idea of what it was like a century ago. People came here by excursion steamers to make merry in Rosherville Gardens. Today, it has some good pubs such as the weatherboarded Railway Bell, and the Edwardian Trocadero. There are a few Regency houses in Lansdowne Square, but nothing much older because a fire gutted the town in 1727.

With Tilbury on the Essex side, Gravesend was fortified for many years, principally against the French who sacked the town in 1380. The Tudor monarchs continued the fortifications, and in the 1860s General (Khartoum) Gordon updated the defences. His earthworks are now a public garden known as Gordon Promenade. Americans come here in search of Pocahontas, buried in the chancel of a tiny riverside church where the present parish church of St George now stands. There is a statue, dating from 1617, to this daughter of a Red Indian chief who, aged thirteen, saved the life of Captain John Smith in Chesapeake in 1608 by begging her father to spare him. Was she in love with Smith? She became the first Red Indian Christian under the name of Rebecca, married John Rolfe, another settler, came to England with him in 1616 and was fêted at the court of James I. She died of fever in 1617 on the Thames returning to Virginia. She was twenty-one.

GREENWICH (*London S.E.10*)

Meaning 'green dwelling or dairy farm'. It is on the south bank, 6 miles east of London. Here is a wonderful mixture of naval and national history, with fine buildings and cultural revival. None the worse for having a middle-class core which has been called 'Nigel and Caroline'. You feel the nautical atmosphere as soon as you touch the pier. Here is the famous tea and wool clipper *Cutty Sark* (launched 1869 – she carried 7,000 yards of canvas) which broke speed records to and from Australia, with an exhibition of figureheads and other sailing relics (open daily weekdays, and Sunday afternoons). Nearby is *Gipsy Moth IV*, the 52-foot ketch in which Sir Francis Chichester sailed solo round the world in 1966–7 (open Monday–Thursday). Elizabeth II knighted him with the same sword that Elizabeth I used to knight Drake. The Trafalgar Tavern in Victorian times was famous for whitebait dinners and lobster omelette, with which a kind of mulled wine called Badminton was drunk. The entire Cabinet used to celebrate the end of a session here, and Dickens and Harrison Ainsworth stood each other whitebait dinners to celebrate the completion of their books.

Royal Greenwich dates from the fifteenth century, when the Manor belonged to Humphrey, Duke of Gloucester, patron of learning and collector of a great library – he called his palace Bella Court. Margaret of Anjou renamed it Placentia when she lived in it. The two Tudors, Henry VII and VIII, made their home there. Cromwell had little use for it, and it was rebuilt by Charles II and William III, mainly to the designs of Wren, with help from Hawksmoor, Vanbrugh and others. It was used as a naval hospital (like Chelsea for pensioners and disabled seamen) until 1873, when it became the Royal Naval College. Only the Painted Hall (ceilings by Sir James Thornhill, with a *trompe l'oeil* effect by which flat pillars seem to be supporting the roof) and the Chapel are open to the public (afternoons except Thursdays). The Chapel (1782) is decorated in Neo-Grecian style, contrasting with the rich colours of the Painted Hall, which is now the Dining Room of the College.

The Queen's House, designed by Inigo Jones for Anne of Denmark, Queen to James I, was completed for Henrietta

Telford's St Katharine's Dock has become a yacht harbour and a popular centre on London River

Maria, wife of Charles I. It is now part of the National Maritime Museum (open Tuesday to Saturday, and Sunday afternoons). In its $3\frac{1}{2}$ miles of galleries the museum displays the world's most comprehensive collection of merchant shipping, shipbuilding, exploration, navigation and Royal Navy exhibits, with models, instruments, paintings, and relics of Nelson (such as the uniform he wore at the battle of Trafalgar). The Barge House contains State ceremonial barges.

The old Royal Observatory is on the hill in Greenwich Park: it marks the prime meridian and tells Greenwich Mean Time. Since 1950 the astronomical work of the observatory has been done at Herstmonceux in East Sussex. Greenwich Park was laid out by Le Nôtre, the landscape gardener of Versailles. Along the western side of the park are some good seventeenth-century and eighteenth-century houses, notably Ranger's House, once belonging to Lord Chesterfield. Blackheath, just beyond, has some fine Georgian architecture, including that famous crescent called The Paragon.

St Alphege's Church (designed by Hawksmoor, assisted by John James 'of Greenwich') stands on the site of an earlier church in which Henry VIII was baptized. Here Thomas Tallis (d.1585) the composer and General Wolfe (1727–59) the victor (but the victim) of Quebec are buried. St Alphege (935–1012), Archbishop of Canterbury and martyr, was beaten to death with the bones of oxen for refusing to pay Danegeld, the annual land-tax, at Greenwich.

The lively Greenwich Theatre should also not be missed.

LAMBETH (*London S.E.11*)

Meaning 'loam-hithe, muddy landing place'. On the right bank, between Vauxhall and Waterloo Bridges. There is a Lambeth Walk, but I have never seen anyone dancing there. However, Lambeth has a lively (and sufficiently Cockney) street market

The Royal Naval College, Greenwich, was once a royal palace and then a hospital for naval pensioners

on weekdays. Lambeth Palace may be visited by arrangement, though the Archbishop's Park is open daily. Cardinal Morton's gatehouse, in red brick, is dated 1490, but the earliest part of the Palace is the thirteenth-century crypt and the chapel above. The Great Hall (70 feet high with a hammer-beam roof) is now a library (started by Archbishop Bancroft in 1610): it contains such rarities as Elizabeth I's prayer book, a letter written by Francis Bacon, Gladstone's diaries and 1,500 manuscripts (some illuminated). In the fifteenth-century Lollards' Tower, built of stone, John Wycliffe's followers (the Lollards) were imprisoned for heresy.

By the gatehouse is St Mary's Church, its foundation as old as the Palace; it was decently rebuilt in 1851. It had some good stained glass, bombed to bits in World War II. It has some monuments and graves, among them that of Captain Bligh of the *Bounty* (d.1817) and the two John Tradescants, father and son. The father founded the first museum and 'physic garden' in South Lambeth. When his son died in 1662 the collections went to the Ashmolean Museum, Oxford.

LIMEHOUSE (*London E.1, E.14*)

Meaning 'lime kilns'. On the north bank, $2\frac{1}{4}$ miles east of Tower Bridge. We think of *Limehouse Nights*, in which Thomas Burke found 'the scum of the world's worst countries', *Limehouse Blues*, Dr Fu Manchu, Sherlock Holmes exploring opium dens – but the East End is so respectable now (though there is trouble with squatters in some of the postwar housing estates). Chinatown has become almost middle-class (but with real Chinese restaurants). Charlie Brown's pub, a well-known sailors' haunt with an intriguing collection of curios, is still in West India Dock Road, but no longer has fights three nights a week.

The last lime-kilns disappeared in 1935, but an equally old tradition survives – service to the seaman. Here are hostels and residential clubs for merchant navy officers, the British Sailors' Society, and well-established shops describing themselves as

177

'complete sea outfitters'. There are even one or two 'bagwash laundries'. Cable Street and Ropemakers' Fields tell of an ancillary industry now defunct. And there are pubs galore. The Grapes in Narrow Street is not the Bunch of Grapes that Dickens took as a model for the Six Jolly Fellowship Porters he wrote about in *Our Mutual Friend* – that was destroyed in the Blitz during World War II. But there are others, such as the Gothic Star of the East in Commercial Road, and the Five Bells and Bladebone in Three Colt Street.

There are three noble Hawksmoor churches in the East End, St George-in-the-East (1715–23), Christ Church Spitalfields (1723–9), and St Anne Limehouse. St Anne (1712–30), badly damaged by wartime bombs, with its splendidly baroque steeple, is appropriately full of the tombs of sea captains.

POOL OF LONDON, The

Situated between London and Tower Bridges; below Tower Bridge is Lower Pool. On the south bank, there is much dereliction along Pickle Herring Street and Shad Thames. On the north, St Magnus the Martyr, in Lower Thames Street, claims our attention with the Tower of London (*see* entry). Almost in mid-stream is HMS *Belfast*, approached by launch from Tower Pier: this veteran 11,500-ton cruiser (open daily) is now a permanent floating naval museum. She took part in the last battleship action in European waters and helped to sink the *Scharnhorst* in 1943.

St Magnus Church (begun by Wren in 1671) no longer smells of fish, as it did when Billingsgate Market was next door. It is truly magnificent: T. S. Eliot described its interior as 'inexplicable splendour of Ionian white and gold'. It stood on the approach to Old (pre-Rennie) London Bridge. The 1712 organ is original. In the older (pre-Wren) church were the graves of Miles Coverdale (d.1569), translator of the Bible and Bishop of Exeter, and Henry Yevele (d.1400), architect of the nave of Westminster Abbey.

RIVERSIDE WALK (*London S.E.1*)

Running along the **South Bank**, between Westminster and Waterloo Bridges. County Hall, by Westminster Bridge, was built by Ralph Knott in 1912–14 as the headquarters for the London County Council which became the Greater London Council (G.L.C.). You can attend sessions of the Council, and visit the Hall, which has an excellent Information Department. It is difficult to describe the architecture, which has been called 'Nordic-palatial'. County Hall covers $6\frac{1}{2}$ acres. After Hungerford Railway Bridge and its footpath comes the Royal Festival Hall (1951, with the river-frontage added 1962–5), one of the two survivors of the 1951 Festival of Britain (the other is the National Film Theatre, underneath Waterloo Bridge). The Festival Hall (designed by R. H. Matthew and J. L. Martin), seating 3,000, is as near acoustical perfection as you can get. The complex contains (for smaller concerts, chamber music and exhibitions) the Queen Elizabeth Hall, the Purcell Room, the Hayward Gallery and restaurants.

Waterloo Station and Bridge, Shell Centre and the South Bank Arts Centre are all interconnected by a concrete system of elevated walkways and tunnels, one of which leads to the National Theatre. It took 128 years for the idea of building a National Theatre to be implemented: the theatre was opened in 1976. It competes with the Royal Shakespeare Company, which now has its own theatre in the City's huge Barbican development. The National Theatre consists of three theatres: the big theatre-in-the-round Olivier, the middle-sized Lyttelton with a conventional stage, and the small Cottesloe for experimental productions; plus foyers for exhibitions and bars for refreshment.

ROTHERHITHE (*London S.E.16*)

Meaning 'landing place for cattle'. Situated on the south bank, between Cherry Garden Pier and Deptford. Once known as Redriff, a district with a long record of service to mariners, many of whom lived here (a few still do; and there are churches to cater for Scandinavian sailors). To see the best of the area, walk down Rotherhithe Street (riverside) as far as St Mary's Church (but look also at Paradise Street and Jamaica Road, almost parallel to it). There used to be a Jamaica Inn (Pepys knew it). The Pilgrim Fathers set sail from Rotherhithe for Plymouth to begin their transatlantic voyage: they probably knew The Ship, an inn which stood on the site of the present Mayflower Inn by the river. The crew of the *Mayflower* were mostly Rotherhithe men, and some of them (with their captain, Christopher Jones) are buried at St Mary's. This fine Georgian church (1715) belongs to a time when Rotherhithe was a boatyard village: it stands unexpectedly amid trees. Its communion table was made from the oak of the sailing ship, the *Fighting Téméraire*. St James's Church (1829, by Richard Savage) in Jamaica Road, Gothic with a 'Grecian' interior, is worth a visit.

Near St Mary's is the old engine house used by Brunel and his son to drain the first (pedestrian) Thames Tunnel opened 1843; it was 1,200 feet long, and surfaced across the river at Wapping. But it didn't pay, and was sold to the East London Railway in 1865. The modern Rotherhithe (road) Tunnel (built 1904–8) connects Lower Road with Commercial Road, Stepney: of its 6,277-foot length, 1,422 feet are under the river.

SOUTHWARK (*London S.E.1*)

Meaning 'southern fortress'. It is on the south bank, situated between Blackfriars and London Bridge and the hinterland. Behind crumbling wharves awaiting demolition (*see also* Bankside above) is a world of history. Southwark became important because of the convergence of roads from the South when London Bridge was the only river crossing. Various bishops had town palaces here: the grandest was Winchester House, used for five centuries from 1107. Clink Street was the site of a prison (destroyed in the Gordon Riots of 1780) used by the bishops to deal with heretics.

An Augustinian priory of St Mary Overy (*over-rie* means 'across the water'), founded 1106, became St Saviour's Church and eventually (in 1905) Southwark Cathedral. Choir and Lady Chapel are Early English, transepts are Decorated and Perpendicular, the nave is nineteenth-century. The Harvard memorial chapel was restored in 1907 in memory of John Harvard, founder of the Massachusetts university, born in the parish in 1607. Here are buried Shakespeare's brother Edmund, Henslowe, Fletcher and Massinger, and Chaucer's contemporary, the poet John Gower (d.1408).

Off Borough High Street is the George Inn (owned by the National Trust), the only surviving galleried coaching inn, built in 1677 (the year after the great Southwark fire) on the site of an earlier inn in whose yard Shakespeare is said to have acted. In the eighteenth century it was the London terminus for mail to and from southeast England. Dickens mentions it in *Little Dorrit*. The coffee-room has Victorian box-pews to sit in. On Talbot Yard, in High Street, stood Chaucer's Tabard Inn (demolished 1629) whence the Canterbury pilgrims set forth on hired horses: the journey cost a shilling to Dartford, another shilling to Rochester, and eight pence for the rest of the way.

TEMPLE, The (*London E.C.4*)

The name is derived from the Knights Templar. Situated on the north bank, between Waterloo and Blackfriars Bridges, and the hinterland. Those Knights Templar were disbanded in 1312, and their land became infested with lawyers and newspapermen, who have a club by Temple Bar called the Wig and Pen. Temple Bar, a Wren-designed arch marking the boundary between Westminster and the City, was removed to Waltham Cross in 1878. This is where the Strand becomes Fleet Street, with its view of St Paul's Cathedral up Ludgate Hill and Dr Johnson's statue looking at it.

Inner and Middle Temple, divided by Middle Temple Lane, feel like a university: squares, courts, passages, gardens going

down to the Embankment, and many seventeenth-century buildings (King's Bench Walk is superb). Temple Church, one of the only five round churches in England, modelled on the Holy Sepulchre of Jerusalem, dates from 1185. The chancel (Early English) was added in 1240. Its choir is famous. As for Fleet Street, it has the showcase-like *Daily Express* building, St Dunstan's-in-the-West (where John Donne was vicar), Wren's St Bride's (the so-called 'journalists' church'), Dr Johnson's House, the Cock Tavern and El Vino, where women have won the right to drink at the bar.

TILBURY (*Essex*)

Meaning 'Tila's fort'. Situated on the north bank, 22 miles from London on the A126. This is now the real Port of London, with docks built for long container ships loading and unloading at very high speeds (for example, 2,000 tons of grain per hour can be unloaded into barges or a silo). The old commercial docks, ahead of their time, were built in the 1880s. There is much desolation round about, but the area is good for birdwatchers who report sightings of Brent geese and eider duck. Tilbury Fort, a superb piece of military engineering (open to visitors), was built *circa* 1670 to resist Dutch and French invasions: appropriately it was designed by a Dutch Frenchman, Bernard de Gomme, as ordered by Charles II. But earlier monarchs — Henry VIII who fortified the place in 1539, and Elizabeth I — were well aware of its strategic importance. It was still regarded as London's first line of defence in the 1860s when General Gordon built Coal House Fort, East Tilbury (*see also* Gravesend, above).

Here, in 1588, Elizabeth I, mounted on a horse in full armour, inspected the Earl of Leicester's troops who were about to sail against the Armada, and made the greatest speech of her life: 'I know I have the body of a weak and feeble woman, but I have

The George Inn, Southwark; the only galleried coaching inn that has survived

the heart and stomach of a king, and of a king of England, too; and think foul scorn that Parma or Spain, or any prince of Europe, should dare to invade the borders of my realm.'

TOWER OF LONDON (*London E.C.3*)

It is between the river and Tower Hill. Monument to in-humanity: sinister by day, almost romantic when floodlit at night. To visit it, you will almost certainly have to queue with small boys who 'want to see the tortures'. The Yeomen Warders who show you round are not called Beefeaters. We cannot enter from the river by the Traitors' Gate today because its portcullis is permanently shut, but that is where anyone who displeased a Tudor monarch entered the Tower. On top of it is the pretty house where the Keeper of the Jewel House lives. The core or keep of the complex is the four-turreted White Tower (yellowish grey, but whitewashed in medieval times). William the Conqueror began building it in 1078 and it was completed in Henry I's reign in 1100, by Ranulph Flambard, Bishop of Durham, who was then imprisoned in it. Another distinguished prisoner was Charles, Duke of Orleans, captured at the battle of Agincourt in 1415.

Tower Green, near the chapel of St Peter ad Vincula, is where Anne Boleyn, Lady Jane Grey, Catherine Howard and so many others were executed, watched from windows by those awaiting the same fate. Horrible ravens emphasize the deathly atmosphere. Each inner tower has its martyrs. The Bloody Tower (were the little princes really murdered here in 1483?) also had Cranmer and Laud as inmates. Sir Walter Raleigh spent many years in it, writing his *History of the World* and studying chemistry before he too went to the block. I have never quite believed the story of the Duke of Clarence drowning in a butt of Malmsey wine, but if it happened, it was in the Bowyer Tower. Bored prisoners carved their names in the stone walls, especially in Bell Tower and St Thomas's Tower. Latter-day prisoners were Lieutenant Norman Baillie-Stewart, the muddled pro-Nazi, and

Rudolf Hess, Hitler's deputy, who was amazed to see British soldiers drilling as smartly as Germans (he had been told that the British were unmilitary). Hooray for Lord Nithsdale, the prisoner who got away: in 1716 he escaped, disguised as a woman.

If you haven't come to see the tortures, you have come for the Crown Jewels. They used to be behind bars in the Wakefield Tower (where for 400 years the Public Records were also housed), but in 1967 they were moved to Waterloo Barracks, by the north wall. They include the Coronation regalia and the largest cut diamond in the world, the Star of Africa. In the Armouries, with a fine collection of weapons, is a suit of armour made for an elephant in the battle of Plassey, 1757. There used to be a Lion Tower by the main entrance, containing (for nearly 500 years) the Royal zoo; but the animals were added to the new Regent's Park Zoo in 1834. The Royal Mint used to be here until 1810: it is now a few hundred yards to the east. There was an Observatory, too, which moved to Greenwich in 1675.

The Tower is open 9.30–5 p.m. (weekdays) and Sunday afternoons. Every night, in the Ceremony of the Keys, it is locked up. The sentry challenges the lockers-up in unchangeable words: 'Whose keys?' 'Queen Elizabeth's Keys.' 'Pre-sent-ARMS.' The Chief Warder says: 'God Preserve Queen Elizabeth.' The sentry replies 'Amen.'

WAPPING (London E.1)

Meaning 'marshy place'. Situated on the north bank, between Tower Bridge and Limehouse. Like Limehouse, it has a reputation (in fiction) for sleaziness and crime; yet if you stroll down Wapping High Street today you will notice one or two smart cars and other signs of gentrification, perhaps influenced by the new area St-Katharine's-by-the-Tower. Behind Wapping lie London Docks, with miles of old wine vaults under them: they

Traitor's Gate; no longer in use, it is the old riverside entrance to the Tower of London

were designed by Asher Alexander (1800–5), who built Dartmoor Prison. The riverfront was then plagued by river Pirates (high tide) and Mudlarks (low tide). At Execution Dock hanged bodies were washed by the tides before being cut down. Captain Kidd, a suppressor of piracy who turned pirate himself, was so treated in 1701. Very appropriate that the Thames River Police Headquarters should be so close at hand.

Many Wapping inns were used by smugglers, notably the Prospect of Whitby (now very much a tourist attraction, with a fine view of the river from its balcony). It gets its name from Yorkshire coal ships that anchored here. Parts of it date back to 1520. It has an aged instrument called a symphonion which plays tunes from The Geisha (1896).

In 1688 Judge Jeffreys, notorious for his conduct of the Bloody Assizes after the suppression of Monmouth's rebellion, pursued by a mob, hid disguised as a sailor, on a ship moored near the Old Stairs; but he was seen in the Red Cow alehouse by a witness he had bullied in court. Tried by the Lord Mayor, he was committed to the Tower where he died (of drink). Among pubs in the area are the Town of Ramsgate, named after the Ramsgate fishermen who used to patronize it when delivering their catch to Billingsgate Market; and The Cuckoo in Wapping Lane (which used to be more prettily known as Welcome to the Cuckoo).

WESTMINSTER (London S.W.1)

Meaning 'abbey in the west'. Westminster is a city, much bigger than (and quite separate from) the square-mile business City I have already described above. It began with Edward the Confessor, who in 1050 founded an abbey on dry land surrounded by marsh, called Thorney Island. The East Saxons had already built a church here.

The Confessor is buried behind the altar in Westminster Abbey, near the Coronation chair and (in Henry VII's 1519 chapel) Elizabeth I's tomb. When the Confessor was canonized

Big Ben and the Houses of Parliament at Westminster

in 1245, Henry III extended the abbey and rebuilt it in the Early English style. Since King Harold, all English monarchs (except Edward V and VIII) have been crowned here. Near the West Door is the tomb of the Unknown Warrior of World War I, buried 11 November 1920. Poets' Corner contains graves or tablets in memory of most of our greatest poets. Cloisters, Chapter House and Museum complete the establishment.

The Abbey acts as the chapel for Westminster School next door: the boys here have the privilege of shouting *Vivat!* at coronations.

Of the ancient Palace of Westminster, a Royal residence until Henry VIII's reign, only Westminster Hall (scene of many trials, such as Guy Fawkes' and Charles I's) and St Stephen's Crypt (built in 1292 and today used by M.P.s for weddings and baptisms) escaped the great fire of 1834. This gave Sir Charles Barry the opportunity of designing the Gothic Houses of Parliament we know today (open on Saturdays 10–4.30 p.m. and public holidays when Parliament is not sitting). When Parliament is sitting, Victoria Tower flies a flag by day and Big Ben shows a night-light. You can be taken round by your Member or join a guided party.

In the near distance is the mighty 284-foot tower of the Byzantine-domed Roman Catholic Westminster Cathedral (1895–1903). The interior may seem austere, but this is because it is still unfinished, awaiting coloured marbles and mosaics of the original design. Eric Gill's sculptures of the Stations of the Cross (1914–18) make a valuable contrast of effect.

Whitehall, almost parallel to the river north of Westminster Bridge, is a general term for Government offices: the name derives from Cardinal Wolsey, who extended York House, the London residence of the archbishops of York and painted it white. All that remains of the house today is the wine cellar, although it was moved in 1935 to make room for the Ministry of Defence. Whitehall Palace, grabbed by Henry VIII, became a

The world's largest movable flood barrier at Woolwich

Royal residence until it was burned down in 1678. Whitehall today also contains the Banqueting House, the Horse Guards, and the Cenotaph (sad and bleak). Downing Street, strangely humble for a Prime Minister and the Chancellor of the Exchequer to live in, leads to St James's Park. No. 10 has been the Prime Minister's official residence since Sir Robert Walpole (1735).

In the shadow of the Abbey is St Margaret's, mostly sixteenth-century, the parish church of the House of Commons and scene of many society weddings. Pepys, Milton and Sir Winston Churchill were all married here.

WOOLWICH (London S.E.18)

Derived from 'wool farm'. It is $3\frac{1}{2}$ miles east of Greenwich on the A206. The world's largest movable flood barrier, with four main gates, each weighing 3,200 tons and spanning 200 feet, can shut off the river here within 30 minutes in the event of a dangerous tidal surge. Let us not forget that other Woolwich wonder, the Free Ferry, which has been connecting Woolwich (south bank) with Woolwich North since 1889 and is now a

vital link for cars and pedestrians between the eastern ends of the North and South Circular Roads. In 1940 the ferry carried out a mini-Dunkirk by rescuing Silvertown people cut off from Essex fire-brigades by bombed buildings. Until 1963 the ferry still used ancient paddle steamers (one was called *Ernest Bevin*). The ferry was nearly abolished soon after it started when in September 1878 it collided with a pleasure-steamer, the *Princess Alice*, and 500 people died.

We think of Greenwich as Naval, and Woolwich (with the Arsenal and the Royal Military Academy – 'the Shop') as Army. 'The Shop' (founded 1805, for Royal Artillery and Royal Engineer cadets) merged with Sandhurst in 1946. Yet Woolwich too has a nautical past. The old shipbuilding yards which built the *Great Harry* in 1512 and the *Royal Sovereign* never came to terms with ships of iron, and in 1869 they lost out to the yards of Devonport in Devon. Much of the docks is now a housing estate. And the site of the old Arsenal, which during World War II employed 40,000 men and women making munitions, is to be used for building a new prison.

CHAPTER SEVEN

Meditation at the Rose Revived

I cannot, after all, leave you at Woolwich; or Tilbury, or Gravesend, even with all that history ringing in your ears. I who first knew the Thames by its Estuary, with flashing lightships by night and pleasure-steamers by day plying between London, Southend, Herne Bay and Margate; who when he became a Londoner thought the grandest sight in the world was the blazing jewelry of the night-river seen from Waterloo Bridge – I seek the peace of a young river.

But where, or what, is the Upper Thames? The term is used inconsistently. Sometimes we mean the whole lock-disciplined river above Teddington Weir. Other times we mean the Isis-Thames above Oxford (what John Buchan called the 'medieval' river). I am with Buchan. Would you believe it, there are some guidebooks that do not take you above Oxford 'because the Upper Thames is so little known'?

There are many matters we have not had time or space to pursue. Bugsby's Hole, for example, a tiny beach near Bow Creek, with Bugsby's Reach: who was (or improbably is) Bugsby? And Cuckold's Point, a sliver of land at Rotherhithe: who was the cuckold, and when, and why? There are isolated facts that don't fit in anywhere. Did you know that in the Thames tunnel from Greenwich to the Isle of Dogs you are not allowed to whistle, carry loaded firearms or ride a tricycle? In which riverside village is a swan buried? Remenham, in the rector's garden: she was a friend of his, and her tombstone reads, 'In loving memory. Died 26 April 1956. Claudine, a swan.' Is it really true that seals have been seen at Teddington, and even (in 1965) at Kingston? And dolphins at Woolwich?

The river begets speculation and legend. We may envy historians who, when facts fell short, thought it their creative duty to invent. Thus Geoffrey of Monmouth in the twelfth century asserted that Oxford was founded in 1099 BC by 'Memphric, King of Britain'. There is nothing like sitting in the garden of a riverside pub for persuading oneself to believe anything. 'If King Canute had had abler successors', runs one train of thought, 'England would have been the centre of a Scandinavian Empire, there would have been no Norman Conquest, and an Anglo-Norse people would have followed Leif Ericson and colonized North America five centuries before Columbus sailed.'

When we are tired of speculation, we can observe. An American family have just tied up among the weeping willows below Newbridge. Unusually, they are in a narrow-boat. They hired it in Maidenhead, took half an hour's instruction in navigation, and here they are, 77 river miles and one week later, within 26 miles of the Source . . . It is clouding over now, and a fine autumn mist comes up. The Americans don't care – 'We're from California, we're sun-crazed anyway . . .'

In the next boat, a two-seater motor-launch, made fast for the night, a young couple sit in oilskins. Two collapsible bicycles are neatly stowed in the stern. Theirs is probably the ideal way to explore the Thames and its valley, with wheeled transport. They too are unperturbed by the weather: they know what a golden dawn can follow an evening like this. Clear voices float on the water: they are reading poetry to each other.

England is sinking at the rate of about a foot a century, and land around London Bridge was 16 feet higher in Roman times. I try to worry about this, but I cannot: it is not my responsibility, it is Thames Water's and the Greater London Council's and the Port of London Authority's. If you want to worry about this or anything else, don't come to the Rose Revived.

Meditation – looking across the river from the Rose Revived, at Newbridge

Index

USEFUL ADDRESSES

The English Tourist Board
4 Grosvenor Gardens
London SW1
Tel: 01-730 0791

The London Tourist Board
26 Grosvenor Gardens
London SW1
Tel: 01-730 0791

The National Trust
42 Queen Anne's Gate
London SW1H 9AS
Tel: 01-930 0211

Thames and Chilterns Tourist Office
8 The Market Place
P.O. Box 10
Abingdon
Oxfordshire
OX14 3UD
Tel: (0235) 22711

Henley-on-Thames Tourist Information Centre
West Hill House
4 West Street
Henley-on-Thames
Oxfordshire
Tel: (04912) 64451

Oxford Tourist Information Centre
St Aldates Chambers
St Aldates
Oxford
Tel: (0865) 726871/2

Thames Water
Nugent House
Vastern Road
Reading
RG1 8DB
Tel: (0734) 593333